Statements on Management Accounting

Supplement 1

The National Association
of Accountants
Montvale,
New Jersey 07645

PRENTICE HALL
Englewood Cliffs, New Jersey 07632

Prentice-Hall International (UK) Limited, *London*
Prentice-Hall of Australia Pty. Limited, *Sydney*
Prentice-Hall Canada Inc., *Toronto*
Prentice-Hall Hispanoamericana, S.A., *Mexico*
Prentice-Hall of India Private Limited, *New Delhi*
Prentice-Hall of Japan, Inc., *Tokyo*
Simon & Schuster Asia Pte. Ltd., *Singapore*
Editora Prentice-Hall do Brasil, Ltda., *Rio de Janeiro*

10 9 8 7 6 5 4 3 2 1

Library of Congress Cataloging-in-Publication Data

Statements on management accounting / the National Association
of Accountants.
   p.   cm.
   Rev. ed. of: Management accounting terminology.   c 1983.
   ISBN 0-13-845538-4
   1. Managerial accounting—United States—Terminology.
I. National Association of Accountants.   II. Management
accounting terminology.
HF5657.4.S73   1991
658.15'11—dc20   91-15521
                                                          CIP

ISBN 0-13-845538-4

9 780138 455385

90000>

PRENTICE HALL
BUSINESS & PROFESSIONAL DIVISION
A division of Simon & Schuster
Englewood Cliffs, New Jersey 07632

Printed in the United States of America

CONTENTS

Statements on Management Accounting

Statement Number 2A
November 30, 1990

PRACTICES AND TECHNIQUES

Management Accounting Glossary

In accordance with the charge to the Management Accounting Practices (MAP) Committee to issue statements on management accounting principles and practices, Statements on Management Accounting are promulgated to reflect official positions of the National Association of Accountants (NAA). The work of the MAP Committee is based on a framework for management accounting, whose principal categories are:

1. Objectives
2. Terminology
3. Concepts
4. Practices and Techniques
5. Management of Accounting Activities

Statements on Management Accounting

Statement Number 2A
November 30, 1990

Practices and Techniques:
Management Accounting Glossary

National Association of Accountants, Inc.

Acknowledgments

The NAA acknowledges with appreciation the direct contributions to SMA 2A made by many people, including members of the MAP Committee and, most notably, Frank C. Minter, chairman of the Subcommittee on SMA Promulgation. He and the members of the subcommittee labored long and hard. Special thanks are due Wagdy Abdallah, NAA project manager and associate professor at Seton Hall University, who persevered through countless iterations reflected in a succession of draft documents. Appreciation is extended to Louis Bisgay, director, management accounting practices, for overseeing the project from inception through completion, and to Lorraine Lupinski for her diligent typing of several drafts. The NAA acknowledges with gratitude the encouragement and guidance provided throughout the course of the project by MAP Committee member Robert N. Anthony, professor emeritus, Harvard Business School. Last, but by no means least, the NAA recognizes the debt owed to the other dedicated professionals who participated in developing this glossary.

Preface

This glossary, Statement on Management Accounting No. 2A (SMA 2A), is the fruit of an extensive effort to develop a glossary of terms used in the practice of management accounting. SMA 2A supersedes SMA 2, "Management Accounting Terminology," issued June 1, 1983. The terms included in SMA 2A are those considered most relevant to potential users of this glossary. The glossary is not intended to cover terms used in all areas of accounting. It does not focus on terms primarily used in governmental accounting, tax accounting, and management information systems. Like other SMAs, this glossary is issued by express authority of the Management Accounting Practices (MAP) Committee, which is responsible for products developed under the supervision of the Subcommittee on SMA Promulgation.

Definitions in the glossary come from a variety of sources, including SMA 2, official definitions found in authoritative accounting literature, textbooks, and definitions suggested by members of the Subcommittee on SMA Promulgation and the MAP Committee. In many cases the definitions represent a combination of several of these sources. Specific attribution is given to definitions taken from official sources, such as the Financial Accounting Standards Board, Cost Accounting Standards Board, etc. All sources that were used in the compilation of the glossary are credited in the section titled *References*.

The NAA believes that the glossary will significantly improve communication about financial matters within the United States of America and, perhaps even more important, internationally. The glossary should benefit practicing accountants, academicians, students, and nonfinancial managers who need to know the language of accountants.

Robert G. Weiss
Chairman
Management Accounting
Practices Committee
National Association of
Accountants

MANAGEMENT ACCOUNTING GLOSSARY

— A —

Abandonment Value

The amount that can be realized by liquidating an asset or project before its economic life has ended. *See* Liquidation Value.

Abnormal Cost

An unusual or atypical cost whose occurrence is usually irregular and unexpected.

Absorbed Overhead

That portion of factory indirect cost that has been allocated to a specific product. The allocation process is usually carried out by the application of an appropriate overhead rate to specific units of production. Also called Applied Overhead.

Absorption Costing

A method of product costing that includes fixed manufacturing overhead in the inventorial costs.

Accelerated Cost Recovery System (ACRS)

A method of depreciation, established by the Economic Recovery Act of 1981, that allows for depreciation over periods of 3, 5, 10, and 15 years. These periods are not intended to represent the useful lives of the assets involved, and in most cases will be much shorter than the actual useful lives. This system eliminates the concept of salvage value from the calculation of depreciation.

Accelerated Depreciation

Any pattern of depreciation that systematically writes off depreciable costs so that progressively smaller amounts are allocated each year.

Accountability

The obligation of a party to answer for the discharge of their responsibility.

Account-by-Account Method

A method of determining fixed and variable costs at the lowest level at which costs are aggregated. The sum of these determinations gives the fixed and variable components of the whole activity or process.

Accounting

The process of classifying, recording, and summarizing—in a significant manner and in monetary terms—transactions and events that are, in part at least, of a financial character and interpreting the results thereof. (Adapted from APB Statement No. 4.)

Accounting Control

The methods adopted within a business to safeguard its assets as well as check the accuracy and reliability of its accounting data and financial records. It includes such controls as the system of authorization and approval, physical control over assets, and internal auditing. Also included are controls to separate duties concerned with record keeping and accounting reports from those duties concerned with operations or asset custody.

Accounting Cycle

The sequence of steps or procedures in the accounting process initiated by an accounting event and completed during each accounting period.

Accounting Entity

An entity for which accounting records are maintained. *Contrast with* Legal Entity.

Accounting Rate of Return

Income for a period divided by average investment during the period. The accounting rate of return is based on income, rather than discounted cash flows, and hence may be a poor decision-making aid.

Accretion

1. Growth as a result of natural causes (for example, growth of timber) or increase by external additions (such as contributions to a pension fund).

2. Also relates to accretion of interest, as in the purchase of a bond at a discount.

Accrual Basis of Accounting

1. The method of recognizing (a) revenues when earned, such as when goods are sold (or delivered) and as services are rendered, and (b) expenses when incurred—both irrespective of the time when cash is received or paid.

2. The method of recording the financial effects on an entity of transactions and other events and circumstances that have cash consequences for the entity in the periods in which those transactions, events, and circumstances occur rather than only in the periods in which cash is received or paid by the entity. (SFAC No.6).

Accumulated Benefit Obligation

The actuarial present value of benefits (whether vested or nonvested) attributed by the pension benefit formula to employee service rendered before a specified date and based on employee service and compensation (if applicable) prior to that date (SFAS No.87). *Contrast with* Projected Benefit Obligation.

Accumulated Depreciation

An amount that offsets a fixed asset and represents depreciation expense that has been charged from the date of acquisition. Also called allowance for depreciation.

Acid-Test Ratio

A ratio that relates quick assets to current liabilities. It is considered a more rigorous measure of a firm's ability to pay off short-term obligations than is the current ratio because no return is presumed from the liquidation of inventories. Also called Quick Ratio.

Acquisition Cost

The cash or cash equivalent value exchanged on the acquisition date to acquire goods or services and have them available for use. Also called Historical Cost or Original Cost.

ACRS

See Accelerated Cost Recovery System.

Activity-Based Cost System

A system that *(a)* identifies the causal relationship between the incurrence of cost and activities, *(b)* determines the underlying "driver" of the activities, *(c)* establishes cost pools related to individual "drivers," *(d)* develops costing rates, and *(e)* applies cost to product on the basis of resources consumed (drivers).

Actual Cost (Basis)

1. Acquisition or historical cost.

2. An amount determined on the basis of cost incurred as distinguished from forecasted cost. Includes standard cost properly adjusted for applicable variance (CASB).

Actual Costing (System)

A method of assigning costs to products using actual costs of direct materials, direct labor, and factory overhead.

Actuarial Gain or Loss

1. A change in the value of either the projected benefit obligation or pension plan assets resulting from experience different from that assumed or from a change in an actuarial assumption (SFAS No.87).

2. The effect on pension cost resulting from differences between actuarial assumptions and actual experience (CASB).

Administrative Expense

Expenses incurred for the general direction of an enterprise as a whole, as contrasted with expense of a more specific function such as manufacturing or selling. Items included vary with the nature of the business, but usually include salaries of top officers, rent, and other general office expense. Also called General and Administrative Expense.

ADR

See Asset Depreciation Range.

All-Inclusive Income Concept

1. The notion that all items of revenues, expenses, gains, and losses are included in the measurement of income rather than being charged or credited to retained earnings.

2. The presumption that net income includes "all transactions affecting the net increase or decrease in equity during the current period, except dividend distributions and transactions of a capital nature" (APB No.9, para. 13).

Allocate

1. To distribute those costs that cannot be directly assigned to the cost objects that presumably caused them.

2. To assign an item of cost, or a group of items of cost, to one or more cost objects. This term includes both direct assignment of cost and the reassignment of a share from an indirect cost pool (CASB).

Allocation Basis

The basis used to assign indirect costs to cost objects. Examples include labor hours, labor dollars, and machine hours.

Allowance for Depreciation

See Accumulated Depreciation.

Allowance Method

An attempt to match all expenses of a transaction with its associated revenues. Usually, this method involves either a debit to expense and a credit to an estimated liability (such as an estimated warranty expenditure), or a debit to a contra revenue account and a credit to a contra asset account (as in some firms' accounting for uncollectible accounts).

Alternative Cost

See Opportunity Cost.

Amortization

The accounting process of reducing an amount by periodic payments or write-downs (SFAC No.6).

Analysis of Variances

See Variance Analysis.

Annualize

To adjust a weekly or monthly rate or amount to reflect a rate or amount for a full year.

Annuity

An agreement providing for a series of economic benefits or cash flows of an amount payable at fixed intervals and normally resulting from an investment in tangible or intangible assets.

Annuity Method of Depreciation

A method of recording depreciation that provides for an imputed interest return on the amount invested in an asset. The amount of depreciation expense increases with the passage of time. Also called Compound Interest Depreciation. *Contrast with* Accelerated Depreciation.

Application Controls

Controls that relate to a specific data-processing activity, such as payroll. They are adopted to safeguard the applications' records and to check the accuracy and reliability of the information generated. Their purpose is to provide reasonable assurance that data are properly processed, recorded, and reported. Application controls are often categorized as "input controls," "output controls," or "processing controls."

Applied Cost

A cost that has been allocated to a cost object.

Applied Overhead

See Absorbed Overhead.

Apportionment

The process of spreading revenues and costs among several time periods or among cost objects.

Appraisal

An estimate of the economic value (usually reflecting the expected market price) of a resource, liability, equity, or entity made by an expert after appropriate physical examination, comparative pricing, and/or engineering review.

Appreciation

An increase in economic worth caused by rising market prices.

Appropriation

An expenditure authorized for the acquisition of assets.

1. In government, the legislative authority that permits government funds to be used for a specific purpose and for no more than a specified amount.

2. In industry, the authorization for specific capital expenditures.

Arbitrage

The simultaneous purchase in one market and sale in another of a security or commodity in hope of making a profit on the price differences in the different markets.

Arm's-Length Price

The price which an unrelated party would have paid for similar property under the same circumstances.

Asset

1. "Probable future economic benefits obtained or controlled by a particular entity as a result of past transactions or events" (SFAC No.3).

2. Any owned physical object (tangible) or right (intangible) having economic value to its owners; an item or source of wealth with continuing benefits for future periods, expressed for accounting purposes in terms of its cost or other value (such as current replacement cost).

Asset Depreciation Range (ADR)

Upper and lower limits set by the Internal Revenue Service for asset lives. An asset may be depreciated for federal income tax purposes over a useful life selected from within this range without further justification.

Asset Turnover Ratio

Net sales for a period divided by average assets during that period.

Assign

To attribute a cost item to one or more cost objects that presumably caused it. Direct costs are assigned directly; indirect costs are allocated. *See* Allocate.

Audit

The systematic examination by analyses, confirmation, and tests of accounting records to confirm with reasonable assurance that they adequately reflect economic actions (status) and operations. It may be conducted by an internal or external auditor.

Average Cost

Total cost divided by total units, the latter representing usable or salable items.

Average Cost Method

An inventory flow assumption in which the cost of units is derived from the weighted average cost of the beginning inventory plus purchases.

Avoidable Cost

An ongoing cost that may be eliminated by ceasing to perform some activity or by improving the efficiency with which such an activity is accomplished. Also called Escapable Cost. *Contrast with* Unavoidable Cost.

— B —

Backlog

Orders on hand that have not been shipped or otherwise converted to revenue.

B and P Cost

See Bid and Proposal Cost.

Bad Debts

Accounts or notes receivable that management determines to be uncollectible after reasonable efforts to collect have not been successful. When such a determination has been made, the receivables account is credited. If the company is on the reserve method, the allowance account is debited. For companies on the direct write-off (charge-off) method, the debit is an expense.

Balance Sheet

The statement of financial position that discloses the assets, liabilities, and equity accounts of an entity as of one particular date.

Bank Overdraft

The amount owed to a bank by a depositor as a consequence of checks drawn in an amount exceeding the depositor's balance in a commercial account.

Bankruptcy

A condition in which a court has granted a company legal protection from creditors because it cannot meet its obligations as they come due. The legal protection of bankruptcy is intended to provide fair treatment to the various classes of creditors and owners.

Barter

An exchange of goods or services for other goods or services rather than for cash.

Baseline Budget

A budget set at the beginning of the year. A comparison of actual performance with baseline performance shows the extent of deviation from the original plan. Comparing the current budget with the baseline budget shows how much of this deviation is attributable to changes in current conditions from those originally assumed.

Basic Standard Cost

A standard cost that is considered to be the historical performance standard. It is not changed unless there are important modifications in the nature of the manufacturing operations.

Basket Purchase

The purchase of a group of assets as a unit (especially capital assets) at a single negotiated price that must subsequently be divided between the various assets or asset groups. Also called a Lump-Sum Purchase.

Batch Costing

A method of cost accounting in which costs are accumulated by batches or runs, as in the petroleum, chemical, and rubber industries. Costs are attached to a specified quantity of raw materials as it enters into a refining or other process. Often, in addition to the cost of the material itself, batch costs include the operating expense of the plant or process during the treatment period.

Benefit-Cost Analysis

A comparison of benefits with costs, usually in the form of a ratio (called the benefit-cost ratio) after both benefits and costs have been stated in comparable units.

Betterment

An expenditure that is expected to materially improve the useful life, quality or quantity of output, or operating costs of an existing fixed asset.

Bid and Proposal Cost (B and P Cost)

The cost incurred in preparing, submitting, or supporting any bid or proposal which effort is neither sponsored by a grant, nor required in the performance of a contract (CASB).

Bill of Materials

A specification of the quantity of direct materials expected to be used to produce a given job or quantity of output.

Book Value

The amount at which an asset or a liability is carried on the books of account, net of any contra account. Also called Net Book Value.

Bottleneck

In general terms, uneven work flow caused by operational constraints or inefficient usage of available resources. In more specific terms, segments of the production process that are slower than other segments, creating work-in-process inventory buildup and/or idle time.

Breakeven Analysis

An analysis of the relationship of cost and revenue. It characteristically emphasizes both the volume at which there is neither profit nor loss and the influence of fixed and variable factors on the profit expectations at various levels of operation. Also called Cost/Volume/Profit Analysis. *See* Breakeven Chart.

Breakeven Chart

A chart showing the profit or loss associated with volume when sales price per unit is constant; some expenses are fixed, and some expenses vary directly with sales. Figures 1 and 2 show examples of two kinds of breakeven charts. Also called Contribution Profitgraph.

Breakeven Point

The volume of revenue at which total revenues and total costs are equal. May be expressed in units (fixed cost divided by contribution margin per unit) or in monetary amounts (fixed cost divided by contribution margin ratio per unit).

FIGURE 1

COST/VOLUME/PROFIT

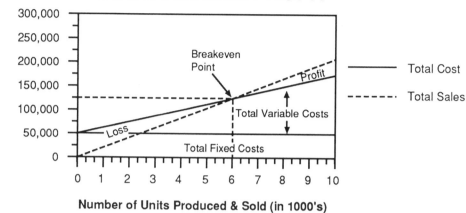

FIGURE 2

PROFIT—VOLUME CHART

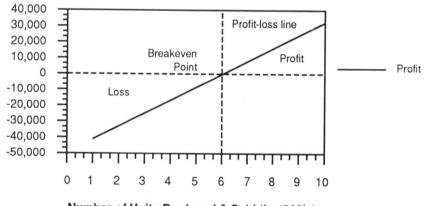

Budget

A statement of planned or expected revenues, expenses, assets, and liabilities. A budget provides guidelines for future operations and appraisal of performance. Also called Profit Plan.

Budgetary Authority

The authority to spend the amount in a budget.

Budgetary Control

The actions necessary to ensure that budgeted amounts are attained, or if unattainable, revised.

Budget Cycle

The recurring sequence of activities involved in the preparation of a budget.

Budgeted Costs

Estimated costs of a specific future period that have been included in the budget.

Budgeting

The process of planning flows of financial resources into, within, and from an entity during a specified future period or for a specified project.

Budget Period

The period for which a budget is prepared and used, which may then be subdivided into control periods. The typical budget period is one year.

Budget Variance

See Variances.

Burden

See Indirect Cost.

Burden Rate

See Overhead Rate.

Business Unit

Any segment of an organization, or an entire business entity that is not divided into segments. Also called a Profit Center (CASB).

Byproduct

A product necessarily obtained during the course of manufacturing, having relatively small importance as compared with that of the main product or products. The cost of a byproduct is commonly regarded as indeterminable; the revenue, if any, from its sale is usually credited to the main product(s) or to a miscellaneous revenue account.

— C —

Capacity

The maximum performance possible under the limiting conditions of the existing physical plant, labor force, method of production, or supply of material.

Capacity Cost

A fixed cost incurred to provide a firm with the capacity to produce or to sell. Also called Standby Costs or Shut-Down Costs.

Capacity Variance

See Fixed Manufacturing Overhead Volume Variance.

Capital

Broadly defined, equity plus long-term liabilities. Otherwise stated as working capital plus noncurrent assets.

Capital Asset

A tangible or intangible asset intended for long-term use and held as such.

Capital Asset Pricing Model (CAPM)

A general framework for analyzing the relationship between risks and rates of return on securities, especially common stocks. Risk is assumed to consist of two parts: unsystematic risk, which is caused by events unique to a firm; and systematic risk, which is the relative volatility of a stock as it moves up and down with the general market.

Capital Budget

A plan of proposed outlays for acquiring long-term assets and the means of financing the acquisition. *Contrast with* Operating Budget.

Capital Cost

See Cost of Capital.

Capital Expenditure

Expenditure for additions to fixed assets intended to benefit future accounting periods (in contrast with other expenditures that benefit the current period). Any expenditure which increases the capacity, efficiency, life span, or economy of the operation of an existing fixed asset.

Capital Gain or Loss

The extent by which the net realized value from sales of a capital asset exceeds (or in the case of a capital loss is less than) the cost of acquisition plus additional improvements, less depreciation and/or depletion charges (where applicable). It can also arise from the exchange of such an asset for that of a different type. The term can have different interpretations for tax purposes depending on the most current legislation.

Capital Intensity Ratio

Sales revenues divided by the average (or ending) book value of property, plant, and equipment. This ratio focuses only on the property, plant, and equipment item. Companies that have a high ratio of plant to sales revenue (i.e. capital-intensive companies) are particularly vulnerable to cyclical fluctuations in business activity. *See* also Capital Turnover Ratio.

Capital Investment

Any outlay of money or its equivalent from which future cash inflows are expected for more than a year. *See* Capital Budget, Capital Expenditure.

Capital Lease

A lease treated by the lessee as both the borrowing of funds and the acquisition of an asset, with the cost being amortized over future periods. Both the liability and the asset are recognized on the balance sheet. Expenses consist of interest on the "borrowing" and amortization of the cost of the asset. The lessor treats the lease as a sale/financing transaction; in other words, the lease is treated as a sale of the asset in return for a series of future revenue payments. Also called Financial Lease.

Capital Leverage

The concept of employing borrowed funds as well as equity funds in a business. The borrowed funds produce more or less return than their interest cost; this excess or shortfall accrues to the providers of equity funds.

Capital Maintenance Concept

A concept in which earnings are said to result only after capital has been maintained or recovered. The concept of capital is therefore critical in distinguishing a return of capital (capital maintenance) from a return on capital (earnings).

There are two different capital maintenance concepts.

1. An entity has maintained its financial capital when its revenues (including gains) have at least equaled its expenses (including losses), both measured according to the concepts of accrual accounting.

2. An entity has maintained its physical capital when its revenues have at least equaled its expenses, with the depreciation on fixed assets being measured on the basis of the replacement cost of these assets.

The FASB's Statements are based on the financial capital maintenance concept.

Capital Structure

The relative proportions of short-term debt, long-term debt, and owners' equity (including minority interest) in the company.

Capital Turnover Ratio

The ratio of annual sales to invested capital. When calculating this ratio, invested capital is usually measured as the sum of equity and long-term liabilities. *See also* Capital Intensity Ratio.

Capitalize

To record an expenditure that is expected to benefit a future period as an asset rather than treating the expenditure as an expense of the period in which it occurs.

CAPM

See Capital Asset Pricing Model.

Management Accounting Glossary

Carrying Cost

Costs of storing and holding inventory, including the cost of capital from the time of acquisition or manufacture until the time of sale or use.

CASB

See Cost Accounting Standards Board.

Cash Basis of Accounting

A basis of keeping accounts that reports cash in the period in which it is received or paid, without consideration of the period to which revenues and expenses are applicable.

Cash Budget

An estimate of the amount and timing of cash receipts and disbursements for a future period, cash requirements at various points within the period, and cash on hand at the end of the period.

Cash Conversion Cycle

The period of time during which cash is converted into inventories, inventories are converted into accounts receivable, and accounts receivable are converted back into cash. Also called Cash Cycle or Earnings Cycle.

Cash Cycle

See Cash Conversion Cycle.

Cash Discount

A reduction in sales or purchase price allowed for prompt payment.

Cash Dividends

Dividends paid in cash, as distinguished from those paid in an entity's stock or bonds, or in property other than cash. Cash dividends become a legal liability of the corporation when they are declared.

Cash Flow

The stream of cash inflows and outflows of an entity or segment of an entity. Analytically, the presentation of cash flow should identify the timing, amount, and source of cash inflows as well as the nature of cash outflows.

Cash Flow Per Share

Net cash flow from operations divided by the number of shares outstanding.

Cash Flow Statement

A statement that classifies cash receipts and payments according to whether they stem from operating, investing, or financing activities. Also called Funds Statement or Statement of Cash Flows (SFAS No.95).

Central Corporate Expense

See Administrative Expense.

Centralized Management

An organizational structure in which senior management maintains significant direction and authority over operations and policies relating to identifiably separate activities or operations. Centralized management allows lower responsibility centers only minimal freedom for decision making. *Contrast with* Decentralized Management.

Certified Internal Auditor (CIA)

An accountant who has satisfied specific requirements of the Institute of Internal Auditors (IIA). In addition to passing the uniform CIA examination administered by the IIA, the CIA must meet certain experiential, moral, and educational requirements.

Certified Management Accountant (CMA)

An accountant who has satisfied specific requirements of the Institute of Certified Management Accountants (ICMA). In addition to passing the uniform CMA examination administered by the ICMA, the CMA must meet certain experiential, moral, and educational requirements.

Certified Public Accountant (CPA)

An accountant who has satisfied the statutory and administrative requirements of his or her jurisdiction to be registered or licensed as a certified public accountant. In addition to passing the uniform CPA examination, he or she must meet certain experiential, moral, and educational requirements; these differ from jurisdiction to jurisdiction.

Chart of Accounts

A systematically arranged list of accounts applicable to a specific entity, giving account names and numbers (if any).

Combined Financial Statements

Financial statements that are combined for a commonly controlled group of companies, or a group of companies under common management influence where the units do not have an investment interest in each other. Intercompany transactions, balances, and profits or losses should be eliminated from combined financial statements.

Comfort Letter

A statement by the independent auditor of a company (usually in connection with a securities offering) in which negative assurance is expressed regarding certain matters of concern to the underwriter.

Committed Costs

Fixed costs arising from plant, equipment and other costs basic to the entity and thus affected primarily by long-term decisions about the desired level of capacity. Committed costs are unlikely to be changed in the short term.

Common Cost

The cost of resources employed jointly in the production of two or more outputs; the cost cannot be directly assigned to any one of those outputs. Assignment is made through one or more consistent allocation procedures. Also called Joint Cost. *Contrast with* Traceable Cost.

Common Stock Equivalent

1. A security whose primary value arises from the owner's ability to exchange it for common shares. This includes stock options, warrants, and convertible bonds or convertible preferred stock whose effective interest rate at the time of issue is less than two-thirds the average Aa corporate bond yield.

2. A security that is not in form a common stock but that usually contains provisions to enable its holder to become a common stockholder. Because of its terms and the circumstances under which it was issued, it is in substance equivalent to a common stock. (APB No.15)

Comparability

The quality of information that enables users to identify similarities in and differences between two sets of economic phenomena (SFAC No.2).

Completed-Contract Method

An accounting method that recognizes revenues and expenses for a contract only when it is finished. However, when a loss on the contract is expected, revenues and expenses are recognized during the period in which the loss is first forecast. *Contrast with* Percentage-of-Completion Method.

Compliance Audit

An audit of specific activities to determine that performance has been in accordance with some specific statutory requirement, contractual agreement, or stated description. For example, audit of a hospital for compliance with Medicare reimbursement regulations; audit by an IRS auditor for compliance with tax laws; audit of a computer service center for compliance with stated systems of internal control. *Contrast with* Performance Audit.

Composite Depreciation

Group depreciation of dissimilar items.

Compound Interest

Interest resulting from the periodic addition of simple interest to principal, establishing the new base as the principal for computation of interest for the next period.

Compound Interest Depreciation

See Annuity Method of Depreciation.

Comprehensive Budget

See Master Budget.

Comprehensive Income Concept

The change in equity (net assets) of an entity during a period from transactions and other events and circumstances from nonowner sources. It includes all changes in equity during a period except those resulting from investments by owners and distributions to owners (SFAC No.6).

Comptroller

An alternate spelling of Controller. Pronounced like controller.

Concepts, Accounting

Essential accounting ideas which permit the identification and classification of phenomena or other ideas. Thus, the concept "asset" separates assets from those items that are not assets.

Condensed Financial Statements

Financial statements in which less important detail is combined to provide a readily comprehensible financial picture.

Conservatism

1. An accounting concept that states that revenues are recognized only when they are reasonably certain, but expenses are recognized when they are reasonably probable.

2. A prudent reaction to uncertainty to try to ensure that uncertainty and risks inherent in business situations are adequately considered (SFAC No.2).

Consistency

1. Treatment of like transactions in the same way in consecutive periods so that financial statements will be more comparable than otherwise. Procedures, once adopted, should be followed from period to period by a reporting entity. If the procedure changes, the change must be disclosed if it is material.

2. Conformity from period to period with unchanging policies and procedures. (SFAC No.2)

Consolidated Financial Statements

Statements showing financial condition or operating results of two or more associated enterprises as they would appear if they were one entity. These statements generally aggregate the accounts of a parent company and the subsidiaries that it owns or controls. The preparation of a consolidated statement would eliminate intercompany accounts, investments, advances, sales, and other items.

Constant Cost

See Fixed Cost.

Constant Dollar Accounting

A method of reporting financial statement elements in dollars, each of which has the same (i.e., constant) general purchasing power, usually as of the date of the current financial statements.

Constraint

An activity, resource, or policy that limits or bounds the attainment of an objective.

Consumer Price Index (CPI)

A price index issued monthly by the Bureau of Labor Statistics of the U.S. Department of Labor. The index attempts to track the price level of a group of goods and services purchased by the average consumer. The CPI is a measure of the general purchasing power of the dollar and is often used in constant dollar accounting.

Continuous Budget

A moving projection of financial operations for a series of weeks, months, or quarters immediately ahead; at the end of each period, the portion of the projection then lapsed is removed and a new projection for a period of similar length is added to the series. Also called Multiple Budget or Rolling Budget.

Continuous Inventory Method

See Perpetual Inventory.

Contra Account

An account that is related to, and reduces the balance in, another account. For example, accumulated depreciation is a contra account for the asset account that shows the cost of the asset being depreciated.

Contract Costing

Measurement of the cost of the goods and services used in connection with performance of a contract.

Contributed Capital

The payments in cash or property made to a corporation by its shareholders *(a)* in exchange for capital stock, *(b)* in response to an assessment on the capital stock, or *(c)* as a gift. Often, though not necessarily, contributed capital equals capital stock plus other paid-in-capital.

Contribution Approach

A method of preparing income statements that separates variable costs from fixed costs to emphasize cost behavior patterns for purposes of planning and control. Contribution is measured by deducting variable costs from revenues.

Contribution Margin

The excess of sales revenues over variable costs; can be referred to as marginal income. Unless another meaning is stated, it is assumed to mean a dollar amount as a total, or it may be stated on a per unit basis. Also called Marginal Contribution. *See also* Contribution Margin Ratio; Unit Contribution.

Contribution Margin Ratio

Contribution margin divided by net sales. It can be measured for a single unit or for the total sales and total contribution margin of the entity.

Contribution Pricing

A method of establishing the price of the product based on variable costs and usually, a profit margin. These variable costs include variable manufacturing costs and selling and administrative expenses. *Contrast with* Full Cost Pricing.

Contribution Profitgraph

See Breakeven Chart.

Controllable Cost

A cost that can be influenced by the action of the responsible manager. The term always relates to a specified manager since all costs are controllable by someone.

Control System

A system intended to facilitate control.

Controller

The individual within an entity who is responsible for the management accounting function. Also called Comptroller.

Controllability Principle

The principle that a manager should be judged only on the performance of items over which the manager has some control.

Control Reports

Reports that compare actual performance in a responsibility center with what performance should have been under the circumstances prevailing. These reports identify reasons for the difference between actual and standard performance and, if feasible, quantify them.

Conversion

The process of converting raw materials and purchased parts into salable finished products.

Conversion Cost

The sum of direct labor, indirect materials, and factory overhead which is directly or indirectly used to transform raw materials and purchased parts into a salable finished product.

Co-Product

A product sharing production facilities with another product. For instance, if an apparel manufacturer produces dress shirts and sport shirts on the same line, these are coproducts. Coproducts are distinguished from joint products and byproducts which, by their very nature, must be produced together, such as the various grades of wood produced in a lumber mill.

Correlation

The extent or degree of statistical association among two or more variables.

Cost

1. In management accounting, a measurement in monetary terms, of the amount of resources used for some purpose. The term by itself is not operational. It becomes operational when modified by a term that defines the purpose, such as acquisition cost, incremental cost, or fixed cost.

2. In financial accounting, the sacrifice measured by the price paid or required to be paid, to acquire goods or services.

    The term "cost" is often used when referring to the valuation of a good or service acquired. When "cost" is used in this sense, a cost is an asset. When the benefits of the acquisition (the goods or services) expire, the cost becomes an expense or loss. *See also* Acquisition Cost.

Cost Absorption

See Absorption Costing.

Cost Accounting

The classification, recording, allocation, summarization, and reporting of current and prospective costs. Included in the field of cost accounting are the design and operation of cost systems and procedures; the methods of determining costs by departments, functions, responsibilities, activities, products, territories, periods, and other units; the methods of determining forecasted future costs, desired or standard costs, and historical costs; the comparison of costs of different periods, and of actual with estimated, budgeted, or standard costs; the comparison of alternative costs; and the presentation and interpretation of cost data to help management control current and future operations.

Cost Accounting Standards Board (CASB)

A board of five members established by the U.S. Congress to "promulgate cost accounting standards designed to achieve uniformity and consistency in the cost accounting principles followed by government contractors and subcontractors under federal contracts." The CASB existed from 1971 to 1980. It was reestablished in the Executive Branch in 1989.

Cost Accounting System

The system within an entity that provides for the collection and assignment of costs to cost objects.

Cost-Based Transfer Price

A transfer price based on costs with no allowances for profit.

Cost Behavior
>The change or lack of change in the amount of a cost item associated with changes in the level of activity.

Cost-Benefit Analysis
>*See* Benefit-Cost Analysis.

Cost Center
>An accounting device for collecting cost elements that have a common cause and that can be assigned to other cost objects according to a common basis of allocation. Many responsibility centers are also cost centers, but some cost centers (such as an occupancy cost center) may not be responsibility centers. Also called Cost Pool. *Contrast with* Responsibility Center.

Cost Concept
>A financial accounting concept stating that assets are normally accounted for at their acquisition costs, rather than at their market value. *See also* Cost Principle.

Cost Driver
>A measure of activity, such as direct labor hours, machine hours, beds occupied, computer time used, flight hours, miles driven, or contracts, that is a causal factor in the incurrence of cost to an entity. *See* Allocation Basis.

Cost-Effectiveness Analysis
>A comparison of costs with a measure of effectiveness, usually in the form of a ratio.

Cost Element
>*See* Element, Cost.

Cost Estimation
>An attempt to measure an historical cost relationship by specifying some underlying relationship between a dependent variable (cost) and one or more independent variables (direct labor hours, machine hours, units produced, etc.).

Costing
>The accumulation and assignment of costs to cost objects such as units of production, departments, or other activities for which management desires a separate measurement or evaluation.

Cost, Insurance, and Freight (CIF)
>A term indicating that the quoted price of a product includes charges for handling, insurance, and freight to a specified destination. Beyond this destination, the purchaser must assume any further handling, insurance, and transportation charges.

Cost Measurement

An assignment and accumulation of monetary amounts for the recognition, classification, and assignment of costs to goods and services acquired or used.

Cost Object

A function, organizational subdivision, contract, or other work unit for which cost data are desired and for which provision is made to accumulate and measure the cost of processes, products, jobs, capitalized projects, etc. (CASB).

Cost of Capital

1. A measure of the cost of using capital. A weighted average of the interest cost of debt capital and the implicit cost of equity capital. It is the minimum rate of return that must be earned on new investments that will not dilute the interests of the shareholders.

2. An imputed cost determined by applying a cost of money rate to a facility's capital (CASB).

Cost of Goods Manufactured

The cost of all goods whose production was completed during a specified accounting period. This includes units started in a prior period and completed in the current period. Costs associated with these goods include work-in-process costs accumulated in prior periods.

Cost of Goods Sold

See Cost of Sales.

Cost of Sales

The cost of products or services whose sales are reported as revenue; that is, cost of goods manufactured (or purchased) plus or minus change in finished goods (or merchandise) inventory. Also called Cost of Goods Sold.

Cost or Market

See Lower of Cost or Market.

Cost-Plus Pricing

A pricing practice in which the selling price is determined by adding a percentage or dollar mark-up to the cost of a product, however defined.

Cost Pool

See Cost Center.

Cost Principle

The accounting principle that holds that historical cost is the appropriate basis for the accounting recognition of asset acquisitions, service acquisitions, liabilities, and equity, as well as for the subsequent tracing of these costs.

Cost System

The system within an entity that collects and assigns costs to intermediate and final cost objects.

Cost to Buy

Direct and indirect costs, measured in terms of cash or cash equivalents, needed to acquire a product. This term often is used in make-or-buy and buy-or-lease analyses.

Cost/Volume/Profit Analysis

See Breakeven Analysis.

CPI

See Consumer Price Index.

Credit

The ability or right to buy or borrow in return for a promise to pay later.

Credit Line

An agreement by a bank to make loans, not to exceed a specified total amount, when needed by a customer. Usually involves a formal contract for which a fee of some sort is charged, but is sometimes informal and of indefinite span. Also the amount of credit a supplier would be willing to provide a customer.

Critical Path Method (CPM)

A method for locating paths formed from all tasks that enter as active elements into estimates of minimum completion times for a project.

Current Assets

Cash and other assets that are expected to be sold, converted into cash, or otherwise consumed during the normal operating cycle of a business or within one year, whichever is longer.

Current Budget

See Operating Budget.

Current Cost

The amount of cash that would have to be paid if the same asset—either an identical asset or an asset with equivalent productive capacity—were acquired currently. Current cost is computed by applying to historical cost one or more index numbers or by substituting for historical prices currently prevailing prices of equivalent goods and services.

Current Cost Accounting

A method of measuring and reporting assets, and expenses associated with the use or sale of assets, at their current cost or lower recoverable amount at the balance sheet date or at the date of use or sale. (SFAS No.33)

Current Exit Value

See Exit Value.

Current Liability

A liability required or expected to be discharged by using current assets within one year or the operating cycle, whichever is longer.

Current Operating Concept

The accounting concept that states that reported income for a period ought to reflect only ordinary, normal, and recurring operations of that period. A consequence is that extraordinary and nonrecurring items are entered directly into the retained earnings account. *Contrast with* All-Inclusive Income Concept and Comprehensive Income Concept.

Current Ratio

Current assets divided by current liabilities. A measure of short-term solvency. Also called Liquidity Ratio.

Current Realizable Value

See Exit Value.

Current Replacement Cost

An amount required currently to acquire *(a)* an asset that is identical (i.e., one of the same age, in the same condition, and with the same service potential) to the existing one, or *(b)* another asset (usually an improved asset) that can give the same service as the existing one.

Current Standard Cost

A standard cost based on anticipated outlays for goods and services and the best performance efficiency reasonably attainable under existing conditions of production.

Current Value Accounting

An accounting approach in which the valuation basis for all assets is current replacement cost (entry value), current exit value, or net realizable value (current exit value). The valuation basis for all liabilities is present value.

Currently Attainable Standard Cost

A standard cost that should be incurred under efficient operating conditions. It allows for ordinary equipment failure, normal lost time, and normal waste or spoilage.

Curvilinear Cost

A continuous, but not linear, functional relationship between activity levels and costs.

Cut-Off Date

The date selected for ceasing to record transactions applicable to a given accounting period.

Cut-Off Rate

See Hurdle Rate.

Cycle Count

A count completed within a given period of time, such as a month or a year. A cycle count is a method of physical inventory verification.

— D —

Data

Facts which, by analysis and association, may be developed into useful information.

Data Base

1. A set of data that is sufficient for a given purpose or for a given data-processing system.

2. A collection of data fundamental to a system or to an enterprise.

Days' Sales in Inventory

A measure of the age or adequacy of inventory. It is calculated by dividing the ending inventory balance, net of any reserves, by average daily cost of goods sold (or cost of goods used, if raw materials inventory is being evaluated) for the period.

Days' Sales Outstanding

A measure of the average number of days it takes to collect receivables (credit sales). It is compared with credit terms extended to customers to evaluate a firm's credit management. It is usually derived as receivables divided by average daily credit sales.

DCF

See Discounted Cash Flow.

DDB

See Double-Declining-Balance Depreciation.

Debt Ratio

A ratio expressing a relationship between debt and shareholders' equity; frequently total debt divided by the sum of debt and equity. Also called Debt/Equity Ratio. *See also* Total-Debt-to-Total-Asset Ratio.

Debt/Equity Ratio

See Debt Ratio

Decentralized Management

An organizational structure in which senior management maintains minimal direction and authority over operations and policies relating to identifiable separate activities and operations. Decentralized management allows great freedom for decision making at the level of lower responsibility centers. *Contrast with* Centralized Management.

Decision Model

A formal framework, which may involve quantitative analysis, for choosing among alternatives.

Decision Table

A systematic layout of alternative approaches to a problem, along with the action and resulting output estimated to flow from each alternative. A decision table can be an aid in decision making.

Decision Tree

A diagram in which the links leading from each node represent alternative choices for decision. Net payoffs (benefits less costs) are assigned to the terminal nodes that may be reached by chains from the initial node.

Defeasance

1. An action that is the economic equivalent to retiring a debt issue but does not require actually locating and retiring the bonds. It involves the establishment of a fund, the income and principal of which will pay interest on the bonds and retire them as they become due.

2. A situation in which a debtor irrevocably places cash or other assets in a trust to be used solely for satisfying scheduled payments of both interest and principal of a specific obligation; the possibility that the debtor will be required to make future payments with respect to that debt is remote. In this circumstance, debt is extinguished even though the debtor is not legally released from being the primary obligor under the debt obligation (SFAS No.76).

Deferred Charge

Expenditures that are not recognized as expenses of the period in which they were made. They are carried forward as assets that will become expenses in future periods. Examples include advance rent payments or insurance premiums. Also called Deferred Cost or Deferred Expense.

Deferred Cost

See Deferred Charge.

Deferred Credit

Generally, revenues received or recorded but not yet earned; can also be referred to as deferred revenue. Also used for certain liabilities, such as deferred income taxes payable and premium on bonds payable.

Deferred Expense

See Deferred Charge.

Departmental Budget

A budget of income and/or expenses applicable to a specific department, function, or process. Examples include a production cost budget, marketing expense budget, personnel budget, purchasing budget, and research and development budget. Also called Functional Budget.

Departmental Overhead

The overhead costs incurred by a department including costs charged to it by service departments.

Depletion

The process of allocating the cost of wasting assets (natural resources) to expense over the periods benefiting from the cost.

Depreciation

The process of allocating the cost of tangible assets to operations over periods benefited (expected life of the asset). Depreciation represents the gradual exhaustion of the service capacity of fixed assets through periodic charges to operations. It is the consequence of such factors as use, obsolescence, inadequacy, and wear.

Design Capacity

See Theoretical Capacity.

Differential Analysis

See Incremental Analysis.

Differential Cost

The cost difference expected if one course of action is adopted as compared with the costs of an alternative course of action; used in decision making. *Contrast with* Sunk Cost.

Direct Charging

The assignment of costs of goods and services to specific cost objects with a reasonable degree of certainty that these cost objects caused the amount so charged.

Direct Cost

A cost that is specifically identified with a single cost object.

Direct Costing

A type of product costing in which the cost assigned to a product includes only the cost of inputs that vary directly with the number of units produced and that are used in the production of the unit. Only the directly variable product costs are charged to inventory. Also called Variable Costing.

Direct Labor Cost

Labor amounts that are caused by a specific cost object.

Direct Labor Hour Rate

An overhead rate used to allocate factory overhead to the units of product produced. It is calculated by dividing the budgeted or estimated overhead cost by the budgeted number of direct labor hours.

Direct Labor Variance

See Variances.

Direct Material Cost

The quantity of material that is specifically identified with a cost object, priced at the unit price of direct material.

Direct Material Variances

See Variances.

Direct Write-off

The practice of charging an asset to expense or loss; that is, a debit to an expense (or loss) account and a credit to an asset account. The alternative is to charge the loss to an allowance account.

Disbursement

The payment of cash. *Contrast with* Expenditure.

Disclosure

An explanation or exhibit attached to a financial statement, or embodied in a report. A disclosure contains a fact, opinion, or detail required or helpful in the interpretation of the statement or report; it may be an expanded heading or a footnote.

Discount Factor

The present value of $1 that is expected to be received n years hence. It is derived from the formula $1/(1 + i)n$ in which i is the interest rate and n is the number of years in the future.

Discount Rate

The interest rate used to convert future cash flows to their present value.

Discounted Cash Flow (DCF)

A method of evaluating future net cash flows by discounting them to their present value. The two methods most commonly used are *(a)* Internal Rate of Return (IRR), and *(b)* Net Present Value (NPV) methods.

Discounted Payback Period

The amount of time expected to elapse before the discounted present value of cash inflows from a project equals the discounted present value of the cash outflows.

Discretionary Cost

A cost whose amount within a time period is governed by a management decision to incur the cost. Most discretionary costs are fixed in the short run, but vary over longer periods. Also called Managed Cost or Programmed Cost.

Discretionary Expense Center

A responsibility center in which most of the costs are discretionary; that is, the "right" amount to spend for its activities is determined through judgement rather than by an engineering study. Examples include personnel and legal departments.

Distribution Expense

Generally, any expense incurred in moving a product from the factory to the customer, including transportation and warehousing expenses. In some industries, it may also include the expense of selling and advertising.

Division

A more or less self-contained business unit that is part of a larger family of business units under common control.

Dollar Value LIFO Method

The LIFO accounting method that uses dollars as the unit of measure rather than quantity of specific goods. It compares the investment in inventory by groups at the beginning of the year when LIFO was adopted with the investment at the end of the year stated in terms of dollars of the same price level. There is no comparison of quantities of individual items, and the relative inventory quantities are determined only by aggregate dollar amounts allocated to the inventories.

Double-Declining-Balance Depreciation (DDB)

A form of declining-balance depreciation. The constant percentage applied to book value in computing the depreciation charge for the year is twice the fraction $1/n$, (n = the service life expressed as years). Salvage value is omitted from the depreciable amount.

Dual Transfer Price

A transfer pricing method in which the price charged to the buying division differs from that credited to the selling division. This method may be useful when the selling division has excess capacity and management does not want the buying division to bear the full cost.

— E —

Early Warning System

A reporting system designed to alert management to potential opportunities and problems before they significantly affect operations. Its purpose is to give management maximum preparation time to take advantage of opportunities or avoid or mitigate potential problems.

Earnings

The excess of revenue over expenses for an accounting period; the net increase in owners' equity of an entity from operating activities for an accounting period. Sometimes used synonymously with net earnings, net income, and income.

Earnings Cycle

See Cash Conversion Cycle.

Earnings Statement

See Income Statement.

Earnings Per Share

Net income to common shareholders (net income minus preferred dividends) divided by the average number of common shares outstanding. The reported amount may or may not include common share equivalents.

Economic Cost

See Opportunity Cost.

Economic Depreciation

The decline in current cost of an asset during a period.

Economic Life

The time period over which the use of an asset is economically justified. It is normally expressed as the period of time that revenues from the productivity of an asset exceed the cost of that productivity. Economic life is typically shorter than physical life and frequently shorter than useful life. *Contrast with* Physical Life.

Economic Order Quantity (EOQ)

The optimal amount of an item to order when inventory is reduced to the reorder point. If "A" represents the incremental cost of placing a single order, "D" represents the total demand for a period of time in units, and "H" represents the incremental holding cost during the period per unit of inventory, then the economic order quantity can be expressed as $Q = \sqrt{2AD/H}$. Also called Optimal Lot Size.

Economic Performance Report

A report of how well a responsibility center has performed as an economic entity. It requires the use of full costs rather than responsibility costs. The report is essentially the same as an income statement for a separate business.

Effective Interest Rate

The internal rate of return or yield to maturity of a bond at the time of issue. If the bond is issued for a price below par, the effective interest rate is higher than the coupon rate; if it is issued for a price above par, the effective interest rate is lower than the coupon rate.

Effectiveness

A measure of how well a responsibility center does what it is supposed to do; that is, the extent to which it produces the intended or expected output. Usually expressed as a comparative judgement (A is more effective than B), rather than as a numerical ratio or amount.

Efficiency

A measure showing the amount of output per unit of input. Often expressed as a percentage of ideal efficiency.

Efficiency Variance

See Variances.

Efficient Market Hypothesis

The hypothesis that security prices always fully reflect all publicly available information concerning traded securities. In efficient capital markets, security prices adjust rapidly and without bias to any newly released information. As a result, there is no way that the investor can outperform the market in an efficient market.

Element, Cost

A component part of costs classified according to the factors for which expenditure is incurred (such as labor and materials). Also called Natural Elements.

Engineered Standards

Cost standards determined by measurements and formulas developed by engineers or other experts rather than by estimates or analyses of historical performance. *Contrast with* Estimated Standards.

Entity

A person, partnership, corporation, or other unit, such as a division or a subsidiary. The accounting entity for which accounting statements are prepared may not be the same as the entity defined by law.

EOQ

See Economic Order Quantity.

Equity Method

A method of accounting for an investment in the stock of another company. A proportionate share of the earnings of the other company is debited to the investment account and credited to a revenue account as earned. When dividends are received, cash is debited and the investment account is credited. Used in reporting when the investor owns sufficient shares of stock of an unconsolidated company and can exercise significant influence over the actions of that company.

Equivalent Production

The number of units of completed output that requires the same costs as actually incurred for production of completed and partially completed units during a period. Used primarily in process costing calculations to measure the output of a continuous process in uniform terms. Also called Equivalent Units.

Equivalent Units

See Equivalent Production.

Escapable Cost

See Avoidable Cost.

Estimated Cost System

A method of accounting in which estimated costs, rather than actual costs, are the basis for credits to work-in-process accounts and debits to finished goods inventory.

Estimated Standards

Cost standards determined by judgmental estimates, history, or the experience in other cost centers. *Contrast with* Engineered Standards.

Estimation Sampling

A statistical technique that uses a representative sample to estimate certain population values.

Exception Reporting

Reporting that focuses on significant deviations from planned or expected performance. The objective is to alert management to correct unfavorable differences in performance.

Excess Capacity

Productive capacity in excess, on a relatively long-term basis, of that needed to supply the demand. It should be distinguished from idle capacity, which relates to short-term imbalances in operational schedules.

Exchange Gain or Loss

See Foreign Exchange Gain or Loss.

Exchange Rate

The price of one country's currency in terms of another country's currency.

Executory Contract

An exchange of promises which neither party has yet performed. An agreement providing for payment by a payor to a payee upon the performance of an act or service by the payee, such as a labor contract. Obligations under such contracts are not generally recognized either as assets or as liabilities.

Exit Value

The price or amount at which an asset could be sold or a liability extinguished. It may take the form of current exit value, expected exit value, or present value. Also called Current Realizable Value.

Expectancy Theory

A theory proposing that the motivation to engage in a certain behavior is determined by (a) a person's beliefs or "expectancies" about what outcomes are likely to result from that behavior, and (b) the attractiveness to the person of those outcomes as a result of the outcome's ability to satisfy the person's needs.

Expected Value

The weighted average of the outcomes of an action, in which the values of the possible outcomes are weighted by their probabilities.

Expenditure

Payment for goods or services received which may be made at either the time the goods or services are received or a later time. *Contrast with* Disbursement.

Expense

1. The cost of goods, services, and facilities used in the current accounting period. Expenses are deducted from revenue to determine net income. The expenses of a period are costs directly or indirectly associated with revenues of the period and cannot be associated with the revenues of future periods.

2. Outflows or other using up of assets or incurrences of liabilities (or a combination of both) during a period from delivering or producing goods, rendering services, or carrying out other activities (SFAC No.3).

Expense Center

A responsibility center in which financial performance is measured only by its expenses. *See* Profit Center.

Experience Curve

A function that shows how total costs (such as manufacturing, marketing, or distribution) per unit decline as cumulative units of output increase. A broader concept than learning curve.

Expired Cost

An expenditure from which no further benefit is anticipated; an expense; a cost absorbed over the period during which benefits were enjoyed or a loss incurred.

Extraordinary Items

1. Events and transactions that are unusual and that occur infrequently. The amount of a material extraordinary item, net of its income tax effect, is separated in the income statement from income from continuing operations.

2. Events and transactions that are distinguished by their unusual nature and the infrequency of their occurrence (APB No.30).

Extraordinary Repairs

Substantial expenditures made to restore a fixed asset to productive capacity after a breakdown due to accident, misuse, neglect, or excessive use. The effect of these expenditures is to restore excessive depreciation of assets over and above that covered by ordinary repairs. The expenditures restore an existing fixed asset to normal operating efficiency and are distinguished from betterment, additions, and improvements, which add to operating capacity.

— F —

Fair Market Value

The exchange price that would prevail for a good or service traded in an active market consisting of a large number of well-informed buyers and sellers dealing at arm's length. It may be estimated in the absence of monetary transactions.

Fairness

The ability of financial statements to convey unambiguous, unbiased information, particularly when accompanied by the representation of a public accountant in order to "present fairly" the detail required by convention for depicting financial position and operating results.

FASB

See Financial Accounting Standards Board.

Favorable Variance

A variance arising when actual or current performance exceeds expected performance; the excess of actual revenues over expected revenues; the excess of expected costs over actual cost.

Feedback

The process of informing users of information about how actual performance compares with the expected or desired level of performance. The hope is that the information will reinforce desired behavior and reduce undesirable behavior.

FIFO

See First-In First-Out.

Final Cost Object

A cost object that has allocated to it both direct and indirect costs; in the cost accumulation system, it is one of the final accumulation points (CASB).

Financial Accounting

The accounting for assets, liabilities, equities, revenues, and expenses of an entity, as a basis for reports to external parties on the entity's historical financial position, results of operations, and cash flow.

Financial Accounting Standards Board (FASB)

An independent board consisting of seven members that, since 1973, is responsible for establishing generally accepted accounting principles for the U.S. Its official pronouncements are called Statements of Financial Accounting Concepts (SFAC), Statements of Financial Accounting Standards (SFAS), Interpretations of Financial Accounting Standards, and Technical Bulletins (TB).

Financial Expense
> A cost incident to the financing of an entity as distinguished from one applicable to other operating activities.

Financial Lease
> *See* Capital Lease.

Financial Leverage
> The extent to which the assets of an entity are financed with debt. The higher the proportion of debt to equity, the greater the financial leverage.

Finished Goods Inventory
> The cost of completed product, ready for sale or other disposition.

First-In-First-Out (FIFO)
> An inventory flow assumption. Under FIFO, the ending inventory cost is computed from the most recent purchases and the cost of goods sold is computed from the oldest purchases, including beginning inventory.

Fiscal Year
> Any accounting period of 12 successive calendar months (or 52 weeks, or 365 days), used by an entity for financial reporting.

Fixed Asset
> A noncurrent, nonmonetary, tangible asset used in the normal operations of a business. *See* Property, Plant, and Equipment.

Fixed Budget
> A budget that states specified amounts of revenues and expenses. Also called a static budget. *Contrast with* Flexible Budget.

Fixed Charge Coverage Ratio
> 1. A ratio that measures the ability of an entity to meet its annual fixed charges, such as interest, rent, and sinking-fund payments, with its regular earnings. Calculated by dividing the sum of *(a)* net income before taxes, *(b)* interest, and *(c)* rent by the sum of *(a)* interest, *(b)* rent, and *(c)* sinking-fund payments adjusted for taxes (i.e., sinking-fund payments divided by 1 minus the tax rate).
>
> 2. The ratio of earnings to fixed charges or the ratio of earnings to combined fixed charges and preferred stock dividends. The term "fixed charges" means the total of *(a)* interest, *(b)* amortization of debt expense and discount or premium relating to any indebtedness, *(c)* such portion of rental expense as can be demonstrated to be representative of the interest factor in the particular case, and *(d)* preferred stock dividends (SEC).

Fixed Charges
> *See* Fixed Charge Coverage Ratio.

Fixed Cost
> A cost or expense element that does not vary with the volume of activity

in the short term. Also called Nonvariable Cost or Constant Cost. *Contrast with* Variable Cost.

Flexible Budget

A budget in which the budgeted amounts may be adjusted to any activity level. It may be a variable budget in which amounts are stated as a fixed amount plus a variable amount of activities. It may be a step budget, in which a series of detailed financial budgets is developed. From this series, a budget appropriate for any level of actual activity can be selected to evaluate actual expense and cost performance. *Contrast with* Fixed Budget.

Flexible Budget Variance

See Variances.

Flow Chart

A graphical representation of the flow of information; a process in which symbols are used to represent operations, data, reports generated, equipment, etc.

FOB

See Free on Board.

Forecast

A prediction of future events or conditions.

Foreign Currency Transaction

Transactions whose terms are denominated in a currency other than the entity's functional currency (SFAS No.52).

Foreign Currency Translation

The process of expressing in the reporting currency of the enterprise those amounts that are denominated or measured in a different currency (SFAS No.52).

Foreign Exchange Gain or Loss

The gain or loss in local currency from holding net foreign monetary items during a period in which the exchange rate changes. *See* Foreign Currency Translation; Foreign Currency Transaction.

Free on Board (FOB)

A term indicating that the invoiced cost to a purchaser includes the cost of delivery, at seller's risk, to an agreed point, beyond which all transportation and delivery costs and risks must be borne by the purchaser.

Freight In

Freight paid on incoming shipments. Usually treated as an element of cost of the goods received unless charged back to the seller.

Freight Out

The cost of freight or shipping incurred in selling products, generally treated by the seller as a selling expense in the period of sale, unless charged to the buyer.

Fringe Benefit

A pension provision, retirement allowance, insurance coverage, or other cost representing a present or future benefit to an employee, in addition to his or her wage or salary.

Full Absorption Costing

A costing system in which direct materials, direct labor, and all elements of manufacturing overhead (fixed and variable) are included (absorbed) in the cost of product.

Full Consolidation

See Consolidated Financial Statements.

Full Cost Pricing

See Contribution Pricing.

Full Costing

The allocation of all costs to products for the purposes of pricing, determining profitability of products, and valuing inventory. In the oil and gas industry, it is the capitalization and subsequent amortization of exploration costs, whether successful or not.

Fully Diluted Earnings Per Share

1. The amount of earnings that may be attributed to each share of common stock given the maximum amount of potential conversions of convertible securities, stock options, warrants, and stock purchase contracts outstanding.

2. The amount of current earnings per share reflecting the maximum dilution that would have resulted from conversions, exercises, and other contingent issuances that individually would have decreased earnings per share and, in the aggregate, would have had a dilutive effect. All such issuances are assumed to have taken place at the beginning of the period (or at the time the contingency arose, if later). (APB No.15)

Function

The general end or purpose to be accomplished by an organizational unit, such as administration, selling, or research. It can also be a group of related activities serving a common end.

Functional Accounting

An accounting system that accumulates costs and assets for each function performed.

Functional Budget

A budget in which expenses and revenues are classified according to functions.

Functional Costing
See Functional Accounting.

Functional Currency
The currency of the primary economic environment in which the entity operates; normally, this is the currency of the environment in which an entity primarily generates and expends cash. (SFAS No.52)

Fund
An asset or group of assets set aside for a specific purpose.

Funds Statement
See Cash Flow Statement.

Future Value
The value at a specified future date of a payment or series of payments calculated at an appropriate interest rate.

— G —

GAAP
See Generally Accepted Accounting Principles.

Gain (or Loss)
The net favorable (or unfavorable) effect of a nonoperating transaction or event. An increase (or decrease) in net assets and equity resulting from a nonoperating transaction or event in which the value of the consideration received exceeds (or is less than) the value of any consideration given. Some entities include gains and losses in revenues and expenses; others classify them as separate elements.

GASB
See Governmental Accounting Standards Board.

General and Administrative Expense
See Administrative Expense.

Generally Accepted Accounting Principles (GAAP)
The body of accounting rules, methods, and procedures endorsed by the accounting profession, either by convention or by authoritative literature, as a guide to the preparation of financial statements.

General Price Level Index
A measure of the aggregate prices of a wide range of goods and services in the economy relative to the prices during a base period.

General Purchasing Power Index
The command of a unit of currency over a wide range of goods and services in the economy. The general purchasing power is inversely related to changes in a General Price Level Index.

Goal

An objective established to coordinate and direct a group of individuals in the pursuit of desired ends.

Goal Congruence

A characteristic of a management control system that is structured so that the goals of individuals are consistent with the goals of the organization as a whole.

Going Concern

The assumption that, in the absence of evidence to the contrary, a firm will continue to exist until (at a minimum) it recovers the cost of its assets through revenues from customers.

Goods Available for Sale

The sum of beginning inventory plus all acquisitions of merchandise, either by purchase or by manufacture, during an accounting period.

Goods-In-Process

See Work-In-Process Inventory.

Goodwill

1. An asset account that appears as the result of acquiring a business entity for an amount in excess of the fair market value of the identifiable net assets.

2. In an economic sense, characteristics of a business entity, not individually identifiable, that permit it to earn above-normal returns on the identifiable assets.

Governmental Accounting Standards Board (GASB)

An independent body responsible, since 1982, for establishing U.S. accounting standards for state and local governmental units. It is part of the Financial Accounting Foundation, parallel to the FASB, and consists of five members.

Grant

A donation or contribution, usually by a superior governmental unit. Such grants may be for specific purposes, for a category, or for a whole block of related uses. Also called Grant-in-Aid.

Grant-in-Aid

See Grant.

Gross Margin

Net sales less cost of sales. Also called Gross Profit. *Contrast with* Profit Margin.

Gross Profit

See Gross Margin.

Gross Profit Ratio
Gross margin (or gross profit) divided by net sales.

Gross Revenue
Total revenue, not reduced by discounts for prompt payment, allowances, returns, or other adjustments. Also called Gross Sales.

Gross Sales
See Gross Revenue.

Group Depreciation
A method of depreciation in which assets with similar characteristics are grouped and a single depreciation expense amount is calculated for the group as a whole. No gain or loss is recognized on disposition of individual assets.

— H —

Half-Year Convention
The practice of taking half of the first year's depreciation in the year in which an asset was acquired. Also could mean a full year's depreciation is taken on assets acquired in the first-half year and none on those acquired in the last half-year.

Hedge
A method of reducing exposures to fluctuations in prices, exchange rates, or interest rates. They are often in the form of futures contracts or purchases and/or call options that transfer the risk of fluctuating prices to other parties. Also, a process of simultaneous sale and purchase of rights to goods and services for delivery at different dates.

High-Low Method
The process for estimating the fixed and variable components of a semivariable cost. The analyst selects one of the highest and one of the lowest pairs of total cost and activity. The variable component is then estimated by dividing the difference between the high total cost and the low total cost by the difference between the high activity and the low activity. The fixed component can be estimated as the difference between high total cost and the product of the variable component and either high or low activity; that is, the variation that the variable component cannot explain.

Highly Inflationary Economy
An economy that has cumulative inflation of approximately 100 percent or more over a three-year period (SFAS No.52).

Historical Cost
The amount originally paid for an asset, unadjusted for subsequent changes in value. Also called Acquisition Cost or Original Cost.

Historical Cost/Constant Dollar Accounting

Accounting based on historical cost valuations measured in dollars that have the same general purchasing power. Nonmonetary items are restated to reflect changes in the general purchasing power of the dollar since the time the specific assets were acquired or liabilities were incurred. A gain or loss is recognized on monetary items as they are held over time periods when the general purchasing power of the dollar changes.

Holding Gain or Loss

The difference between the end-of-period price and the beginning-of-period price of an asset held during the period. Realized holding gains and losses are not ordinarily reported separately in financial statements. Unrealized gains are not usually reflected in income at all. Some unrealized losses, such as on inventory or marketable securities, are reflected in income or equity as the loss occurs.

Human Resource Accounting

The process of accounting for the investment in and benefits derived from the use of human resources in a business. Not permitted in GAAP financial statements, and rarely used in management accounting.

Hurdle Rate

The minimum acceptable rate of return that companies will consider from a prospective project or investment, disregarding nonfinancial considerations. The hurdle rate is generally in excess of a company's cost of capital. Also called Required Rate of Return or Cut-Off Rate.

— I —

IAS

See International Accounting Standard

ICMA

See Institute of Certified Management Accountants.

Ideal Standard Cost

The minimum cost that would result if all productive inputs were combined to achieve the maximum feasible output. Because of its premise of technological perfection, such cost is meaningful only in a relative and not in a practical sense. Also called Perfection Standard Cost.

Idle Capacity

The difference between the available capacity of a production unit and its actual utilization level.

Idle Capacity Cost

The variance attributed to failure to use facilities at projected rates.

Idle Time

Lost time of workers or machines arising from lack of business or material, a breakdown of equipment, faulty supervision, or other causes whether or not avoidable.

IFAC

See International Federation of Accountants

Imposed Budget

A budget that is decided by higher level management without the participation of the manager of the unit to whom that budget relates. Also called Top-Down Budget. *Contrast with* Participative Budgeting.

Imputed Cost

A cost properly attributed to a cost object even though no actual transaction occurred that would be recognized in the accounting records.

Imputed Interest

An amount of interest assumed to be included in the face amount due on a note when that note does not carry an explicit rate of interest, or carries a rate that is lower than market.

Improvement

An expenditure that extends the useful life of an asset, or increases the functions that it performs, beyond the life or function of the asset at the time it was acquired. An improvement is capitalized. *Contrast with* Maintenance; Repair.

Income

The difference between revenues and expenses.

Income from Continuing Operations

Revenues, expenses, and changes in accounting estimates less applicable income taxes for the accounting period—except for results from discontinued operations (including income from operations net of applicable income taxes and gain/loss net of applicable income taxes on the disposal of a discontinued segment); extraordinary gains (losses) net of applicable income taxes; and the cumulative effect of a change in accounting principle. Also called Net Operating Profit (APB No.30).

Income from Discontinued Operations

Income (loss) less applicable income taxes from the operations of a segment of the business that has been discontinued during the period (or that is in the process of being discontinued). The amount is reported on a separate line of the income statement (separated also from the gain or loss from disposal of the segment) between income from continuing operations and extraordinary items (APB No.30).

Income Statement

A financial statement that reports revenues, expenses, gains, and losses for an accounting period, usually compared with amounts in one or more earlier periods. Also called Earnings Statement.

Income Tax

An annual tax levied by the federal government and other governments based on income.

Incremental Analysis

A method of analyzing managerial decision problems that emphasizes incremental rather than the total costs and benefits associated with an action (or set of alternative actions). Also called Marginal Analysis or Differential Analysis.

Incremental Budgeting

A budgeting process in which justification is generally required only for increments (or decrements) to previous budgeting levels.

Incremental Cost

1. The difference in cash flow, both as to amount and as to timing, between two alternative courses of action.

2. The additional cost caused by some specific project or group of projects as compared with the cost of some specific base case or reference standard. Also called Marginal Cost.

Incremental Margin

The difference between incremental revenues and incremental expenses (or incremental costs).

Incremental Revenue

The additional revenue, either as to amount or as to timing, that results from pursuing an alternative course of action. Also called Marginal Revenue.

Incurred Cost

A cost arising from cash paid out or an obligation to pay for an acquired asset or service; a loss that has been sustained and must be paid for.

Indebtedness

A debt owing; any liability; an aggregate of liabilities.

Independent Research and Development Cost (IR&D)

As used in government contracting, the cost of effort which is neither sponsored by a grant, nor required in the performance of a contract, and which falls within any of the following three areas: *(a)* basic and applied research, *(b)* development, and *(c)* systems and other concept formulation studies (CASB).

Indirect Cost

1. A cost item that is common to two or more cost objects and cannot be identified specifically with any one of these cost objects in an economically feasible manner. All costs other than direct materials and direct labor. Also called Overhead Cost and Burden.

2. Any cost not directly identified with a single final cost object, but identified with two or more final cost objects or with at least one intermediate cost object (CASB).

Indirect Cost Pool

A grouping of incurred costs identified with two or more cost objects but not identified specifically with a single final cost object (CASB).

Indirect Labor Cost

Labor costs that are not identifiable directly with a single cost object, such as supervision. (Often used in the narrower sense of labor not specifically used on a product.)

Indirect Materials Cost

The cost of materials that do not enter directly into the production of a product. Examples are supplies consumed in cleaning, oiling, and maintenance generally; replacement of small parts.

Indirect Method (Statement of Cash Flows)

A method of calculating cash flows that starts with net income and adjusts for noncash changes. This method may be used to prepare the statement of cash flows.

Indirect Production Cost

A production cost that is not assignable directly to a single cost object.

Institute of Certified Management Accountants (ICMA)

An affiliate of the National Association of Accountants that administers the program leading to the Certified Management Accountant designation. The ICMA evaluates credentials of CMA candidates, develops and conducts examinations, grants certificates to successful candidates and monitors their compliance with continuing professional education requirements.

Intangible Asset

A type of noncurrent asset that has no physical substance and whose value comes from rights or advantages conferred upon the owner. Examples are patents, copyrights, trademarks, brand names, licenses, and goodwill. Generally, accounting recognition is given to intangible assets that are acquired as opposed to those that are developed internally. The consumption of an intangible asset is recognized through amortization.

Interdivisional Profit

The difference between the selling price and the cost of products sold by one division to another division of the same entity. The selling price is generally referred to as the transfer price.

Interest

The cost incurred or amount earned for the use of borrowed capital. Less commonly, the cost incurred for the use of both borrowed capital and equity capital.

Interim Financial Reports

Financial statements prepared for periods shorter than one year, such as monthly or quarterly.

Internal Accounting Control

Procedures and practices designed to give management reasonable assurance that assets are safeguarded from unauthorized use or disposition and that financial controls are sufficient for the preparation of reliable financial statements.

Internal Audit

An appraisal activity within an entity that measures and reports on the extent to which various organizational policies are followed and goals are met. Internal auditing reviews and analyzes the integrity of financial, operating, and systems activities, or any other activity that management requires. Internal auditing is concerned with the effectiveness and reliability of operating reports to management and functions primarily as a service to management.

Internal Control

The whole system of controls (financial and otherwise) established by management to carry on the business of the enterprise in an orderly and efficient manner, to ensure adherence to management policies, safeguard the assets, and ensure as far as possible the completeness and accuracy of the records.

Internal Rate of Return (IRR)

The discount rate that equates the net present value of a stream of cash outflows and inflows to zero. Also called Time-Adjusted Rate of Return.

International Accounting Standard (IAS)

A standard issued by the International Accounting Standards Committee (IASC).

International Federation of Accountants (IFAC)

An entity whose purpose is to develop and enhance a coordinated worldwide accounting profession with harmonized standards.

Interdivision Transfer

A product that is transferred from one division (the selling division) to another division (the buying division) of the same company. Also called an Intracompany Transfer.

Intracompany Profit

The profit on sales from one company to another within a consolidated or affiliated group (SFAS No.71).

Intracompany Transfer

See Interdivision Transfer.

Inventoriable Cost

A cost incurred that is included in the inventory value of purchased or manufactured products. It is a product cost (asset), as opposed to a period cost (expense).

Inventory

1. As a noun raw materials, supplies, goods on hand, goods in process of manufacture, and goods in transit and owned, in storage, or consigned to others.

2. As a verb to account, list, and price items in inventory; to take a physical inventory.

Inventory Control

An approach to safeguarding and assuring the effective and efficient acquisition and use of inventory. Inventory control systematically relates accounting documents to a physical review of factory and distribution operations.

Inventory Pricing

See Inventory Valuation.

Inventory Profit

That portion of profit determined on the basis of historical cost (especially FIFO and average cost) attributable to the increase in replacement cost of the inventory up to the time of sale.

Inventory Turnover

A ratio that measures the number of times a firm's average inventory is sold during a year. It is calculated by dividing cost of sales by average inventory.

Inventory Valuation

The measurement of the cost assigned to items in inventory.

Invested Capital

The amount of capital contributed to a business by equity investors, either directly or through the retention of earnings.

Investment

An expenditure to acquire property or other assets in order to produce revenue; the asset so acquired; i.e., an expenditure made in anticipation of future income.

Investment Center

A responsibility center whose performance is measured in the amount of income it earns relative to the investment in its assets.

Investment Turnover Ratio

The ratio of annual revenue to total assets.

IRR

See Internal Rate of Return.

— J —

JIT

See Just-In-Time Inventory System.

Job Cost Sheet

A detailed record of the amount of material, labor, and overhead costs incurred on a specific job or job lot.

Job Order Costing

A method of cost accounting that accumulates costs for individual jobs or lots. A job may be a manufactured item or a service, such as the repair of an automobile or the treatment of a patient in a hospital. *Contrast with* Process Costing.

Joint Cost

The cost of simultaneously producing or otherwise acquiring two or more products (joint products) that must, by the nature of the process, be produced or acquired together. The cost of beef and hides of cattle are joint costs. Also called Common Cost. *Contrast with* Traceable Cost..

Joint Product

Two or more products so related that one cannot be produced without producing the others. All the products have relatively substantial value and are produced simultaneously by the same process up to a split-off point.

Joint Variance

See Variances.

Joint Venture

1. An arrangement whereby two or more parties undertake an economic activity that is contractually subject to joint control (IAS Exposure Draft No.35).

2. "Corporate joint venture" refers to a corporation owned and operated by a small group of businesses (the "joint venture") as a separate and specific business or project for the mutual benefit of the members of the group (APB No.18).

Journal

A record of original entry that records transactions in chronological sequence.

Journal Voucher

A document that describes (and sometimes authorizes) an individual transaction, leading to an entry in a journal.

Justification

A narrative analysis of the need for funds.

Just-In-Time (JIT) Inventory System

A system whose purpose is to produce or procure the right parts at the right time, as they are needed rather than when they can be made. It is a "pull" manufacturing system that moves goods through a shop based on end-unit demand. Just-In-Time focuses on maintaining a constant flow of components and products rather than batches of work-in-process inventory.

— L —

Labor

Services provided by an entity's employees. It is distinguished from services, which are provided by external parties.

Labor Related Costs

Costs that are related to the number or cost of employees, other than the compensation earned by them. Examples are social security taxes, pension costs, and other fringe benefits paid by the employer.

Labor Time Variance

See Labor Efficiency Variance.

Last-In-First-Out (LIFO)

A method of inventory valuation and costing. It is based on the assumption that costs of the earliest inventory purchases are applicable to the goods on hand, and that the costs of the latest inventory acquired is applicable to cost of sales. LIFO attempts to match current costs of obtaining inventory against current revenues.

Lead Time

The time expected to elapse between the date an order is placed and the date the goods or services are received.

Learning Curve

A mathematical expression of the phenomenon that incremental unit costs to produce decrease as managers and labor gain experience from practice and as better methods are developed.

Least-Squares Method

A statistical method for defining a line that reflects the relationship between variables, such that the sum of the squares of the vertical distances from the points to the line is less than the sum of squares would be from any other straight line. This method is sometimes used to analyze fixed/variable cost behavior, with each point on a graph representing the cost/volume relationship for an individual time period. Also called Linear Regression.

Ledger
A book of accounts; any book of final entry.

Legal Entity
An entity, such as a partnership, corporation, or trust that is defined as such as a matter of law. *Contrast with* Accounting Entity.

Leveraged Lease
A lease classified and accounted for as a single net investment by the lessor. A leveraged lease *(a)* involves three parties (a lessee, a long-term creditor, and a lessor); *(b)* involves financing that is nonrecourse to the general credit of the lessor; and *(c)* requires an initial net investment by the lessor that typically declines during the early years of the lease and rises during the later years of the lease.

Liability
Probable future sacrifices of economic benefits arising from present obligations of a particular entity to transfer assets or provide services to other entities in the future as a result of past transactions or events. The amount that an entity owes to an outside party (SFAC No.3).

Liability Method
An asset and liability approach for financial accounting and reporting for income taxes, focusing on the balance sheet. Income tax expense shown in the financial statements represents the taxes paid or to be paid on pretax income for the period shown in those statements. Differences between the tax expense shown and taxes currently payable resulting from temporary differences are deemed (and presented in the balance sheet as) liabilities (for taxes payable in the future) or assets (for taxes reduced in the future). Deferred taxes under the liability method are computed at the rates expected to be in effect when the timing differences are expected to be included in the taxable income. Adjustments of the liability or asset accounts for deferred taxes are made whenever tax rates change.

Life Cycle Accounting
The accumulation of costs for activities that occur over the entire life cycle of a product, from inception to abandonment by the consumer. It is a measure of the total costs over the product's life including design and development, acquisition, operation, maintenance, and service. Service costs include marketing, distribution, administration, and after-sales service costs.

LIFO
See Last-In-First-Out.

LIFO Layer

A quantity of inventory acquired at approximately the same time and at the same unit cost. It is used to find the cost of sales under the LIFO method and represents an increase in inventory levels since LIFO was first adopted.

LIFO, Dollar Value Method

See Dollar Value LIFO Method.

LIFO Reserve

An unrealized holding gain in ending inventory, measured as the difference between LIFO and FIFO costs.

Linear Assumption

The assumption that the relationship between costs and volume is linear. Although not necessarily precisely correct, the assumption is usually close enough to reality to express the relationship by a straight line, rather than using curves, which are more complex.

Linear Programming

A mathematical tool used to find the combination of products that will maximize profits or minimize costs. It is used when there are several products that can be produced, but there are constraints on either the resources available in the production processes or on maximum and minimum product quantities required.

Linear Regression

See Least-Squares Method.

Line of Business

A set of operations directed to the production and sale of a distinctive type of goods or services to customers.

Line of Business Reporting

See Segment Reporting.

Line Item Budget

A budget that classifies items of expense by the nature of the expense, such as salaries, fringe benefits, travel, etc. *Contrast with* Program Budget.

Liquidation Value

The market price in cash or cash equivalents that could be obtained in the event of an immediate requirement to discontinue ownership of an asset. *See* Abandonment Value.

Liquidity

A measure of the relationship between cash or near-cash assets to an entity's need for these items in order to pay maturing obligations.

Liquidity Ratio

See Current Ratio.

Logistics Cost

The cost of planning, implementing, and controlling all inbound, in-process, and outbound goods and inventory from the point of origin to the point of consumption. Logistics consists of the integration of purchasing, transportation, and warehousing functions to provide the most efficient flow of materials and products in the most cost-effective manner in meeting customer needs.

Long-Range Plan

A plan or program prepared for a period of several future years, usually at least 3 years, and in some cases as long as 40 years.

Loss

See Gain (or Loss).

Lower of Cost or Market

A method of valuation that results in an asset being valued at either acquisition cost or market value, whichever is lower. Market value is defined as current replacement cost (whether by purchase or reproduction) or net realizable value, whichever is lower.

Lump-Sum Purchase

See Basket Purchase.

— M —

Machine Hour Rate

A rate for allocating costs to cost objects based on the number of hours that a machine is used in producing that cost object.

Maintenance

Expenditures necessary to achieve the originally anticipated useful life of a fixed asset. Maintenance restores or prevents destruction of parts of a property that deteriorate faster than the whole property unit.

Make-or-Buy Decision

The decision either to produce a good or service with an entity's own resources or to buy it from an outside supplier.

Managed Cost

See Discretionary Cost.

Management Accounting

The process of identification, measurement, accumulation, analysis, preparation, interpretation, and communication of financial information used by management to plan, evaluate, and control within an entity and to assure appropriate use of and accountability for its resources. Management accounting also comprises the preparation of financial reports for nonmanagement groups such as shareholders, creditors, regulatory agencies, and tax authorities.

Management Audit

An independent examination and evaluation of the actions of management according to various standards of good performance.

Management by Exception

A principle of management that states that attention should be focused primarily on those aspects of actual performance that differ significantly from expected performance.

Management by Objectives (MBO)

The joint formulation by a manager and his or her superior of goals and plans for achieving the overall objective of the unit for a forthcoming period. The manager's actual performance is then measured in relation to the agreed upon goals and plans.

Management Control

An organized, integrated process and structure through which management attempts to achieve enterprise goals effectively and efficiently. It encompasses an entity in its entirety, provides well-defined units of measurement and evaluation, and emphasizes continuous comparisons of actual with planned or budgeted performance.

Management Information System (MIS)

A system that provides past, present, and prospective information about internal operations and external intelligence. It supports the planning, controlling, and operational functions of an entity by providing timely information to help decision makers.

Manufacturing Cost

See Production Cost.

Manufacturing Overhead Cost

See Production Overhead Cost.

Manufacturing Resource Planning II (MRPII)

A system that integrates all the functions required to operate a successful manufacturing operation. The operation begins with a timed master production schedule derived from a realistic sales forecast. The system will plan the entire manufacturing process by taking into account inventory levels, lead times, capacity, rejections, safety stocks, etc., from the ordering of materials to the delivery of finished goods to the warehouse.

Margin of Safety

The excess of actual or budgeted sales over breakeven sales. Usually expressed in dollars; may be expressed in units of product or a ratio.

Marginal Analysis

See Incremental Analysis.

Marginal Contribution

See Contribution Margin.

Marginal Cost

See Incremental Cost.

Marginal Revenue

See Incremental Revenue.

Marketable Securities

A balance sheet title for negotiable financial instruments, excluding investments accounted for by the equity method. Marketable securities may be classified as current or noncurrent assets.

Market-Based Transfer Price

A transfer price based on the price found in the external market, rather than on internal company data.

Marketing Cost

The cost of locating customers, persuading them to buy, delivering the products, and collecting sales proceeds. Also called Selling Cost.

Markon

See Markup.

Markup

The relationship between the cost and selling price of a product. The term markon is also used, sometimes as a synonym and other times for a different relationship. For example, a markon (or markup) of 40% can either mean that the selling price is 140% of the cost or the cost is 60% of the selling price.

Master Budget

A budget that consolidates all budgets into an overall plan and control document, typically encompassing one year. It also includes *pro forma* financial statements—including an income statement, balance sheet, and cash flow statement—as well as operating and sales budgets. It may also include all or part(s) of the capital budget that are to be accommodated during the budget period so that it can serve as a basis for coordinating all activities. Also called Comprehensive Budget.

Matching

The process of recognizing cost expirations (expenses) in the same accounting period as that in which the related revenues are recognized.

Materiality

The concept that accounting should separately recognize only those events that are relatively important for understanding an entity's statements. Statement of Financial Accounting Concepts No. 2 states that accounting information is material if "the judgment of a reasonable person relying on the information would have been changed or influenced by the omission or misstatement."

Material Requirement Planning (MRP)
A system that translates a production schedule into requirements for each component needed to meet that schedule.

Material Price Variance
See Variances.

Material Quantity Variance
See Variances.

MBO
See Management by Objectives.

Merchandise Budget
The planning of sales, inventories, reductions, markdowns, employee discounts, stock shortages, purchases, freight-in, handling, storage, and gross margins for a merchandising enterprise.

Method Variance
A change in production method or technique that causes a variance from standard cost.

MIS
See Management Information System.

Mixed Cost
A cost composed of fixed and variable elements.

Mix Variance
See Variances.

Monetary Items
1. Monetary assets or liabilities, fixed in terms of currency; usually contractual claims to fixed amounts of money. Examples of monetary assets and liabilities are cash, accounts and notes receivable, and accounts and notes payable. Under certain circumstances, a monetary asset or liability may become nonmonetary. For example, a marketable bond being held to maturity would qualify as a monetary asset because its face amount is fixed in terms of currency. However, if the same bond were being held for speculation, it would possibly be classified as a nonmonetary asset because the amount that would be received when the bond is sold is not determinable and therefore not fixed in terms of currency.

2. Money or a claim (an obligation) to receive (or pay) a sum of money, the amount of which is fixed or determinable without reference to future prices of specific goods and services (SFAS No.89).

Moving Average Method

An inventory costing method in which the average cost of the units on hand is recomputed immediately after each purchase of additional units. Subsequent removal of units from stock are valued at this new average price until it is changed by the next purchase.

MRP

See Material Requirement Planning.

MRP II

See Manufacturing Resource Planning II.

Multiple Budget

See Continuous Budget.

— N —

Natural Elements

See Element, Cost.

Negative Goodwill

The difference between the purchase price of an acquired company and the higher sum of the fair market value of the identifiable net assets acquired. APB Opinion No. 16 requires the valuation of acquired noncurrent assets (except investments in marketable securities) be reduced until the purchase price equals the adjusted valuation of the fair market value of the net assets acquired.

Net Assets

Total assets less total liabilities. It is also equal to owners' equity.

Net Book Value

See Book Value.

Net Earnings

See Net Income.

Net Income

Income for a period after subtracting expenses from all sources for that period. Also called Net Earnings.

Net Operating Profit

See Income from Continuing Operations.

Net Present Value (NPV)

The difference between the present value of all cash inflows from a project or investment and the present value of all cash outflows required to obtain the investment, or to finance the project at a given discount rate.

Net Profit Margin

The profit margin on sales, computed by dividing net earnings by sales revenue. It indicates the profit per dollar of sales.

Net Realizable Value

1. As used for inventories, the estimated selling price in the ordinary course of business less the reasonably predictable cost of completion and disposal.

2. As used for receivables, the net amount of accounts receivable after deducting the allowance for bad debts.

Net Sales

Gross sales less returns and allowances, freight-out, and often cash discounts allowed. In recent years, the trend has been to report as net sales the net amount finally received, or expected to be received, from the customer.

Net Working Capital

See Working Capital.

Net Worth

An obsolete term for owners' equity.

Noncurrent Assets

All assets other than current assets.

Noncontrollable Cost

A cost that is not controllable by a particular manager.

Nonmanufacturing Costs

All costs incurred other than those to produce goods.

Nonmonetary Items

Assets and Liabilities other than monetary ones. Examples are inventories; investment in common stocks; property, plant, and equipment; and liabilities for rent collected in advance (APB No.29).

Nonvariable Cost

See Fixed Cost.

Normal Capacity

The average output level required to meet customer demand over several periods of time.

Normal Costing

The process whereby cost objects are assigned the sum of direct materials and labor resources consumed plus an allocation of overhead based on normal capacity.

Normal Spoilage

Costs incurred because of spoilage that cannot be eliminated in a cost effective manner; these costs should be assigned to cost objects as elements of product cost.

Normal Standard Cost

The cost expected to be incurred under reasonably efficient operating conditions with adequate provisions for an average amount of rework, spoilage, and the like.

NPV

See Net Present Value.

— O —

Objectivity

A trait of financial reporting that emphasizes the verifiable, factual nature of events or transactions and minimizes personal judgments in the measurement process.

Obsolescence

The loss in usefulness of an asset caused by progress of the arts or by changing laws or social customs. It is distinguished from exhaustion, wear and tear, and deterioration in that these terms refer to a functional loss arising out of a change in physical condition.

Operating Budget

A plan for the revenues and expenses associated with operating activities of a given period. Also called Current Budget. *Contrast with* Capital Budget.

Operating Capacity

The number of units of output that plants can produce when working on a normal operating schedule. The company's sales are often stated as a percentage of operating capacity.

Operating Cycle

The average time between the acquisition of materials or services and the final cash realization from the sale of products (SFAS Nos.6 & 78).

Operating Expenses

Expenses incurred in the course of ordinary activities of an entity. Frequently, this classification includes only selling, general, and administrative expenses, thereby excluding cost of goods sold, interest, and income tax expenses.

Operating Lease

A lease accounted for by the lessee without showing an asset for the lease rights (leasehold) or a liability for the lease payment obligations. Rental payments of the lessee are shown as expenses of the period. The asset remains on the lessor's books, where rental collections appear as revenues.

Operating Leverage

The extent to which a firm's operations involve fixed operating expenses (fixed manufacturing, selling, and administrative expenses). Being highly leveraged means that a relatively small change in sales results in a large change in net operating income.

Operational Auditing

A process of obtaining and evaluating evidence about operating procedures and events as compared with established criteria of good performance. Operational auditing may result in recommendations to improve the effectiveness and efficiency of operations and internal controls.

Operations Research

An analysis of an entity's operations involving the application of scientific techniques, often in the form of mathematical formulas or models, to solve operating problems or improve operating efficiency.

Opportunity Cost

The value of the alternatives forgone by adopting a particular strategy or employing resources in a specific manner. Also called Alternative Cost or Economic Cost.

Optimal Lot Size

See Economic Order Quantity.

Option

A legal right to buy or sell something at a specified price, usually within a specified period of time.

Ordering Cost

The cost of preparing a purchase order, and the special processing and receiving costs related to the number of orders processed.

Original Cost

See Acquisition Cost and Historical Cost.

Out-of-Pocket Cost

A cost that requires the use of cash, either immediately or in the near future.

Out-of-Stock Cost

The estimated decrease in future profit as a result of losing customers because quantities of inventory currently on hand are insufficient to meet customers' demands.

Overabsorbed Overhead

See Overapplied Overhead.

Overapplied Overhead

The excess of overhead applied to production over the actual expenses incurred. Also called Overabsorbed Overhead.

Overhead Cost

See Indirect Cost.

Overhead Rate

The ratio of overhead costs for a period of time related to the amount of some measurable causal factor during the same period of time. For example, the expected or standard overhead costs divided by the expected or standard productive effort. Also called Burden Rate.

— P —

Paid-In Capital

The amount paid by investors in exchange for stock. The amount in excess of the stock's par or stated value is called additional paid-in capital.

Par Value

1. The specific amount printed on the face of some stock certificates.

2. A measure of minimum legal capital of corporations required by some state laws.

Participative Budgeting

A type of budgeting which allows managers to participate in the preparation of those budgets applying to them. *Contrast with* Imposed Budgeting.

Payback Period

The period of time necessary to recoup the cash cost of an investment from the cash inflows attributable to the investment.

Payback Reciprocal

One divided by the payback period. This number approximates the internal rate of return on a project when the project life is more than twice the payback period, and the cash inflows are approximately equal in each period throughout the payback period.

Payroll Cost

Payments to employees for labor services. Payroll costs are usually composed of two components. One includes cash paid to employees and amounts withheld from employees' paychecks such as income taxes, Federal Insurance Contributions Act (Social Security), union dues, as well as payments to retirement or other plans that will result in future cash payments to employees. The other component of payroll costs is taxes and tax-like payments an employer incurs as a legal condition of employment. Examples include the employer's share of FICA and unemployment insurance paid to state and federal governments.

Pension Expense

The cost of a pension plan for a given period. The following components are included in the net pension cost recognized for a period by an employer sponsoring a defined benefit pension plan:

1. Service cost component (of net periodic pension cost), which is the actuarial present value of benefits attributed by the pension benefit formula to employee services rendered by employees during that period. The service cost component is a portion of the projected benefit obligation and is unaffected by the funded status of the plan.

2. Interest cost.

3. Actual return on plan assets component (of net periodic pension cost), which is the difference between the fair value of plan assets at the end of the period and the fair value at the beginning of the period, as adjusted for contributions and payments of benefits during the period.

4. Amortization of unrecognized prior service costs.

5. Gain or loss (including the effects of changes in assumptions) to the extent recognized.

6. Amortization of the unrecognized net obligation (and loss or cost) or unrecognized net asset (and gain) existing at the date of initial application of this section (SFAS No.87).

Percentage-of-Completion Method
A method of measuring income for a given accounting period on a contract, such as a construction contract, that is worked on over several periods. Revenue is measured as the amount earned in the period for the work done in that period. Expense is measured by relating the percentage of cost incurred for the work done in the period to the total estimated cost of the project. *Contrast with* the Completed-Contract Method.

Perfection Standard Cost
See Ideal Standard Cost.

Performance
A general term applied to part or all of the conduct or activities of an entity over a period of time, often with reference to some standard such as past or projected costs, an efficiency base, management responsibility or accountability.

Performance Audit
An audit to evaluate the efficiency and effectiveness of activities conducted. *Contrast with* Compliance Audit.

Performance Budget
A budget classified by activities to be performed and by personal responsibility against which the results of actual performance are compared.

Performance Measurement
A quantification of the effectiveness and efficiency with which the objectives of a responsibility center have been accomplished.

Performance Report

A report comparing actual performance with expected or historical performance. The purpose of the report is to identify significant differences as a basis for management consideration and action.

Period Cost

An expenditure or loss that is charged to the current period rather than as a cost of the products produced in that period. *Contrast with* Product Cost.

Periodic Inventory

A method for determining inventory values dependent upon a physical inventory taken at the end of each period, with the resulting inventory value entered on the books; additions to inventory during the period are charged to a purchases account and not to inventory, as in a perpetual inventory system. Inventory book value does not change until the next physical inventory is made. Cost of sales for a period is calculated by *(a)* adding beginning inventory value (the physical inventory value determined at the end of the last period) to the period's net purchases or costs of goods manufactured, and *(b)* subtracting the ending inventory value derived from the end-of-period physical inventory.

Perpetual Inventory

A record that shows additions and deletions for an item of inventory; therefore, the amount on hand at any time. With a perpetual inventory, cost of sales is the total of deductions from inventory during the period.

PERT

See Program Evaluation and Review Technique.

PERT Cost

A PERT system that contains the estimated costs and estimated times of each work package. *See* Program Evaluation and Review Technique.

Physical Budget

A budget expressed in units of materials, number of employees, or number of labor hours or service units, rather than in monetary amounts.

Physical Control

The application of physical internal control procedures to the resources of an entity in order to ensure their efficient and effective use in accordance with policy.

Physical Inventory

A physical count (or other physical measure) of all inventories on hand. The physical inventory verifies the book balance and is usually an annual procedure.

Physical Life

An estimate of the period over which a depreciable asset will maintain its functional capacity whether or not it will be so used by the entity. *Contrast with* Economic Life.

Planning and Control Process

General name for the techniques of management comprising the setting of organizational goals and strategic plans; capital budgeting; operations budgeting, comparison of plans with actual results; performance evaluation and corrective action; and revisions of goals, plans, and budgets.

Planning, Programming, and Budgeting System (PPBS)

A comprehensive management system designed to *(a)* improve policy making and the allocation of resources, especially in the public sector, and *(b)* plan programs that will be consistent with specific objectives, analyzing costs and effectiveness of programs, and continuously reexamining program results in relation to anticipated outcomes to determine the need for changes in established programs and objectives.

Plant

Land, buildings, machinery, equipment, furniture and other fixed assets used to produce products.

Plantwide Overhead Rate

A single overhead rate for an entire plant used to allocate overhead costs to products produced in the plant.

Pooling-of-Interests Method

A method of accounting for a business combination in which the effect of transactions between the entities is eliminated: the remaining balances in the balance sheet accounts of the separate entities are then added together to produce the balance sheet. *Contrast with* Purchase Method.

Post-Employment Benefits

1. Post-employment includes the period of time after termination but before retirement, during which disability and other benefits may be provided (SFAS No.81). Post-employment benefits are payments to which participants may be entitled under a pension plan, including pension benefits, death benefits, and benefits due upon termination of employment (SFAS No.87).

2. Post-employment benefits are payments to which participants may be entitled under a pension plan, including pension benefits, death benefits, and benefits due upon termination of employment (SFAS No.87). Post-employment includes the period of time after termination but before retirement, during which disability and other benefits may be provided (SFAS No.81).

3. Payments to which participants may be entitled during the period after termination, before retirement, and after retirement. These payments may

include pension benefits, death benefits, benefits due upon termination of employment, health benefits, and life insurance.

PPBS

See Planning Programming Budgeting System.

Practical Capacity

A realistic expectation of the production level of an entity over a period of time. It may be measured as ideal capacity less an allowance for the estimated effect of downtime for operating interruption and maintenance.

Predetermined Overhead Rate

The rate at which manufacturing overhead is applied to production, based on the ratio of total budgeted overhead expenses for a period of time to the expected total of some relevant measure of activity for the same period, such as machine hours or direct labor hours.

Preoperating Costs

The costs of preparing to operate: costs of designing, tooling, recruiting, and training the labor force before production starts; moving; preparation of facilities; and related general and administrative costs. Also called Start-Up Costs.

Prepaid Expenses

Payments made for services to be received after the date of payment. Usually such services are consumed in the near future in the ordinary conduct of the business. Examples include prepaid rent, unexpired insurance, prepaid wages, and salaries.

Present Value

The value today (or at some specific date) of an amount or amounts to be paid or received later (or at other, different dates), discounted at some discount rate.

Price-Earnings Ratio

The market price (can be an average or at a point in time) of a stock divided by the earnings per share.

Price Level Adjusted Statements

Financial statements expressed in terms of dollars of constant purchasing power. Nonmonetary items, from historical cost statements, are restated to reflect changes in general price levels since the time specific assets were acquired and liabilities were incurred. A gain or loss is recognized on monetary items as they are held over time periods when the general price level changes.

Prime Cost

The cost of direct materials and direct labor.

Process Costing

A method of cost accounting that first collects costs by cost centers and then allocates the total costs of each cost center equally to each unit flowing through it during an accounting period. *Contrast with* Job Order Costing.

Product

Anything that is produced. Goods are tangible products; services are intangible products.

Product Cost

The direct material, direct labor, and production overhead cost of a product. Goods are charged to inventory at their product cost. *Contrast with* Period Cost.

Production Budget

The planned cost of producing goods during a given period.

Production Cost

The material, labor, and overhead cost of producing products and services. Excludes distribution and selling costs. Also called Manufacturing Cost.

Production Overhead Cost

A product cost other than direct materials and direct labor. It includes, for example, supervision, building maintenance, and power. Also called Manufacturing Overhead Cost.

Production Volume Variance

See Variances.

Productivity

The relationship between "output" (the quantity of goods and services produced) and "inputs," (the amounts of labor, material, and other costs used to produce the goods and services). Usually measured in terms of output per worker per hour but conceptually it should include all conversion costs, not only labor.

Product Mix

The proportion of each product, all of which constitute the products produced or sold. *See* Mix Variance (Variances).

Profit Center

A responsibility center whose financial performance is measured by the difference between its revenue and its expenses or cost. *Contrast with* an Expense Center.

Profit Margin

The ratio of income to revenue. Income may or may not include extraordinary items and may be stated before or after income taxes. Also called Return On Sales. *Contrast with* Gross Margin.

Profit Plan

See Budget.

Profit Planning and Control

A systematic approach for developing information used for planning, coordinating, and controlling enterprise activities to achieve profit objectives.

***Pro forma* Budget**

A projected financial statement or budget that is prepared according to a set of assumptions regarding what will happen in a specified future period or periods. It differs from a budget, which is usually an agreed upon plan, whether or not the assumptions made are the most likely.

Program Budget

A budget that is structured to show the expenses (and often revenues) of the principal programs that the entity will undertake. *Contrast with* a Line Item Budget.

Program Evaluation and Review Technique

A technique for planning and controlling the work on a project. It breaks the project down into work packages and shows the estimated time required to complete each work package; it also sets priorities for work packages.

Programmed Cost

See Discretionary Cost.

Progress Payment

A payment of an interim billing based upon partial completion of a contract.

Project Budget

A budget of costs classified by resources and function for a specific project over the project's life; this life may span several operating budget time periods.

Projected Benefit Obligation

The actuarial present value as of a date of all benefits attributed by the pension benefit formula to employee service rendered prior to that date. The projected benefit obligation is measured using assumptions about future compensation levels if the pension benefit formula is based on those future compensation levels (pay-related, final-pay, final-average-pay, or career average-pay plans). Contrast with accumulated benefit obligation, where the obligation is measured using employee compensation prior to the measurement date of the obligation. (SFAS No.87)

Property, Plant, and Equipment

A balance sheet classification for fixed assets used in business operations. Property, plant, and equipment items are normally grouped and reported at acquisition cost using separate disclosure of accumulated depreciation or depletion in order to arrive at a net figure. Also called Plant Assets, Operational Assets, or Fixed Assets.

Prorate

To allocate; to charge an indirect cost to the several cost objects that are assumed to have caused this cost. More generally, to divide a total among several elements.

Provision

A term used for an estimated liability or expense when the exact amount is not known. An example would be a provision for income taxes.

Purchase Method

A method of accounting for a business combination. The acquiring firm adds the assets and liabilities of the acquired firm to its balance sheet. Assets and liabilities are added at their fair value. If the purchase price exceeds the amount of acquired assets less liabilities, the excess is reported as goodwill. This method is used for all business combinations that do not qualify for the pooling-of-interests method. *Contrast with* Pooling-of-Interests-Method.

Purchasing Budget

A projection, classified by types of material, of the cost and time needed to provide budgeted material requirements.

— Q —

Qualitative Factors

Factors that are relevant to a decision but which are not expressed numerically. *Contrast with* Quantitative Factors.

Quality Assurance

The function or an organizational unit responsible for providing assurance that products or services are consistently maintained at a high level of quality. It encompasses preventing product defects (job training, quality circles, procedures); ensuring that products conform to specification (inspection, testing); monitoring internal quality failures (rework, yield losses) and external failures from customer/warranty complaints. This function is broader than the traditional quality control function of setting standards and testing for adherence to standards.

Quality Control

A process, which may include statistical sampling, that monitors the quality of operations. Techniques include precise specifications, random inspection procedures, and disciplined reviews of deviations from specification.

Quantitative Factors

Those factors that can be expressed in numerical terms, such as projected alternative costs of direct materials, direct labor, and factory overhead. *Contrast with* Qualitative Factors.

Quantity Discount

An allowance given by a seller to a buyer because of the size of an individual purchase transaction, or the total size during a specified period. This practice is not a violation of U. S. federal laws dealing with price discrimination provided the allowance granted represents a reduction in costs.

Queue

A line of customers, a file, or a list of items waiting for service.

Quick Assets

Current assets minus inventories and prepaid expenses; therefore, cash, cash equivalents, accounts receivable, and marketable securities.

Quick Ratio

See Acid Test Ratio.

— R —

Rate Variance

See Variances.

Ratio Analysis

The computation of significant financial and other ratios and the comparison of these ratios with those of prior years, industry averages, or standards. The purpose of this analysis is to obtain evidence about economic actions and events.

Realization

The process of converting noncash resources and rights into money. This term is most precisely used in accounting and financial reporting to refer to sales of assets for cash or claims to cash. The related terms "realized" and "unrealized" therefore identify revenues, gains, or losses on assets sold and unsold, respectively (SFAC No.6).

Receivable Turnover

A measure of asset utilization determined by dividing total annual credit sales by the average receivable balance.

Recognition

The process of formally recording an item in the financial statements of an entity. Thus, an asset, liability, revenue, expense, gain, or loss may be recognized (recorded) or unrecognized (unrecorded) (SFAC No.6).

Reciprocal Method of Allocation

A method for allocating service department costs by including the mutual services rendered among all departments. It is also referred to as the cross allocation method, matrix allocation method, or double distribution allocation method.

Recovery Value

Estimated revenue from the resale or scrapping of a fixed asset; salvage.

Regression Analysis

A statistical analysis tool that quantifies the relationship between a dependent variable and one or more independent variables. *See* Least-Squares Method.

Reinvestment Rate

The rate of return at which cash flows from an investment are expected to be reinvested.

Relevant Cost

A cost that should be considered in choosing among alternatives. Only those costs yet to be incurred (future costs) that differ among the alternatives (differential costs) are relevant in decision making.

Relevant Range

The range of economic activity within which estimates and predictions are valid. This range is normally viewed in the context of variable budgets and cost/volume/profit analysis. Outside of this range, the relationship assumed may need to be reexamined in a breakeven analysis.

Reliability

1. In statistics, the degree of confidence that a sample estimate of a population parameter is within a certain range of the results that would be obtained from a complete census of the entire population.

2. In accounting, the quality of information that assures that information is reasonably free from error and bias and faithfully represents what it purports to represent (SFAC No.2).

Reorder Point

The quantity level of an inventory item that triggers an order to replenish the item.

Repair

1. The restoration of a capital asset to its full productive capacity, or a contribution thereto, after damage, accident, or prolonged use, without an increase in the asset's previously estimated service life or productive capacity.

2. The activity of putting assets back into normal or expected operating condition (CASB).

Replacement

The exchange or substitution of one fixed asset for another that has the capacity to perform the same function. Within reasonable limits, the new asset may perform the function more or less efficiently than the retired asset, and it may have the capacity to perform the function for a longer or shorter period of time, but the intent of the exchange must be to substitute assets having similar service capacity.

Replacement Cost

The current cost of replacing an existing asset with one of equivalent productive capacity. The term is also used in a more general sense as the cost at current prices, in a particular locality or market area, of replacing an item of property or a group of assets.

Replacement Cost Method of Depreciation

The computation of depreciation cost or expense for a period using the replacement cost of an asset rather than its historical cost.

Reporting Currency

The currency in which an entity prepares its financial statements (SFAS No.52).

Reproduction Costs

The cost required to restore an existing asset to its original condition.

Required Rate of Return

The minimum acceptable rate of return on an investment. Also called Hurdle Rate.

Research and Development Cost

Outlays made in an attempt to discover new knowledge (research) or to use the results of research to develop new or improved products or processes (development). Unless such costs are incurred under contractual arrangements for others, under U.S., GAAP state they must be charged as expenses when incurred.

Reserve

Formerly, used in the sense of "allowance," as an allowance for bad debts or accumulated depreciation; this usage is obsolete. Currently, used primarily to segregate part of retained earnings, such as for a reserve for contingencies.

Residual Income

A means of measuring performance of an investment center that stresses profit responsibility and the financial management efficiency of the investment center manager. Residual income is typically computed as the difference between investment center profits and a charge for capital resources committed to the unit.

Responsibility Accounting

A system of accounting that assigns revenues, costs, and/or capital to responsibility centers.

Responsibility Budget

A budget that sets forth approved plans structured in terms of the persons responsible for carrying them out. It is a control device in that it is a statement of performance expected of each responsibility center manager against which actual performance can be compared.

Responsibility Center

An organizational unit headed by a manager who is responsible for its activities. Responsibility centers can be measured as revenue centers, expense centers, profit centers, or investment centers. *Contrast with* Cost Center.

Retained Earnings

Net income over the life of a corporation less cash or stock dividends. Thus, retained earnings represents the total earnings of a corporation that have been retained in the business and not transferred to contributed capital because of stock dividends or distributed to owners as cash. Appropriations of retained earnings do not diminish the amount of retained earnings; they merely subdivide the existing amount.

Return on Equity (ROE)

The ratio of net profit after taxes to net equity. Indicates the rate of return on the shareholders' investment. Also called return on owners' equity.

Return on Investment (ROI)

The ratio of income to the investment used in earning that income. Income may be expressed either as net income before income taxes, or income before extraordinary items. Investment my be expressed either as shareholders' equity, total permanent capital, or total assets. The specific meaning used must be deduced from the context.

Return on Sales

See Profit Margin.

Revenue Center

A responsibility center in which management control is focused on the revenue that the center earns.

Revenues

Inflows or other enhancements of assets of an entity or settlements of its liabilities (or a combination of both) during a period from delivering or producing goods, rendering services, or other activities that constitute the entity's ongoing major or central operations (SFAC No.6).

Risk

A measure of the variability of the return on investment. For a given expected amount of return, most people prefer less risk to more risk. Therefore, in rational markets, investments with more risk usually promise, or are expected to yield, a higher rate of return than investments with lower risk.

Risk-Adjusted Discount Rate
See Risk-Adjusted Rate of Return.

Risk-Adjusted Rate of Return
In capital budgeting, a rate of return that is adjusted for the expected risk of the proposed project. The net present value of a project whose risk is expected to be greater than average is found by using a higher than average discount rate. Also called Risk-Adjusted Discount Rate.

Risk Analysis
A method used in capital budgeting for identifying, disclosing possible consequences of, quantifying, and placing an economic cost on the relative risk of a project.

Robotics
Technology dealing with the design, construction, and operation of robots. A robot is a machine that performs mechanical functions similar to certain physical functions that are performed by human beings. These functions involve the arms, legs, eyes, nose, and/or ears.

ROE
See Return on Equity.

Rolling Budget
See Continuous Budget.

ROI
See Return on Investment.

— S —

Safety Stock
A quantity of inventory held to meet unanticipated demand during the time between placement of an order and its receipt into inventory, or unanticipated delays in receiving the replenishment.

Sale
A revenue transaction in which goods or services are delivered to a customer in return for cash or an obligation to pay.

Sale and Leaseback
The sale of property by an owner and its subsequent lease back to the seller.

Sales Allowance

A reduction in the originally agreed upon price for goods or services, usually because the product is not fully satisfactory.

Sales Budget

An approved plan, classified by responsibility, product, and/or area, of the net revenue expected to be earned by an entity in a period of time. Sometimes stated as orders booked, rather than, or in addition to, sales revenue.

Sales Discount

A reduction in the stated selling price, usually as a reward for prompt payment. *Contrast with* a Trade Discount.

Sales Forecast

A prediction of sales using various data and methods such as trend projections, regression/correlation analyses, operations research techniques, computer simulation, or less rigorous prediction procedures.

Sales Mix Variance

See Variances.

Sales Volume Variance

See Variances.

Salvage Value

The net cash inflow expected from the sale of resources no longer useful to the firm.

Segment

1. One of two or more divisions, product departments, plants, or other subdivisions of an entity reporting directly to a home office, usually identified with responsibility for profit and/or producing a product or service. The term includes government-owned contractor-operated (GOCO) facilities, and joint ventures and subsidiaries (domestic and foreign) in which the entity has a majority ownership. The term also includes those joint ventures and subsidiaries (domestic and foreign) in which the entity has less than a majority of ownership, but over which it exercises control (CASB).

2. As defined by APB Opinion No. 30, "a component of an entity whose activities represent a separate major line of business or class of customer. . . .[It may be] a subsidiary, a division, or a department, . . .provided that its assets, results of operations, and activities can be clearly distinguished, physically and operationally for financial reporting purposes, from the other assets, results of operations, and activities of the entity." In SFAS No. 14 a segment is defined as "A component of an enterprise engaged in promoting a product or service or a group of related products and services primarily to unaffiliated customers. . .for a profit."

3. Within an entity, a component that markets and/or produces a product or a group of related products and services primarily to unaffiliated customers (SFAS No. 14-modified).

Segment Margin

The contribution margin of a business segment less fixed costs assigned to that segment. It is a measure of long-run profitability.

Segment Reporting

Annual disclosure of financial information disaggregated to a firm's reportable industry segments, its foreign operations and export sales, and its major customers as prescribed by SFAS No.14 and SEC Regulations. Also called Line of Business Reporting.

Selling Costs

Any expense or class of expense incurred in selling or marketing. Examples include sales representatives' salaries, commissions, and traveling expense; advertising; selling department salaries and expenses; samples; credit and collection costs. Shipping costs are also often classified as selling costs.

Semifixed Cost

A cost that includes both variable and fixed elements. Also called Semivariable Cost.

Semivariable Cost

See Semifixed Cost.

Senior Indebtedness

Indebtedness that has preferential rights ahead of some or all other indebtedness of the enterprise. *Contrast with* Subordinated Indebtedness.

Service Capacity

The greatest number of service units that a machine, operation, or plant can produce within a specified period of time; productivity capacity.

Service Cost Center

A cost center that furnishes services to other units within an entity. A service cost center usually charges its customers for these services.

Service Department

An entity unit that provides services to other departments. A service department is usually the same as a service cost center; however, service cost centers need not be entity units.

SFAC

See Statements of Financial Accounting Concepts.

SFAS

See Statements of Financial Accounting Standards.

Shadow Price

The potential value of having available more of the scarce resource that constrains the production process; for example, the value of having more time available on a machine tool critical to the production of two products. This value is called a shadow price or the dual value of the scarce resources. It is one output of a linear programming analysis.

Shareholders' Equity

The owner's equity in a corporation. Also called Stockholders' Equity.

Shrinkage

The loss of raw materials, work in process, or finished goods in terms of weight or volume due to the nature of the product or the methods employed for production, transportation, and storage. Shrinkage can also result from theft or shoplifting as well as from evaporation or general wear and tear. Once it has occurred, shrinkage usually cannot be restored.

Shut-Down Costs

Those fixed costs that would be incurred even if there were no production. They include taxes on the factory building, insurance on the factory building, and guards' salaries. Also called Standby Costs.

SIAS

See Statements of International Accounting Standards.

Significance

The magnitude, as measured by a departure from some norm or standard, that is sufficient to raise doubt that the deviation is the result of chance, random, or compensating factors.

Simulation

A method of studying an operational problem, whereby a model of the system or process is subjected to a series of manipulations to reflect varying assumptions.

Slack

In budgeting, the difference between the costs or expenses actually required in the operation of a responsibility center and the costs or expenses that have been proposed or approved in the budget. The term is occasionally applied to revenues as well as to costs or expenses.

Social Accounting

The identification, measurement, and reporting of the social costs and benefits of economic activity. It is concerned with the positive or negative impact (social benefits or social cost) of an entity's activities upon the financial, physical, or emotional well-being of those who are directly associated with the entity (such as investors, employees, beneficiaries of services, suppliers, customers, or clients), and of those who are affected by the entity's activities by reason of geographic proximity or otherwise.

Span of Control

The extent of a supervisor's jurisdiction, often represented in entity charts by subordinate lines of authority extending to activities or subunits.

Specific Identification

A method for valuing ending inventory and cost of goods sold that identifies actual units sold and in inventory and then sums the actual costs of those individual units. It is usually used for items with large unit values, such as precious jewelry, automobiles, and fur coats.

Split-Off Point

The point of production beyond which the cost of separate products can be measured. Up to this point, the products were either joint products or byproducts.

Spot Rate

The exchange rate for immediate delivery of currencies exchanged (SFAS No.52); the rate of interest or price being charged currently.

Standard Cost

1. Any cost computed with the use of pre-established measures (CASB).

2. The anticipated cost of producing a unit of output; a predetermined cost to be assigned to products produced. Standard cost implies a norm, or what costs should be.

Standard Cost System

A product cost system that uses standard costs rather than actual costs. It may be based on either absorption or direct costing principles, and may apply either to all cost elements or to some of them.

Standard Labor Rate

Base pay, incentives, premiums, fringe benefits, and labor-related taxes estimated to be attainable under the planned working conditions. In some systems, fringe benefits and labor-related taxes are excluded.

Standard Price

A unit price established for materials or labor used in standard cost systems.

Standby Capacity

The volume that can be obtained from fixed assets that have been retired from active service but not disposed of.

Standby Costs

See Capacity Cost; Shut-Down Costs.

Start-up Costs

See Preoperating Costs.

Statement of Cash Flows

See Cash Flow Statement.

Statements of Financial Accounting Concepts (SFAC)

Statements issued by the Financial Accounting Standards Board that set forth objectives and fundamentals used as the basis for development of financial accounting and reporting standards (FASB).

Statements of Financial Accounting Standards (SFAS)

Accounting standards established and published by the Financial Accounting Standards Board (FASB).

Statements of International Accounting Standards (SIAS)

International Accounting Standards established and published by the International Accounting Standards Committee (IASC).

Static Budget

See Fixed Budget.

Step-Down Allocation Method

The method of allocating service department costs that begins by allocating one service department's costs to production departments and to all other service departments. A second service department's costs, including costs allocated from the first, are then allocated to production departments and to all other service departments except the first one, and so on. In this fashion, the costs of all service departments are ultimately allocated to production departments.

Step Variable Cost

A cost that increases by steps with increased volumes of activity.

Stockholders' Equity

See Shareholders' Equity.

Stock-Out Costs

The contribution margin or other measure of profits not earned because a seller has run out of inventory and is unable to fill a customer's order. It may be an extra cost incurred because of a delay in filling an order.

Storage Capacity

The maximum storage space available in an entity's existing physical plant.

Strategic Plan

The overall goals and objectives of an organization. *Contrast with* Tactical Plan.

Strategic Planning

The process of discovering, evaluating, and selecting the strategies that management decides the entity should undertake. Strategies are broad, major plans, usually without specific time limits. *See* Tactical Plan.

Suboptimization

A decision that increases the current profit of a responsibility center but decreases the profit of the entity.

Subordinated Indebtedness

Indebtedness that can be repaid only after some or all other indebtedness is repaid. *Contrast with* Senior Indebtedness.

Subsidiary

A corporation that is controlled, directly or indirectly, by another corporation. The usual condition for control is ownership of a majority (over 50%) of the outstanding voting stock. The power to control may also exist with a lesser percentage of ownership, for example, by contract, lease, or agreement with other stockholders or by court decree (APB No.18).

Subsidiary Ledger

A supporting ledger consisting of a group of accounts, the total of which is in agreement with a control account. Examples: a customers' ledger; a creditors' ledger; a factory ledger; an expense ledger; a plan ledger; a branch or departmental ledger.

Sum-of-Years'-Digit (SYD) Depreciation Method

A depreciation schedule obtained by *(a)* summing the digits (1,2,3. . .n) of the years of an asset's depreciable life, and *(b)* finding the depreciation rate for each year as the fraction that the year's digit, in reverse order, is to the total sum. For example, for an asset with a life of four years, the sum of 1,2,3, and 4 = 10. The depreciation rate in year 1 is 4/10 = 40%. It is an accelerated depreciation method that gives results close to those found with the double-declining balance method. The sum-of-years'-digit is no longer widely used.

Sunk Cost

A past cost which cannot now be revised and hence cannot (or should not) enter into current decisions for increasing or decreasing present profit levels (aside from any income tax effects). *Contrast with* Differential Cost.

Surrogate

A substitute that is believed to behave in approximately the same manner as the variable or other item of interest; a proxy; used because data on the variable itself are not available.

— T —

Tactical Plan

A plan for achieving the entity's objectives covering a relatively short time period, usually one year. *Contrast with* a Strategic Plan.

Take-or-Pay Contract

An agreement between a purchaser and a seller that unconditionally requires the purchaser to pay specified amounts periodically in return for products or services. The purchaser must make specified minimum payments even if it does not take delivery of the contracted products or services (SFAS No.47).

Target Costing

A cost management tool designed to reduce the overall cost of a product over its entire life cycle. The target is a predetermined cost that should result in an acceptable price to customers as well as an acceptable return to the organization.

Task Control

A detailed control of individual work and procedures. A task control system consists of three interrelated parts: *(a)* an identification of points and activities; *(b)* the selection of control techniques and methods appropriate for each identified area, point, or activity to correct or prevent departures from plans; and *(c)* constant review to assure that the system is adequate for control and that employees do not override the control system.

Theoretical Capacity

The maximum possible output of a machine or other production unit per time period assuming no interruptions, delays, or downtime during that period. It is usually achievable only for relatively short periods of time. Also called Design Capacity.

Time-Adjusted Rate of Return

See Internal Rate of Return.

Times Interest Earned

The ratio of earnings before interest, income taxes, and extraordinary items (EBIT) to annual interest expense. A widely used measure of the entity's ability to make interest payments when they are due.

Top-Down Budget

See Imposed Budget.

Total-Debt-to-Total-Asset Ratio

A variation of the debt ratio.

Traceable Cost

A cost that can be identified with or assigned to a specific product or service. *Contrast with* Common Cost; Joint Cost.

Trade Discount

A reduction in the stated selling price based on quantities ordered or purchased. *Contrast with* Sales Discount.

Transaction Gains or Losses

Gains or losses that result from a change in exchange rates between the functional currency and the currency in which a foreign currency transaction is denominated. They represent an increase or decrease in *(a)* the actual functional currency cash flows realized upon settlement of foreign currency transactions, and *(b)* the expected functional currency cash flows on unsettled foreign currency transactions (SFAS No. 52).

Transfer Price

The price at which goods and services are transferred from one profit center to another. It should be distinguished from a cost accounting charge from one cost center to another in that the transfer price usually includes a profit component, whereas the cost accounting charge does not.

Translation Adjustments

Adjustments that result when an entity's financial statements are translated from the entity's functional currency into the reporting currency (SFAS No.52).

Transportation Cost

The cost of freight, cartage, handling charges, and the like, relating to goods either purchased, in-process, or sold.

Treasury Stock

Fully paid capital stock reacquired by the issuing company through gift, purchase, or otherwise, and available for resale or cancellation; neither gain nor loss is recognized. The amount is shown as a deduction from shareholders' equity. Also called Treasury Shares.

Trend

Long-term movements of a time series that are characterized by steady or slightly varying rates of change.

Trial Balance

A listing of all account balances in a general ledger. All accounts with debit balances are totaled separately from accounts with credit balances; the two totals should be equal. Trial balances are taken as a partial check of the arithmetic accuracy of entries previously made.

Trust Fund

A fund held by one person (trustee) for the benefit of another, usually pursuant to the provisions of a formal trust agreement. The investment of the principal of a trust established under the law is restricted by statutory provisions in the various states.

— U —

Unallowable Cost

Any cost that, under the provision of any pertinent law, regulation, or contract, cannot be included in prices, cost reimbursements, or settlements under a contract to which it is allocable (CASB).

Unavoidable Cost

A cost that must be continued under a program of business retraction. *Contrast with* Escapable Cost.

Uncertainty

The likelihood that an actual amount will be different from its estimate or forecast.

Unconsolidated Subsidiary

A subsidiary whose financial results are not consolidated with those of the parent company. For guidance regarding unconsolidated subsidiaries under GAAP, refer to SFAS No. 94.

Underabsorbed Overhead

See Underapplied Overhead.

Underapplied Overhead

The excess of actual manufacturing expenses incurred over the amount of manufacturing overhead applied to production. Also called Underabsorbed Overhead.

Unexpired Cost

The cost of an asset on hand now that will be consumed in future accounting periods.

Unfavorable Variance

The amount by which actual cost exceeds standard or budgeted cost, or the amount by which actual revenue is less than standard or budgeted revenue.

Uniformity

The concept that states that like economic events should be accounted for in the same manner by all entities.

Unit Contribution

The difference between the selling price and the variable cost of one unit of a product. *See* Contribution Margin.

Unit Cost

The cost of one unit of a product or of one unit of a cost element of a product. It is usually obtained by dividing a total cost by the total number of units.

Units-of-Production Depreciation Method

A depreciation method in which the depreciation rate is determined by dividing the net cost of the asset by the number of units of service that asset is estimated to produce over its life. Depreciation expense for one year is found by multiplying this unit cost by the number of units produced in the year. Sometimes used in the depreciation of dies, trucks, buses (cost per vehicle mile), and aircraft engines (cost per operating hour).

Unrecovered Costs

The portion of original investment not previously charged to expense through the process of amortization, depreciation, or depletion.

Unusual Items

Items in which the underlying event or transaction possesses a high degree of abnormality and is a type clearly unrelated to, or only incidentally related to, the ordinary and typical activities of the entity, taking into account the environment in which the entity operates. *See* Extraordinary Items (APB No.30).

Useful Life

The service capacity, normally expressed in time periods or production units, of an asset used in its original form for entity activities. The useful life ends when the asset is physically unable to provide service or when it has become obsolete, whichever occurs earlier.

Utility

The relative satisfaction or need gratification derived from a good or service.

Utilization Cost

The economic sacrifice involved in using an available resource or service to perform some act.

Utilization Variance

See Variances.

— V —

Value

Attributed worth, expressed in money and applied to a particular asset, such as the value of an automobile; to services rendered, such as the value of a person's labor; to a group of assets, such as the value of a company's patents; or to an entire business unit, such as the value of a plant or business enterprise.

Value-Added Analysis

A review of operational activities and processes to determine the extent to which activities and processes add value or utility to consumers of a product or service. Value-added analysis focuses on eliminating wasteful activities.

Variable Budgeting

See Flexible Budget.

Variable Costing

See Direct Costing.

Variable Cost

An operating expense, or operating expenses as a class, that vary directly, and proportionately, with sales or production volume, facility utilization, or some other measure of activity. Examples include materials consumed, direct labor, power, factory supplies, depreciation (on a production basis), and sales commissions. *Contrast with* Fixed Cost.

Variable Overhead Variance

See Variances.

Variance Analysis

1. In accounting, the investigation of the causes of the variances between actual cost and standard or budgeted cost.

2. In statistics, the investigation of departures from a measure of central tendency.

Variances

Budget Variance

A deviation of actual results from budgeted results, such as actual revenues earned or costs incurred compared with the amount expressed in the budget.

Capacity Variance

See Fixed Manufacturing Overhead Volume Variance.

Direct Labor Efficiency Variance

The difference between the standard and actual number of direct labor hours multiplied by the standard labor cost per hour. Also called Labor Time Variance or Labor Quantity Variance.

Direct Labor Mix Variance

The variance that results from a difference in the actual mix of labor inputs from the standard mix of labor inputs.

The formula is: [(Actual labor mix percentage minus budgeted labor mix percentage), multiplied by (actual total units of labor inputs used)], multiplied by (budgeted individual price per unit of labor input minus budgeted average price per unit of labor input).

Direct Labor Rate Variance

The difference between the actual wage rate per hour and the standard wage rate per hour, multiplied by the number of actual hours of direct labor.

Direct Labor Yield Variance

The variance caused by using more or fewer units of labor for a given quantity of outputs than was budgeted. It is calculated as: (Standard units of labor inputs allowed for actual outputs minus actual units of labor inputs used) multiplied by (budgeted average price per unit of labor input).

Direct Labor Variance

The difference between the standard direct labor cost and the actual direct labor cost incurred.

Direct Material Price Variance

The difference between the actual unit price for purchased parts and materials and the standard unit price, multiplied by the actual number of units acquired (or used in production).

Direct Material Quantity Variance

The difference between the standard and actual quantity of a raw material used to produce a given output; usually priced at standard cost. Mathematically it is: (standard quantity minus actual quantity) multiplied by standard price.

Direct Material Variances

The difference between the standard direct material cost of the actual production or output and the actual cost of direct material.

Fixed Manufacturing Overhead Budget Variance

The difference between the budgeted fixed manufacturing overhead and the actual fixed manufacturing overhead.

Fixed Manufacturing Overhead Volume Variance

The over- or underabsorbed fixed production costs that result when actual production volume is higher or lower than planned volume. The difference between budgeted fixed manufacturing overhead costs and the fixed manufacturing overhead costs applied to products. Also called Capacity Variance and Utilization Variance.

Flexible Budget Variance

The difference between actual amounts and the flexible budget amounts for the actual level of activity.

Joint Variance

A variance caused jointly by both price variance and quantity variance. It may be stated mathematically as: (actual unit price minus standard unit price) multiplied by (actual quantity minus standard quantity).

Mix Variance

A variance that results when actual proportions of the components of revenues or costs are different from the proportions used in arriving at the budgeted or planned revenue or cost, or the standard cost.

Production Volume Variance

See Fixed Manufacturing Overhead Volume Variance.

Rate Variance

The variance in cost associated with a difference between the standard unit cost and the actual unit cost of product inputs. Typically, it is measured as the difference between the standard rate per unit (for instance, per hour) and the actual rate per unit, multiplied by the actual quantity of units (hours) used.

Sales Mix Variance

The difference between budgeted and actual sales caused by a difference between the budgeted and actual proportions of products with different profit margins.

Sales Volume Variance

The difference between budgeted and actual sales caused by differences in the volume of products sold. It is found by multiplying the difference in quantity by the average budgeted revenue per unit of quantity. An alternative, and usually more informative variance, is found by multiplying the difference in quantity by the average budgeted gross margin per unit.

Utilization Variance

See Fixed Manufacturing Overhead Volume Variance.

Variable Manufacturing Overhead Efficiency Variance

The difference between actual direct labor hours incurred and the standard direct labor hours allowed for actual production, multiplied by the standard variable overhead rate per direct labor hour (or per some alternate appropriate basis).

Variable Manufacturing Overhead Spending Variance

The difference between actual variable overhead costs and budgeted variable overhead costs at the actual volume.

Variable Manufacturing Overhead Variance

The difference between actual and standard variable overhead costs.

Yield Variance

The difference between the actual quantity of material used for a given amount of product and the standard quantity of the material required for that amount of product, priced at the standard cost per unit of material.

Verifiability

The ability, through consensus among measures, to ensure that information represents what it purports to represent or that the chosen method of measurement has been used without error or bias (SFAC No.2).

— W —

Warranty Cost

A cost incurred, or expected to be incurred, in connection with the sale of goods or services that will result from a further performance by the seller after the sale has taken place.

Weighted Average Cost

An inventory costing method under which an average unit cost is computed periodically by dividing the sum of the cost of beginning inventory, plus the cost of acquisitions, by the total number of units included in these two categories (CASB).

Working Capital

The excess of current assets over current liabilities. Sometimes erroneously used as a synonym for "current assets"; if so, the excess is referred to as "net working capital." Some analysts exclude the current portion of long-term debt from their definition of working capital.

Work-In-Process

See Work-In-Process Inventory.

Work-In-Process Inventory

The costs incurred to date on products for which production has begun but has not yet been completed; the product can be either goods or services. Also called Work-In-Process or Goods-In-Process.

Work Measurement

Careful analysis of a task, its size, the method used in its performance, and its efficiency. The objective of work measurement is to determine the workload in an operation and the number of worker hours needed to perform that work efficiently.

— Y–Z —

Yield Variance

See Variances.

Zero-Based Budgeting

A budget that is developed by analyzing the amount of each element of cost that should be incurred under a variety of assumptions for the budget period and then selecting what appears to be the optimum "decision packages" from these alternatives. The first package is the amount developed "from scratch"; that is, the amount required for the lowest possible level of activity. *Contrast with* Incremental Budgeting.

Zero-Based Review

A systematic way of analyzing ongoing programs. In a zero-based review, the cost estimates are built up "from scratch," or zero, rather than taking the current level of costs as the starting point, as is often done in the annual budgeting process.

REFERENCES

Anthony, Robert N. *A Review of Essentials of Accounting,* 4th ed. Reading, Massachusetts: Addison-Wesley Publishing Company, 1988.

Anthony Robert N. and James S. Reece. *Management Accounting: Text and Cases,* 8th ed. Homewoood, Illinois: Richard Irwin, 1988.

Anthony, Robert N., John Dearden, and Norton Bedford. *Management Control Systems,* 6th ed. Homewood, Illinois: Richard Irwin, 1988.

Anthony, Robert N. and James S. Reece. *Accounting: Text and Cases,* 8th ed. Homewood, Illinois: Richard Irwin, 1988.

Black, Homer A. *Cost Accounting.* Homewood, Illinois: Richard Irwin, 1978.

The Canadian Institute of Chartered Accountants. *Terminology for Accountants,* 3rd ed. Toronto, Canada, 1983.

The Chartered Institute of Management Accountants. *Management Accounting: Official Terminology of the CIMA.* London, England, 1982.

Cherrington, J. Owen, E. Dee Hubbard, and David H. Luthy. *Cost and Managerial Accounting.* Dubuque, Iowa: William C. Brown Publishers, 1985.

Cooper, W.W. and Yuji Ijiri, eds. *Kohler's Dictionary for Accountants,* 6th ed. Englewood Cliffs, New Jersey: Prentice Hall, 1983.

Davidson, Sidney, Clyde P. Stickney, and Roman L. Weil. *Accounting: The Language of Business,* 7th ed. Sun Lakes, Arizona: Thomas Horton and Daughters, 1987.

Horngren, Charles T., and George Foster. *Cost Accounting: A Managerial Emphasis,* 6th ed. Englewood Cliffs, New Jersey: Prentice Hall, 1987.

Gray, Jack and Diane Matson. "Early Warning Systems." *Management Accounting,* (August 1987): 50–55.

McNair, C.J., William Mosconi, and Thomas Norris. *Meeting the Technology Challenge: Cost Accounting in A JIT Environment.* A Joint Study by National Association of Accountants and Coopers & Lybrand, 1988.

Financial Accounting Standards Board (SFAS & SFAC)

Statement of Financial Accounting Concepts No.2, "Qualitative Characteristics of Accounting Information," Financial Accounting Standards Board, Norwalk, Conn. 1980.

Statement of Financial Accounting Concepts No.6, "Elements of Financial Statements of Business Enterprises," Financial Accounting Standards Board, Norwalk, Conn. 1985.

Statement of Financial Accounting Standards No.2, "Accounting for Research and Development Costs," Financial Accounting Standards Board, Norwalk, Conn. 1974.

Statement of Financial Accounting Standards No.6, "Classification of Short-Term Obligations Expected to Be Refinanced," Financial Accounting Standards Board, Norwalk, Conn. 1975.

Statement of Financial Accounting Standards No. 14, "Financial Reporting for Segments of a Business Enterprise," Financial Accounting Standards Board, Norwalk, Conn. 1976.

Statement of Financial Accounting Standards No. 33, "Financial Reporting and Changing Prices," Financial Accounting Standards Board, Norwalk, Conn. 1979.

Statement of "Financial Accounting Standards No. 47, Disclosure of Long-Term Obligations," Financial Accounting Standards Board, Norwalk, Conn. 1981.

Statement of Financial Accounting Standards No.52, "Foreign Currency Translation," Financial Accounting Standards Board, Norwalk, Conn. 1981.

Statement of Financial Accounting Standards No.71, "Accounting for the Effects of Certain Types of Regulation," Financial Accounting Standards Board, Norwalk, Conn. 1982.

Statement of Financial Accounting Standards No.76, "Extinguishment of Debt," Financial Accounting Standards Board, Norwalk, Conn. 1983.

Statement of Financial Accounting Standards No.78, "Classifications of Obligations That Are Callable by the Creditor," Financial Accounting Standards Board, Norwalk, Conn. 1983.

Statement of Financial Accounting Standards No.87, "Employers' Accounting for Pensions," Financial Accounting Standards Board, Norwalk, Conn. 1985.

Statement of Financial Accounting Standards No.89, "Financial Reporting and Changing Prices," Financial Accounting Standards Board, Norwalk, Conn. 1986.

Statement of Financial Accounting Standards No.94, "Consolidation of All Majority-Owned Subsidiaries, " Financial Accounting Standards Board, Norwalk, Conn. 1987.

Statement of Financial Accounting Standards No.95, "Statement of Cash Flows," Financial Accounting Standards Board, Norwalk, Conn. 1987.

Accounting Principles Board (APB)

Accounting Principles Board Opinion No.4, "Accounting for the Investment Credit," American Institute of Certified Public Accountants, New York, N.Y. 1964.

Accounting Principles Board Opinion No.9, "Reporting The Results of Operations," American Institute of Certified Public Accountants, New York, N.Y. 1966.

Accounting Principles Board Opinion No.15, "Earnings Per Share," American Institute of Certified Public Accountants, New York, N.Y. 1969.

Accounting Principles Board Opinion No.18, "The Equity Method of Accounting for Investments in Common Stock," American Institute of Certified Public Accountants, New York, N.Y. 1971.

Accounting Principles Board Opinion No.29, "Accounting for Nonmonetary Transactions," American Institute of Certified Public Accountants, New York, N.Y. 1973.

Accounting Principles Board Opinion No.30, "Reporting the Results of Operations—Reporting the Effects of Disposal of a Segment of a Business, and Extraordinary, Unusual and Infrequently Occurring Events and Transactions," American Institute of Certified Public Accountants, New York, N.Y. 1973.

Securities And Exchange Commissions (SEC)

Guidelines, Rules, & Regulations, Regulation S-K, Washington, DC. 1988, pp. 240-241.

Cost Accounting Standards Board (CASB)

Code of Federal Regulations (4), Chapter III, Subchapter G- Cost Accounting Standards, Washington, D.C., January 1988.

International Accounting Standards (IAS)

International Accounting Standards Committee, Exposure Draft 35, "Financial Reporting of Interests in Joint Ventures," London, England, December 1989.

NATIONAL ASSOCIATION OF ACCOUNTANTS
MANAGEMENT ACCOUNTING PRACTICES COMMITTEE
SUBCOMMITTEE ON SMA PROMULGATION
1989–1991

Frank C. Minter,* *Chairman*
Accounting Chairman and Professor
Samford University
Birmingham, Alabama

Robert W. Backes
*Manager of Accounting Implementation
    and Control*
Schering-Plough Corporation
Madison, New Jersey

Dennis C. Daly
Academic Specialist
Department of Accounting
Michigan State University
East Lansing, Michigan

Lee D. Dobbins
*Director, Professional Development
    Activities*
ITT Corporation
New York, New York

James C. Hawley
*Group Controller Pharmaceutical and
    Dental Products Group*
3M Company
St. Paul, Minnestoa

Neil E. Holmes*
Vice President
The Marley Company
Mission Woods, Kansas

Thomas E. Huff
Wharton School and Financial Consultant
University Associates, Inc.
New Canaan, Connecticut

Philip B. Livingston
Vice President and Controller
Kenetech Corporation
Livermore, California

Raymond H. Peterson
Consultant
Peterson's Consultants
Petaluma, California

L. Hal Rogero, Jr.*
Vice President, Administration
Publishing Paper Division
Mead Corporation
Escanaba, Michigan

Donald J. Trawicki
Partner (Retired)
Deloitte & Touche
Short Hills, New Jersey

Barrington C. Turner
Policy Liaison Division
Defense Contract Audit Agency
Alexandria, Virginia

Robert F. Wurzelbacher
Director, Product Supply–Finance
The Procter & Gamble Company
Cincinnati, Ohio

*Also a member of the MAP Committee.

NAA Staff
Louis Bisgay
Director
Management Accounting Practices

Wagdy Abdallah
Manager
Management Accounting Practices

NAA Staff
Louis Bisgay
Director
Management Accounting Practices

Wagdy Abdallah
Manager
Management Accounting Practices

Statements on Management Accounting

Statement Number 4L
February 7, 1990

PRACTICES AND TECHNIQUES

Control
of Property,
Plant, and Equipment

In accordance with the charge to the Management Accounting Practices (MAP) Committee to issue statements on management accounting principles and practices, Statements on Management Accounting are promulgated to reflect official positions of the National Association of Accountants (NAA). The work of the MAP Committee is based on a framework for management accounting, whose principal categories are:

1. Objectives
2. Terminology
3. Concepts
4. Practices and Techniques
5. Management of Accounting Activities

Statements on Management Accounting

Statement Number 4L
February 7, 1990

Practices and Techniques:
Control of Property, Plant, and Equipment

National Association of Accountants, Inc.

Acknowledgments

The National Association of Accountants is grateful to all who contributed to the publication of Statement 4L, "Control of Property, Plant, and Equipment." Appreciation is extended to members of NAA's Management Accounting Practices Committee and to its Subcommittee on SMA Promulgation, which guided development of the Statement. Special thanks go to Michael J. Sandretto for his research and writing associated with the project.

INTRODUCTION

1. This document is a recommendation for managerial issues involving control of property, plant, and equipment (See paragraph 48, below, for a definition of these assets). Assets referred to in this document include both (1) owned and leased assets, and (2) assets used internally in the business, such as personal computers. Asset control is important to the management accountant because

   (1) capital is costly, and proper asset control can reduce the need for additional capital expenditures;

   (2) proper asset control can improve the efficiency of an organization by limiting the need for equipment repairs and by maintaining high product quality; and

   (3) control is a major function of management accountants.

STATEMENT OF SCOPE

2. Proper asset control includes

   (1) budget authorization to acquire assets, supported by an explanation of the purpose and the objectives of the acquisition;

   (2) internal review programs to

      a. evaluate acquisition programs (if acquisitions are significant);

      b. verify the annual depreciation expense and the ending asset account balances; and

      c. confirm the existence of assets and detect unused, underutilized, or improperly maintained assets.

3. Part I of this Statement recommends practices for planning the acquisition of property, plant, and equipment. Part II recommends general accounting methods to control property, plant, and equipment.

4. This Statement is limited to management accounting; it does not specifically address accounting for taxes or tax rules and regulations that apply to plant, property, and equipment.

PART I. PLANNING THE ACQUISITION OF PROPERTY, PLANT, AND EQUIPMENT

5. Organizations have systems to control assets. These systems, both formal and informal, are necessary to ensure adequate productive and administrative capacity, to prevent theft or loss, to avoid premature deterioration (aging) of a firm's assets, and to avoid operating with economically inefficient production processes.

THE CAPITAL EXPENDITURES BUDGET AS A
CONTROL DOCUMENT

6. Most organizations have a formal system to approve capital asset additions. The process normally begins when managers at various organizational levels prepare a list of proposed capital expenditures (often referred to as a capital expenditures budget) as part of an annual corporate business plan. If the business plan also includes longer-term estimates of revenue and expense, such as a five-year business plan, then these managers normally include proposed capital additions for those later periods as well.

7. In most cases a proposed project should be included in the capital expenditures budget only after performing, at minimum, a preliminary economic analysis. This analysis typically shows that the project is justified because it satisfies certain economic criteria, or because it satisfies noneconomic criteria such as legal or regulatory requirements.

8. Capital projects fall into two broad categories: Productive-type projects, and administrative-type projects. Most capital projects are for space or equipment used in productive-type activity. Examples include machine tools, warehouse space, and moving equipment. Computer systems to process accounting and production transactions would also fall into this category. These investments are made only if an economic evaluation shows that expected benefits are greater than projected costs. The second category, administrative-type projects, typically includes space and equipment needed to satisfy legal or regulatory requirements for pollution or safety equipment. It also includes remodeling needed to maintain employee morale, such as with regard to a cafeteria, or to maintain an image, such as a reception area. Administrative-type projects are usually subjected to far less rigorous economic analysis (See Para. 15-17).

9. A statement of corporate objectives, or of corporate strategy, normally serves as the basis for a preliminary capital expenditures budget. It typically includes economic projections, a statement of strategy, a discussion of objectives for various segments of the business, and capital limitations. These corporate objectives are used to evaluate performance in the subsequent audit phase. In addition, they may identify an overall spending limit for each of the two broad categories of capital projects.

10. A preliminary capital expenditures budget is initiated by operating management, then submitted to successively higher levels of management for review and preliminary approval. Projects may be added or deleted throughout the review process. Projects are usually initiated by managers who are responsible for the activities that would use the assets to be acquired. Depending on the size of the firm, senior managers may focus on

individual capital projects, or only on the overall level of the capital budget, and whether it meets strategic objectives.

11. The preliminary capital expenditures budget is reviewed by either the chief executive officer, the board of directors, or a committee of executives or directors. The preliminary budget is usually returned to initiating managers for reconsideration, then returned through more senior levels of management in an iterative process until it is given final approval by senior management.

12. At the point the budget receives final approval it becomes both a policy statement and a control document, rather than a discussion document.

13. Final approval of the capital expenditures budget is usually not authorization to acquire an asset. Several months before the projected start of a project, the person initiating the project submits detailed justification for the expenditure. That justification may be reviewed by a division or group planning/finance staff, then approved by someone with proper authorization. For example, a division general manager may have authority to approve expenditures up to $50,000. Expenditures of more than $5,000,000 may require approval of the board of directors.

14. Most firms permit managers to invest in projects not included in the annual capital expenditures budget. This flexibility permits managers to take advantage of attractive investments that become available or to make required investments that were not anticipated during the budget process. However, most firms require additional controls on projects not included in the capital expenditures budget. Many firms require that a division or plant substitute a new project for one that was approved in the capital expenditures budget. Others require that projects added during the year be approved by someone in the organization with one level of signing authority higher than normal. For example, if a firm authorizes division managers to approve capital expenditures of up to $50,000 and group vice presidents to approve capital expenditures of up to $100,000, then a $40,000 project not included in the annual capital expenditures budget would need approval by a group vice president.

Administrative-type Projects

15. Many firms classify certain projects as noneconomic or administrative-type investments. For example, in terms of economic analysis, a court order requiring a firm to add pollution control equipment, or a decision by a plant manager to remodel a cafeteria, are more similar to operating expenses than to capital expenditures.

16. Administrative-type projects, if material, should also have measurable objectives so that the investments can be evaluated in the review phase of the budgeting process.

17. Decisions involving administrative-type projects are economic, and eco-

nomic analysis can conceivably be used to justify their acquisition. However, the difficulty in quantifying the intangible aspects of some projects, such as remodeling a cafeteria or repaving a parking lot, and the strategic analysis needed to decide whether to remain in business for some projects, such as replacing a broken press, often make the cost of economic analysis far greater than the value of the benefits.

PART II. GENERAL ACCOUNTING METHODS TO CONTROL PROPERTY, PLANT, AND EQUIPMENT

PROJECT CONTROL

18. Only properly authorized expenditures should be charged to a capital asset account. If an acquisition requires more than a single expenditure, as in the case of a construction project or a complex piece of equipment, expenditures should be controlled with a project or asset work order against which costs are charged.

Interim Project Control and Cost Overruns

19. If a project is of sufficient size, progress reports should periodically compare interim project costs with the original planned costs. Many firms prepare these reports monthly or quarterly. Larger firms often have formal reporting requirements for cost overruns. Major dollar overruns and major percentage overruns must be reported to designated individuals or committees within a certain period after they are detected.

Large Project Control

20. The control needed for a large project depends upon whether the project is a fixed-price or a time-and-materials type project. Control of fixed-price type contracts is generally limited to determining whether the project was completed on schedule and as planned. This evaluation, which may require input from the engineering department, determines whether the completed project is of specified quality and of correct scope. Changes to fixed-price contracts, however, should be controlled in the same manner as changes to time-and-material contracts.

21. Control of time-and-material contracts includes the work described in paragraph 20, but also includes on-site control of expenditures and charges. Control of a time-and-material contract begins with a review of the contract. The contract must be auditable; it must describe all the contractor's accounting policies and techniques; it must limit the contractor's discretion in allocating fringe benefits, overhead costs, and idle time to the project.

22. Once a project is complete, the project account should be closed so that costs can no longer be charged to it.

POST-ACQUISITION AUDITS

23. Post-acquisition audits, or reviews, are used to review the objectives of the budget and to determine whether those objectives were met. Many firms audit all capital expenditure projects while others audit selected projects or all projects above a certain dollar value.

24. All acquisitions should at least be evaluated informally by the manager who initially approved the investment. As part of the corporate oversight responsibility, a corporate officer or the audit committee of the board of directors should compare the actual and projected results for selected investments.

25. Post-audits provide feedback to the senior managers who approve investment decisions. Although managers involved in a project generally know the results of an investment, senior managers often do not, so a post-audit provides information to senior managers. Post-audits also provide a check on overly optimistic forecasts of a project's projected benefits.

26. Post-audits should evaluate whether the capital was invested as planned and, possibly more important, should evaluate the investment decision. The type of project will determine which phase to emphasize. Where project costs are difficult to estimate, such as software development, a post-audit of project costs is often more important. Where product demand and market share are difficult to estimate, as in the case of projects to develop and produce a new product, the post-audit of the investment decision, including revenue projections, is usually more crucial.

27. The post-audit to evaluate whether capital was invested properly is usually conducted between six months to one year after a project's completion. That analysis typically includes some or all of the following factors:

    (1) Was the scope correct? Did the firm obtain what was proposed in the capital expenditures request?

    (2) Was the project completed on time and within budget?

    (3) Was the quality of the plant or equipment as planned?

    (4) Was the quality and quantity of the output as planned?

    (5) Were funds spent for authorized purposes? Answering this question may require an audit to determine whether any excess funds were spent for unauthorized purposes.

28. The post-audit to evaluate the actual economic effects of the investment decision is typically undertaken between two and three years after the project is complete. Factors to be considered include these:

    (1) Was revenue per unit as planned?

(2) Was cost per unit as planned?

(3) Did the project achieve the desired market share?

(4) Was the return on the investment as planned?

29. The same criteria used to justify approval of an investment should be used to evaluate the completed project. If net present value (NPV) was used to justify approval, it should also be used to evaluate the completed project. (See paragraph 49, below, for a definition of NPV.)

30. The capital investment review process should be detailed in the firm's budget manual or a comparable document. The manual should include the timing of these reviews, which projects should be reviewed, and who should conduct the reviews. The budget manual should also describe the technical aspects of the review process, such as whether the review should include an NPV analysis, a comparison of planned and actual investment, a comparison of planned and actual revenues and expenses, and a comparison of the planned and actual impact on production quantity and quality.

CONTROL OF EXISTING ASSETS

31. A manager should be assigned responsibility to oversee the maintenance of each significant asset or group of assets.

32. Tangible capital assets are usually less difficult to control than most other assets because they are often highly visible, difficult to remove, and have a limited resale market. Small, easily portable assets, such as personal computers and audio visual equipment, require more specific controls due to their ease of movement.

33. Asset schedules should be reviewed to ensure that depreciation expense and accumulated depreciation have been properly computed. Assets that are fully, or almost fully, depreciated may be near the end of their physical or economic life. Such assets should be reviewed both to determine whether they will need to be replaced and also to determine whether depreciable lives are reasonable.

34. Individuals should be assigned responsibility to selectively inventory capital assets within their departments, possibly through cycle counts combined with a complete inventory every few years. These periodic reviews should classify assets according to whether they are active or surplus, and whether there is any asset impairment. Assets susceptible to loss because of their size or marketability, such as personal computers, should be inventoried at least annually, and in some cases more frequently.

COMPUTERIZED SYSTEMS FOR ASSET CONTROL

35. Commercial software packages for controlling assets are widely available. These systems can greatly simplify the often tedious work of computing

depreciation expense and of maintaining separate asset and depreciation records for financial and tax reporting. These systems also provide asset control, since most permit an organization to record the location of an asset, and some support input from bar code scanners.

36. The availability of commercial software packages may also influence a firm's choice of base unit (see Statement on Management Accounting No. 4J, "Accounting for Property, Plant, and Equipment"). With low cost-computers and software, it is no longer necessary to combine many capital assets into a larger base unit. To provide better cost control, a firm may choose to implement a computer system and initially record capital assets in more detail. Asset records must also be in sufficient detail to satisfy the tax compliance requirements of the Internal Revenue Service and other taxing authorities.

RETIREMENTS, UNUSED, AND UNDERUTILIZED ASSETS

37. Organizations should use a formal system to ensure that retirements are properly authorized and recorded. Assets should also be periodically reviewed to locate unused or underutilized equipment or facilities. These assets should be analyzed for possible sale or retirement. Any unneeded assets should be physically disposed of because

    (1) they occupy space,

    (2) they may be subject to personal property tax,

    (3) they may be included in the insurable base, and

    (4) their sale may provide the firm with cash.

38. Firms that routinely have assets that are unused or underutilized should consider establishing a methodology to dispose of such assets. Other divisions or subsidiaries within the company should be notified of available assets before disposing of those assets externally. A control should also be established in the purchasing process to ensure, before purchases are made, that there are not similar unused assets available within the organization. A firm should also determine if the nonuse or under- utilization of these assets is temporary or permanent before deciding on disposition.

REPAIRS

39. Repair costs should be evaluated in total and as a percent of business activity. Unusually low repair costs may indicate that needed repairs are avoided to reduce costs. Unusually high repair costs may indicate that assets are being used improperly, and/or that they will soon need major overhaul or replacement.

40. Where there is high cost associated with failure to properly maintain equipment, such as with airplanes or nuclear power plants, the primary

focus should be on ensuring that repairs have been made. In lower-risk environments, such as buildings or production equipment, managers should balance the cost of too-frequent repairs with the economic costs associated with poorly maintained assets, such as lower quality output and lost production due to equipment failures.

RISK PROGRAMS

41. Investments should be evaluated for the risk involved, and those risks should be periodically reviewed and monitored. Proper risk control involves (1) risk analysis, (2) risk mitigation, and (3) risk management.

Risk Analysis

42. Risk analysis considers the risks involved in an investment. This includes both the risk to the capital equipment, (e.g., the risk of locating a plant in a hurricane or earthquake zone) and the risk involved in selling a product produced by the equipment (e.g., health risks from selling a chemical, or product liability risks from selling a product bought for infants).

Risk Mitigation

43. Risk mitigation considers steps that can be taken to reduce risk. Examples include fire suppression systems, safes, security systems, and alarms. Risk mitigation also includes major steps, such as (1) specifying that a building be built to withstand an earthquake of up to a certain intensity, and (2) limiting business risks by considering the possible obsolescence of acquired equipment.

Risk Management

44. Once an investment has been undertaken, an organization should take steps to manage the risks associated with it. For example, periodic reviews are important to identify changing risks and to determine whether insurance coverage is adequate. It has become increasingly important to consider the risk of buying property that may contain toxic chemicals, and to consider the risk in producing products whose production process generates toxic waste.

45. An organization should periodically review its assets, including changes in market values and replacement costs, to determine insurance needs. The amount of self-retained risk should be carefully documented. Deductibles in insurance policies will reduce the cost of an insurance policy; however, the maximum coverage, when less than the market value of the insured assets, represents self-retained risk. An organization should also review insurance coverage after major capital additions or acquisitions and before new product introductions.

PLANNING FOR ASSET REPLACEMENT

46. Organizations should have formal programs to plan for longer-term asset replacements. Such a program should review both leased and owned equipment. That program should consider when, or whether, leases should be renewed and whether owned assets should be replaced by leased assets.

PLANNING FOR ASSET MAINTENANCE

47. Organizations should plan for long-term routine and nonroutine maintenance. Equipment overhauls should be tied into regular plant maintenance schedules. Firms should also periodically evaluate whether equipment requires major repair. This review should include not only obvious equipment, such as pumps and motors, but also less obvious items, such as pipes and wiring. The review of maintenance plans should be an ongoing process.

DEFINITIONS

48. Property, Plant, and Equipment. Assets that are used in operations, that have an economic life of more than one year, and that have physical substance. Property, plant, and equipment are sometimes referred to as fixed assets.

49. Net Present Value (NPV). The present value (discounted value) of future after-tax cash flows, less the initial cost of an investment.

REFERENCES

Babad, Yair M., and Kathryn M. Cullen. "Criteria for Selecting Accounting Software: Part III." *Journal of Accounting and EDP* (Spring 1986): 35-44.

Brealey, Richard A., and Stewart C. Myers. *Principles of Corporate Finance.* New York: McGraw-Hill, 1988.

Carmine, Jr., F. Thomas. "Fixed Asset Management: Another Use for the Personal Computer." *The Virginia Accountant* (December 1984): 42-43.

Cook, John W., and Gary M. Winkle. *Auditing*, Third Edition. Boston: Houghton Mifflin Company, 1984. See pp 460-65.

Corr, Arthur V. *The Capital Expenditure Decision*. New York: National Association of Accountants, and Ontario: The Society of Management Accountants of Canada, 1983.

"Finance: The Capital Investment Decision—How to Make it." *Financial Executive* (July/August, 1988): pp. 40-47.

Grobstein, Michael, Stephen E. Loeb, and Robert D. Neary. *Auditing: A Risk*

Analysis Approach. Homewood, Ill.: Richard D. Irwin, Inc., 1985. See pp. 392-403.

International Federation of Accountants. Exposure Draft No. 2: *Proposed International Management Accounting Practice on Internal Control of the Capital Expenditure Decision.* New York: International Federation of Accountants, 1958.

Kell, Walter G., William C. Boynton, and Richard E. Ziegler. *Modern Auditing,* Third Edition. New York: John Wiley & Sons, 1986. See pp. 519-25.

Kraus, Jerome. *How U.S. Firms Measure Productivity.* New York: National Association of Accountants, 1984.

Locke, Susan A. "Should You Set Up an Accounting System for Capital Assets?". *Touche Ross Public Sector Review* (August 1986): 1-4.

Meschke, Marvin F. "Keeping Track of Office Assets Via Computer." *Management Accounting* (July 1984): 38-41.

Myers, Stewart C. "Finance Theory and Financial Strategy." *Midland Corporate Finance Journal.* (Spring 1987): pp. 6-13.

National Association of Accountants. Statement on Management Accounting No. 4J: *Accounting for Property, Plant, and Equipment.* New York: National Association of Accountants, 1990.

National Association of Accountants. Statement on Management Accounting No. 4A: *Cost of Capital.* Montvale, N.J.: National Association of Accountants, 1984.

National Association of Accountants. Statement on Management Accounting No. 4H: *Uses of the Cost of Capital.* Montvale, N.J.: National Association of Accountants, 1987.

Robinson, Leonard A., James R. Davis, and C. Wayne Alderman. *Accounting Information Systems: A Cycle Approach.* New York: Harper & Row, 1982. See pp. 483-92.

Stettler, Howard F. *Auditing Principles: A Systems-Based Approach.* Englewood Cliffs, N.J.: Prentice-Hall, Inc., 1982. See pp. 476-99.

Sullivan, Jerry D., Richard A. Gnospelius, Philip L. Defliese, and Henry R. Jaenicke. *Montgomery's Auditing,* Tenth Edition. New York: Ronald Press, 1985. See pp. 703-33.

Van Horne, James C. *Financial Management and Policy.* Englewood Cliffs, N.J.: Prentice Hall, Inc., 1989.

NATIONAL ASSOCIATION OF ACCOUNTANTS
MANAGEMENT ACCOUNTING PRACTICES COMMITTEE
SUBCOMMITTEE ON SMA PROMULGATION
1989-1990

Statements on Management Accounting

Statement Number 4M
September 7, 1990

PRACTICES AND TECHNIQUES

Understanding Financial Instruments

In accordance with the charge to the Management Accounting Practices (MAP) Committee to issue statements on management accounting principles and practices, Statements on Management Accounting are promulgated to reflect official positions of the National Association of Accountants (NAA). The work of the MAP Committee is based on a framework for management accounting, whose principal categories are:

1. Objectives
2. Terminology
3. Concepts
4. Practices and Techniques
5. Management of Accounting Activities

Statements on Management Accounting

Statement Number 4M
September 7, 1990

Practices and Techniques:
Understanding Financial Instruments

National Association of Accountants, Inc.

Acknowledgments

The National Association of Accountants is grateful to all who contributed to the publication of Statement 4M, "Understanding Financial Instruments." Appreciation is extended to members of NAA's Management Accounting Practices (MAP) Committee and its Subcommittee on SMA Promulgation. Special thanks to go to Michael J. Sandretto, University of Illinois, for his research and writing associated with the project, and to the members of the MAP Committee's review panel: John E. Stewart, John J. Perrell III, and MAP Committee chairman Robert G. Weiss.

Introduction

1. This document provides background information about financial instruments and discusses methods used to evaluate them. It considers financial transactions engaged in to raise capital, to invest funds, or to reduce economic risk (hedge). The primary focus of this document is on the economic analysis used to evaluate particular financial instruments. It is a reference to be used when an accounting professional is called upon to evaluate financial instruments. Technical financial tools, tax and legal issues, internal controls, and financial accounting regulations are discussed briefly from a management perspective, and further references for those topics are listed in the bibliography.

2. This document also contains a comprehensive glossary of current terminology.

Statement of Scope

3. To properly evaluate a financial instrument it is necessary to understand the objectives of an organization, the economic risks and benefits offered by the financial instrument under consideration, and the alternatives. Although the objectives of a specific organization are a primary factor, this Statement considers those objectives only in a general manner.

4. Part I of this Statement discusses reasons for the introduction of additional types of financial instruments. Part II considers general uses of financial instruments. Part III discusses the risks that an organization faces by owning or issuing financial instruments. Part IV considers specific risks and features of individual financial instruments, categorized by groups, while Part V provides a basic introduction to hedging. Part VI considers internal control issues; it is followed by a glossary and a bibliography.

5. This Statement covers the most commonly used financial instruments. New financial instruments are continually developed, but in many cases they may differ from the financial instruments discussed in this document in relatively minor ways. The general risks and benefits discussed in this document will, in most instances, apply to newly developed financial instruments.

6. This Statement is limited to management accounting. It is not a comprehensive review of financial accounting rules (GAAP) or of tax rules and regulations.

PART I: ADDITIONAL FINANCIAL INSTRUMENTS

7. Since the mid-1970s the variety of financial instruments has increased significantly. These additional instruments were made available for a

variety of reasons ranging from increased complexity of commerce to feasibility because of changes in regulations, communications, and computing power.

8. Changing Regulatory Environment. Financial institutions and financial markets are in various stages of deregulation in the United States, Japan, Germany, the United Kingdom, and other nations. Deregulation allows financial institutions to develop financial instruments that were once prohibited. As institutions in one nation introduce a new type of financial instrument there is pressure on other governments to permit similar financial instruments.

9. Because of changes in government regulation, financial institutions have been pressured or required to increase their capital. To meet regulatory capital requirements, financial institutions use innovative methods to raise capital, to hedge, and to utilize off-balance sheet financing techniques.

10. Modified Rules and Regulations for Taxes and Financial Accounting. As tax rules and regulations are changed, new financial instruments are introduced to minimize taxes in various situations. Similarly, as financial accounting rules change, financial instruments are developed to achieve certain income statement and balance sheet results.

11. Increased Competition Among Financial Institutions. Deregulation has led to additional competition among investment banks, commercial banks, insurance companies, and merchant banks. This competitive pressure has led to innovation in developing financial products that respond to a variety of client needs and to innovation in marketing them to financial, industrial, and not-for-profit clients.

12. Greater Economic Volatility. Until the early 1970s foreign exchange rates were fixed, interest rate volatility was low, credit conditions changed slowly, and commodity prices were comparatively stable. Under floating exchange rates, deregulated financial markets, and less stable commodity price and credit conditions, the volatility that firms face in terms of interest and exchange rates and market prices has increased markedly. Firms often seek to limit their exposure to these risks; many financial instruments have been developed to meet that need.

13. Internationalization of Commerce. Firms increasingly conduct trade in foreign countries, have customers, suppliers, and subsidiaries in other countries, and are more likely to borrow or invest funds in other countries. These operating and financing activities pose numerous risks, and many financial instruments were developed to limit those risks.

14. Improvements in Technology. Rapid telecommunication and improved computing technology permit firms to analyze and use financial instruments that were previously too complex to evaluate in the time available. These developments include satellite transmission of prices, the accessibility of large financial databases that are continually updated, and high-speed

computers to process that information. This technology facilitates global financial markets, because it is now possible to execute a financial transaction at almost any time of day somewhere in the world, and there are proposals to implement around-the-clock trading at exchanges within the United States.

PART II: GENERAL USES OF FINANCIAL INSTRUMENTS

15. To meet the various needs of organizations, financial instruments are available with features that were previously unavailable (such as interest rate swaps) or with only some of the features of traditional debt and equity instruments. For example, zero-coupon bonds, which repay principal but do not currently pay interest, are equivalent to only the principal portion of a traditional debt instrument. Because of the greatly expanded choice of features in financial instruments, it is important for a firm to consider its objectives before entering a financial transaction.

16. Raise Funds. This is one of the most common reasons to enter into a financial transaction. The choices have expanded to include put-able common stock, dutch auction preferred stock, and numerous other new instruments. In addition, instruments such as swaps and futures can be used to effectively convert a debt issue with a floating interest rate into a combined debt package with a fixed interest rate payment. Such a combination can be arranged either at the time of the debt issue or at a later date.

17. Invest Funds. This is another straightforward reason to enter a financial transaction. As in the case of raising funds, there are now far more choices among financial instruments. They include mortgage-backed securities that have been separated into many classes, or tranches. Such packaging offers maturity features often unavailable with other investments, but the instruments are often extremely difficult to evaluate.

18. Reduce Financing Costs. Firms may use asset-based financing to reduce financing costs. Although asset-based financing was often used in the past, there are now far more alternatives. Another alternative is an interest rate swap to take advantage of arbitrage opportunities in interest rates in various markets. As an example, an industrial firm wanting to obtain medium-term fixed-rate debt may be able to do so only at great cost. Floating-rate debt, however, may be readily available. To take advantage of a financial institution's ability to issue fixed-rate medium-term debt at more favorable terms, an industrial firm may swap its floating-rate interest payments for a financial institution's fixed-rate interest payments.

19. Hedge the Exposure to Risk. Firms now have a variety of financial instruments to limit their exposure to foreign exchange risk, interest rate risk, and other operating and financial risks. These instruments include futures,

forwards, options, caps, and swaps. In addition, it is now relatively simple to evaluate the cost of such instruments.

20. Accounting, Tax, or Regulatory Objectives. Some financial transactions are designed to minimize taxes, to impact (or not impact) reported earnings, or to minimize debt for financial or regulatory accounting purposes. While these issues are frequently not the main reason for making a financial transaction, they are often a major consideration.

PART III: GENERAL RISKS OF OWNING OR ISSUING FINANCIAL INSTRUMENTS

21. The risks that an organization faces when it enters an operating or a financial transaction are likely more numerous and more complex than in the past. These risks are greater because of increasingly complex commerce, reduced government regulation, and greater international competition.

III. A. Economic Risks

22. Financial Risk. The risk from financial leverage. If two firms are identical except that one is financed primarily with equity and the other primarily with debt, the firm with more debt is more risky to both equity and debt holders (although equity holders have the potential for larger gains in a more leveraged firm). The difference in risk is considered financial risk.

23. Interest Rate Risk. The risk from fluctuating interest rates. For a borrower, increasing interest rates are the primary risk for a floating-rate debt instrument, while for an investor/lender increasing interest rates are one of the primary risks (together with default risk) in a fixed-rate debt instrument. In some cases financial instruments exist, and are used, to reduce interest rate risks.

24. For an investor, the longer the period until repayment of interest and principal, the greater the interest rate risk. Thus, a zero-coupon bond, which does not currently pay interest, is the debt instrument with the greatest amount of interest rate risk. Similarly, a bond that sells at a discount has a greater interest rate risk than an equivalent bond with an identical maturity date that sells at par.

25. Default Risk. The risk that a borrower will be unable to meet its financial obligations. This is often measured by the ratings from Standard and Poor's or Moody's ratings services. The top four ratings in each service indicate investment grade bonds. An investment grade rating typically qualifies bonds for certain institutional portfolios. Investment grade bonds typically carry a lower effective interest rate and are usually easier to market than lower rated bonds.

26. Bonds that do not qualify for an investment grade rating are considered

high-yield or noninvestment grade bonds. At one time such bonds consisted primarily of debt from firms that were too small to be classified in the top four ratings. Such firms were usually highly stable and included many well managed and conservatively financed utilities. The effective interest rates paid by such institutions were typically well above interest rates on investment grade bonds even though the bonds were only slightly more risky.

27. In the early 1980s investment banks emphasized the relatively high interest rates paid by noninvestment grade bonds. At the same time, the supply of noninvestment grade bonds changed dramatically. From a market that consisted primarily of stable, conservatively managed and financed smaller firms, the market developed into one with bonds from firms that had been acquired with very little equity. These changes subjected debt-holders to a default risk considerably greater than for earlier noninvestment grade issues.

28. Prepayment Risk. The risk that an investment in a fixed-rate debt instrument will be repaid early. For example, an investment in a pool of mortgages may offer an attractive long-term interest rate. If interest rates decline, however, the borrowers are likely to repay their loans early. The investor must then reinvest funds at far less attractive interest rates.

29. In some cases the interest and principal payments for an investment pool of mortgages is subdivided into interest-only and principal-only investment pools. In the case of an interest-only pool, if mortgages are prepaid, the interest payments may be far lower than anticipated. In other cases potential cash flows from a mortgage pool are reserved for investors purchasing the residual cash flows. If prepayments exceed some level, owners of the rights to the residual cash flows may receive nothing. Thus, prepayment risk ranges from the need to reinvest cash flows at unexpectedly low interest rates, to the possibility of receiving far lower payments from an I/O pool, to the possibility of receiving no payment at all.

30. Currency Risk. The risk from fluctuating currency rates. A firm may purchase a machine tool from a supplier in Japan at a price of 50 million yen, payable in 90 days. If the value of the yen increases, the firm will be required to pay more for the machine tool than anticipated. The area of foreign exchange risk has been one of the most active areas for the development of financial products that limit risk.

III. B. General Risks

31. Sovereign Risk. There is a risk that a foreign government will default on its loans, expropriate property, impose confiscatory taxes or export/import duties, restrict payments, or take other action that will harm a firm. Firms often produce only part of a product in any one country to minimize these risks. In the case of natural resource developments, such minimization actions are not feasible.

32. Regulatory Risk. Financial transactions are sometimes undertaken to reduce taxes, to impact reported accounting income, or to remove liabilities from the balance sheet. There is a risk that laws, rules, or regulations will change in response to financial instruments developed to achieve such results. The Financial Accounting Standards Board (FASB) is engaged in a major multiyear project dealing with financial instruments. The Emerging Issues Task Force of the FASB often affects accounting rules for financial instruments on a short-term basis. The International Accounting Standards Committee is also working on a major project, as are accounting committees in other nations.

33. Internal Control-Complexity Risks. Many financial instruments are difficult to evaluate because they are so complex or because the firm's accounting or internal audit department has only limited information about the instrument. This is particularly true of some hedge transactions, of transactions that involve multiple currencies, and of transactions involving thinly traded financial instruments. Such instruments pose considerable problems for internal control.

34. Other internal control risks include extension beyond established financial limits, concentration on a particular industry or region, and theft or fraud.

III. C. Market Risks

35. Liquidity Risk. Liquidity is the ability to quickly buy or sell a security in quantity with little effect on price. Most equity securities traded on the New York Stock Exchange (NYSE) are reasonably liquid. The average spread (difference between the "bid" price and the "asked" price) for a stock that sells for $60 per share typically ranges from 1/8 to 1/4 ($.125 to $.25) for the 500 largest corporations traded on the NYSE. The bids or asks (offers) are often for only a few thousand shares, but in most cases trades of 20,000 shares or more can be carried out with little effect on price, particularly if a block trader from an investment bank or brokerage firm is permitted to handle the trade. Few other markets approach that liquidity.

36. Equity securities traded on the American Stock Exchange (AMEX) or traded over-the-counter often have spreads of 1/2 (.$50) or more on a $10 stock. The size of the bids or offers for such securities are often for only 100 or 200 shares, and block traders are frequently unable to trade large orders without significant price changes. With some exceptions, such as Tokyo, Bonn, and London, liquidity can be a serious problem in foreign equity markets.

37. Many options are also illiquid. The Standard and Poor's 100 index option is one of the most liquid option contracts in the United States, but "out of the money" S&P 100 index options, often priced at $2.00 or less, frequently trade with a spread of 1/4 or more. Although that is only $.25, it is 12.5% for a one-way trade. During periods of high economic uncertainty, such

spreads occasionally exceed 1/2. The options markets for commodities and for equity securities of very large corporations are also reasonably liquid most of the time. Common stock options for most corporations traded on the major options exchanges are relatively illiquid.

38. Liquidity is also a problem with most debt securities except for U.S. Government securities, a few other major U. S. Government-backed debt issues, and debt issues of large corporations. In the case of debt securities for large corporations, liquidity is not a major problem, but bond dealers have an advantage of better price information than their customers, so it is necessary to exercise caution when trading such securities. In other instances, particularly in the case of noninvestment grade bonds, a customer may be able to trade only through one dealer. In such cases liquidity is often a serious problem. Illiquidity can also be a serious consideration for unlisted options, swaps, caps, mortgage-backed securities, and other specialized financial instruments.

39. A second definition of liquidity refers to the ability of an enterprise to repay its debt. (Default risk, para. 25.)

40. <u>Fair Market Risk.</u> The NYSE, the AMEX, a few foreign equity markets, and markets for U.S. Government securities are widely regarded as fair markets. Investors can expect to trade in those markets at the posted bid and asked prices and in the volumes quoted. In many other markets investors often find that their trades are not executed at the posted prices. Recent investigations of certain U.S. options and futures markets have uncovered examples of problems in markets that are allegedly unfair.

41. <u>Options Risks.</u> There are well understood risks with purchased options. The investor may lose all or part of the initial investment; the market for many options is thin, so there are often serious liquidity risks; some options markets are allegedly unfair.

42. The risks to written options are also reasonably well understood but can be far greater than the risks for purchased options. The most obvious risk is that a written call option has the potential for unlimited loss. The maximum loss for the writer of a put option is the exercise price of the underlying security, less the amount received for sale of the option. These risks were highlighted by the market decline of October 1987.

43. A less obvious risk to the writer of an option is the risk that an option will be exercised early. While it is rare for an option to be exercised early (other than early exercise of a call option for common stock, immediately prior to a dividend), it does occur. If an investor is using a written option in a supposed hedging strategy, it is possible that the hedge will be eliminated and will need to be reestablished at a higher cost.

44. <u>Margin Risks.</u> Many financial instruments are purchased on margin. If the investor suffers an unrealized loss on the investment, additional funds, determined by the amount of such loss, must be deposited with the broker.

If such additional deposits are not made, a position will be "closed out" without the investor's approval.

PART IV: SPECIFIC RISKS AND FEATURES OF INDIVIDUAL FINANCIAL INSTRUMENTS

45. This section is separated into six subsections: (A) Debt Instruments, (B) Futures and Forwards, (C) Swaps, (D) Options, (E) Equity and Equity-like Features, and (F) Caps, Floors, and Collars. Each subsection begins with a general discussion of issues.

IV.A. Debt Instruments

46. Traditional debt issues are straightforward from both an accounting and a finance perspective; some newly devised instruments raise complex and unsettled issues. One issue is whether a financing is a sale of assets (e.g., receivables) or merely a secured loan: (1) In some situations a financial transaction designed to raise funds triggers an immediate gain or loss and may remove assets (and related liabilities) from a firm's balance sheet. In some cases gains or losses are recognized in the income statement; in other cases they are reported as a component of shareholders' equity (e.g., conversion of convertible debt). (2) A similar transaction structured differently may have no effect on a firm's income statement or shareholders' equity section.

47. Other factors also influence how a financial transaction is considered for accounting and tax purposes. These include the type of transaction (e.g., investment or hedge) and the type of organization (operating entity, financial institution, or dealer in financial instruments). Because of the wide range of existing and potential financial structures, the issues described in this and the preceding paragraph are unsettled for many financial instruments and transactions.

IV.A.1. Standard Debt Issues

Treasury Bills (T-bills)

48. T-bills consist of 90-day, 180-day, and 365-day debt issues (actually 13-, 26-, and 52-week, or 91-, 182-, and 364-day bills). The 90- and 180-day bills are issued weekly while 365-day bills are issued monthly. They are among the most liquid investments in the world and among the lowest in credit risk (essentially risk-free) and have low interest rate risk because of the short term until maturity.

49. T-bills are noninterest-bearing securities; they sell at a discount from their

face value that reflects their effective interest rate. T-bills are usually quoted in the financial pages at both a bid and an ask discount percent (discount if maturity were in 360 days) and at an annual yield: 7.92 bid, 7.85 ask, 8.12 yield for a 90-day T-bill, for example (see Para. 50-52).

50. The yield quoted in the financial pages and by bond dealers is a bond-equivalent yield typically computed using a 365-day year. The bond-equivalent yield for a period of less than six months is the simple rate of interest (uncompounded). For periods of greater than six months the bond-equivalent yield is the interest rate that would be earned if the interest were compounded semiannually.

51. The price of the 90-day T-bill described above is computed as follows:

Price = $10,000 * (1 – ask yield x (days to maturity / 360))
       = $10,000 * (1 – .0785 * (91/360)) = $9,801.56

52. The bond-equivalent yield on the above T-bill would be computed as a simple rate of interest because the period is for less than six months:

{((1/.980156)–1) x (365/91)} – 1 = .0812

53. The annual compound interest rate on the above T-bill is computed as follows:

$$(1/\text{price})^{(365/\text{days to maturity})} - 1$$

The annual compound interest rate on the above T-bill is:

$$(1/.980156)^{(365/91)} - 1 = .08371$$

Whether a bond-equivalent yield or a compound interest rate is quoted, the interest rate is greater than the ask discount, which in this example is 7.85%.

54. T-bills mature at face value. The difference between the discount (purchase price) and the face value is interest income subject to federal income tax but not to state or local income taxes. Contracts to purchase U.S. Government securities call for delivery and payment on the first business day following the trade date (regular-way delivery).

55. T-bills are sold at auction whereby potential bidders can submit either competitive or noncompetitive bids. Noncompetitive bids by private investors are accepted in full (up to a limit). The remainder of the offering is allocated to competitive bidders, beginning with the highest bid, until the issue is fully allocated. The lowest accepted price is referred to as the stop-out price. Noncompetitive bidders receive the weighted average price paid by competitive bidders.

56. Liquidity. While T-bills and other Treasury securities are highly liquid instruments, for most other debt instruments there is considerably less information on the bid and asked prices than for equity securities traded on the NYSE. In some cases investors have paid more or received less for debt securities than if they had traded with another broker or dealer. Whenever

trading debt securities it is prudent to call two or more broker/dealers for quotes on a particular debt issue. This is considerably more important for non-Treasury issues, where illiquidity and lack of timely and accurate market information are far more serious problems.

Treasury Notes

57. Treasury notes are interest-bearing general obligations of the U.S. Government, issued with maturities of from two to 10 years, in denominations of from $1,000 to $500 million. Two-year notes are issued monthly while three- to 10-year notes are issued quarterly. Treasury notes pay a fixed rate of interest in semiannual installments and are issued and quoted as a percentage of their face value. Secondary market quotes are shown in thirty-seconds of a point. A quote of 103.16 for a $1,000 note indicates a price of 103 16/32, or $1,035.00.

58. When Treasury notes or Treasury bonds are traded prior to maturity the seller is paid simple interest for the actual number of days since the last interest payment date. For example, the seller of a 6.35% $10,000 Treasury note held for 37 days would receive $10,000 * .0635 * .5 (one-half year) * (37/days from last interest payment until next interest payment). This is in contrast to the 30-day month 360-day year used to compute interest on municipal and corporate bonds.

59. The primary risk in holding Treasury notes and bonds is that the interest rate will increase causing the market price of the debt security to decline. A particular advantage of these securities is that most do not have a call feature, so the purchaser is assured of a constant yield to maturity. This feature is often a major advantage for pension plans.

60. As in the case of Treasury bills, Treasury notes (and bonds) are sold at auction, and investors may submit either competitive or noncompetitive bids. The bidding process for Treasury notes and bonds is somewhat different from the process for Treasury bills. Competitive bidders submit bids for a yield. The Treasury then sets the coupon on the security to the nearest 1/8% so that the average price charged to successful bidders is 100 or less. Each successful bidder is then charged a price so that the yield to maturity equals the submitted yield bid.

Treasury Bonds

61. Treasury bonds are fully registered bonds that pay a fixed rate of interest semiannually. They are currently issued with maturities of 30 years in denominations of from $1,000 to $1 million. In the past Treasury bonds were also issued with maturities of 15 and 20 years. As in the case of Treasury notes, Treasury bonds are issued and quoted as a percentage of face value and secondary market quotes are shown in thirty-seconds of a point.

62. Some older Treasury bonds contain call features. Because of the demand

for stripped Treasury bonds (bonds whose interest payment coupons have been stripped from the principal portion of the bond and sold separately), beginning in 1985 the Treasury eliminated the call feature from Treasury bonds so that, at the purchaser's option, Treasuries may be issued in stripped form.

Federal Agency Notes (Agency Securities; Agencies)

63. Agencies of the federal government, such as the Government National Mortgage Association (GNMA), and government-sponsored enterprises (GSEs), such as the Federal National Mortgage Association ("Fannie Mae") or the Federal Home Loan Mortgage Corporation (FHLMC), issue both short-term and long-term debt. These notes and bonds are actively traded but offer slightly higher yields than Treasury securities because they are less marketable and, other than GNMA, are not backed by the "full faith and credit" of the federal government. Further, they may subject the investor to the additional risk of an uncertain maturity due to prepayments. Most investors consider the credit risk of agency notes to be minor.

64. Debt issues from the major GSEs are highly liquid, but illiquidity may be a serious problem with the debt issues from the minor agency issuers. The interest income from a few agency debt issues is subject to state and local income taxes, but most agency issues are exempt from state and local income taxes.

Certificates of Deposit

65. Certificates of deposit (CDs) are short-term debt obligations issued by banks or savings and loan institutions. CDs are insured for the first $100,000 by the federal government. CDs for larger amounts that are issued by large, conservatively financed banks and that are negotiable are usually considered to be highly liquid and to have low credit risk.

66. The CD-equivalent yield is a benchmark interest rate against which other investments are often compared. Unlike the T-bill equivalent yield, which is based on a 365-day year-count, the CD-equivalent yield is based on a 360-day year-count. That is, if a T-bill is to be outstanding for 365 days, a 10% yield would pay 10% of the investment, compounded semiannually. If a CD is to be outstanding for 365 days, a 10% yield would pay 10% multiplied by (365/360) of the investment. The CD-equivalent yield is compounded semiannually only for CDs with a maturity of more than one year. Thus, for securities with a maturity of more than a year, the CD-equivalent yield is slightly higher than the Treasury equivalent yield.

Commercial Paper

67. Large, secure, well-known organizations are able to obtain short-term funds by issuing unsecured debt known as "commercial paper." Although commercial paper was originally issued primarily by industrial corporations and

finance companies, it is now also issued by banks, foreign entities, and government agencies. Because of their high credit rating, these organizations are able to sell an issue directly to investors, or to investors through a dealer. Maturities range from a few weeks to 270 days, but most commercial paper matures in 30 days (registration with the SEC is not required for issues not exceeding 270 days).

68. While commercial paper is usually sold with a maturity of 30 days, most institutions intend to "rollover" the debt into a subsequent 30-day issue of commercial paper. Although commercial paper is unsecured, firms often back up an issue with a guaranteed line of credit from a major bank to ensure that the firm will have funds to repay the issue in the event that the firm is unable to "roll" its paper. Although there is no general secondary market for commercial paper, most dealers or organizations will repurchase an issue that they have sold.

69. Most commercial paper is rated by at least one of the major credit rating services (e.g., Moody's or Standard and Poor's). Because of the requisite high credit rating of organizations that issue commercial paper and because many issues are backed by bank guarantees, credit risk is usually small. Commercial paper trades at a higher yield than Treasury issues primarily because of the greater credit risk but partially because most commercial paper is relatively less liquid. The commercial paper market is currently larger than the market for Treasury bills.

70. Asset-Based Commercial Paper. This is commercial paper issued by a shell company whose only assets are trade receivables or term receivables such as auto loan or credit card receivables. Asset-based commercial paper often provides corporations funds at a lower cost than other alternatives, such as factoring or bank financing.

Corporate Bonds

71. Corporate bonds are long-term debt obligations that typically pay a stated interest rate for the life of the bond. This stated interest rate is often called the coupon rate, because in the past corporate bonds were typically issued with coupons attached that could be clipped off and exchanged for a fixed semiannual interest payment. The stated, or coupon, interest rate is also called the nominal interest rate; the actual, or effective, interest rate depends upon the price paid for a bond. The interest rate for corporate bonds is computed on a 30-day month and a 360-day year.

72. Corporate bonds issued by large U.S. corporations were, in the past, among the least risky investments available. The interest rate risk was low because interest rates were generally stable, and the default risk was low because of the large safety factor provided by conservative financing practices. More recently even corporate bonds issued by large conservative firms are subject to default risk because of the possibility of added debt resulting from takeovers. For example, the bonds of RJR Corporation suffered a signifi-

cant price decline when the firm was acquired in a highly leveraged buyout. As another example, the bonds of Interco collapsed in value after Interco issued significant amounts of debt, then paid a large cash dividend to equity holders to protect against a hostile takeover.

73. High-Yield Bonds. Bonds that do not qualify for one of the top four rankings of Moody's or Standard and Poor's rating services. These bonds are not considered investment grade so are not considered acceptable for certain investment portfolios and can be only a small percentage of the total investments of other investment portfolios. As described in paragraphs 25-27, prior to about 1980 the high-yield bond market consisted of bonds issued by conservatively managed corporations that were too small to qualify for one of the top four ratings. During the 1980s that market changed to one where most of the bonds were issued by thinly capitalized corporations that had been acquired through leveraged buyouts. In addition, as described in the preceding paragraph, bonds classified as investment-grade issues can suddenly become high-yield or junk bonds as a result of a takeover or a defense against a takeover.

74. Convertible Bonds. Bonds that offer investors an opportunity to exchange a bond for a stated number of shares of common stock in the issuing corporation on or subsequent to some future date. The number of shares of common stock that a bond may be exchanged for is termed the conversion ratio. For example a bond with a conversion ratio of 2:1 may be exchanged for two shares of common stock. In some cases a cash payment may be required to exercise the conversion privilege.

75. Debentures. Corporate bonds of large stable firms often issued without specific collateral. These debenture bonds are backed by the good faith and credit of a corporation.

76. Mortgage Bonds. Bonds secured by a mortgage on specific real assets (buildings and land) owned by a corporation. These bonds may be closed-end mortgage bonds, in which case the proceeds from the sale of mortgaged property must be used first to repay the first issue of mortgage bonds. Mortgage bonds may also be open-ended bonds, in which case the corporation is allowed to issue additional bonds at a later date that receive the same preference in the event of default as the earlier issue of mortgage bonds.

77. Equipment Trust Certificate. A secured bond usually sold by railroads and airlines to finance the purchase of rolling stock and airplanes. The bonds are designed to be repaid more rapidly than the equipment declines in value, to ensure adequate security in the event of default.

78. Collateral Trust Bond. A bond backed by other financial instruments. Commonly a corporation will back a collateral trust bond issue with the common stock of one or more of its subsidiaries.

79. Guaranteed Bond. A bond whose payment of interest and repayment of principal is guaranteed by a company other than the issuing corporation.

80. Call Provisions. Many corporate and municipal bonds contain call provisions that permit the borrower to purchase outstanding bonds on or after a certain date, usually by paying the bondholders a certain call premium. A call provision offers the borrower some protection against a decline in interest rates after the bond is issued. That protection, however, causes callable bonds to sell at a discount to an equivalent noncallable bond to compensate for the risk borne by the bondholders.

81. Restrictive and Protective Covenants. Most bonds contain certain restrictions on the activity of the borrower or offer certain protective covenants to bondholders. Common examples of restrictive covenants are limitations on additional debt that is not subordinate to a particular bond issue and limitations on off-balance sheet financing such as leases. Protective, or positive, covenants prevent the borrower from taking action that would benefit shareholders at the expense of bondholders. A common example would be maintenance of a minimum net worth in order for a corporation to pay dividends.

Municipal Bonds

82. Municipal bonds are issued by states, territories, possessions, and political subdivisions of the United States. Political subdivisions include counties, cities, and special districts for schools, waste disposal, and other political purposes.

83. The interest income from most municipal bonds is exempt from U.S. federal taxation and in some cases from state and local income taxes. States generally exempt from state income tax any bonds issued by a political entity within their own state. Bonds issued by a territory, commonwealth, or possession of the United States are exempt from federal, state, and local income taxes. Such bonds are referred to as triple tax exempts. (This paragraph is prior to consideration of the alternative minimum tax in the United States, which must also be considered.)

84. Municipal bonds are interest-paying debt issues that pay interest semiannually as a stated percent of the face value of the bond. Since 1983 all U.S. municipal bonds have been issued in registered form. (Registered bonds pay interest to bondholders whose names appear on a list, or register, of bondholders. In contrast, bearer bonds pay interest to whoever mails in a coupon that was originally physically attached to the bond.)

85. Risks. Municipal bonds carry the normal risks associated with bonds, but because many are issued by specific funding units, there may be significant risk of default or of delayed payment. In addition, many municipal bonds are relatively illiquid.

IV. A. 2. Repos And Reverse Repos

Repurchase Agreements (Repos, Buy-backs)

86. Repos are among the investments with the greatest liquidity in the United States (although because they are not negotiable they are not considered liquid investments). In form, repos are the purchase of a security combined with an agreement that the seller will repurchase the security on a specified date at a specified price. The difference between the two prices reflects the interest, or "repo" rate. Repos may be for any term but are most commonly used for very short-term investments by corporations, financial institutions, and pension funds that enter repo agreements with banks or other government securities dealers.

87. An "overnight repo" is probably the most common transaction; the "overnight repo rate" is usually slightly lower than the federal funds rate (the rate of interest paid on a bank's excess deposits in the Federal Reserve and the rate of interest at which those funds are loaned to other banks). Longer-term repos may be for a fixed period, in which case they pay higher rates, or may be "open repos" that pay the current "overnight repo rate" each day. Open repos may be terminated on one day's notice by either party.

88. While the term "repo" implies a sale of a security, depending on circumstances a repo may range from a sale to an unsecured loan to a secured loan. If the purchaser takes delivery of the securities the argument to view the transaction as a sale is strengthened (although it is not considered a sale for accounting purposes). If the seller/borrower transfers securities to a custodial agent and signs an agreement with the custodian stating that the securities are collateral for a repo-loan, then the purchaser/lender has a secured loan. If the seller/borrower simply holds securities for the benefit of the purchaser/lender, then the repo is likely to be viewed as an unsecured loan, although the legal issue is unsettled. Most repos are probably set-asides for the benefit of the purchaser/lender. That is, the securities are set aside for a particular customer but are not delivered to that customer. The purchaser must consider the credit risk of the entity holding the security when evaluating a set-aside repo transaction.

89. Most repos involve U.S. Government securities but can also involve commercial paper, certificates of deposit, or other negotiable instruments. A "dollar repo" is an agreement to repurchase substantially the same mortgage-backed securities of a particular federal agency.

90. Margin. Because there is some interest rate risk in a repo transaction, the party selling or pledging the securities is required to value the securities at a yield that is slightly less than their market bid yield. The difference between the market value of the securities sold and the margin value is referred to as a haircut and varies by the length of the repo agreement and

by the type of collateral. A one-week repo backed by T-bills has a standard haircut of 10 basis points.

91. <u>The Repo Rate.</u> The interest payment for a repo transaction is determined by the following add-on interest formula:

Interest payment =
Principal x repo rate x (days outstanding/360)

Reverse Repurchase Agreements (Reverse Repos)

92. A reverse repo is simply the opposite side of a repo transaction. From the buyer's standpoint a repo is a simultaneous purchase and agreement to resell, while a reverse repo is a simultaneous sale and agreement to repurchase. The terms repo and reverse repo are frequently used differently by the two parties to a repurchase transaction. What is a repo to one party is a reverse repo to the other party to the transaction.

IV. A. 3. Repackaged Debt Issues

Zero-Coupon Bonds (P/O Strips, CATS, TIGRs)

93. A zero-coupon bond is a debt instrument that pays principal only. Originally zero-coupon bonds were created by financial institutions that purchased U.S. Treasury notes or bonds, then separated those bonds into two repackaged issues. One package contained only the bond itself (the principal payment, or the principal-only strip) while the other package contained only the interest coupons (the interest payments, or the interest-only strip). A zero-coupon bond consists of the principal payments (no interest coupons, hence, zero-coupon), so it sells at a steep discount from the face value of the issue.

94. Corporations began issuing zero-coupon bonds both because of the great demand for such issues and because anomalies in U.S. tax laws made zero-coupon bonds less costly to issue than other debt instruments. Changes in the tax laws have reduced the tax advantages of issuing zero-coupon bonds for corporations. In 1985 the U.S. Treasury decided to take advantage of the demand for zero-coupon bonds by offering to strip 10-year notes and 30-year bonds (and 20-year bonds, if issued). Because of these changes it is now less common for corporations to issue zero-coupon bonds.

95. A zero-coupon Treasury bond is essentially risk-free in terms of credit risk, but zero-coupon bonds are the most risky of all debt issues with respect to interest-rate risk. The entire repayment of debt consists of a single terminating payment, so a change in long-term interest rates affects the entire payment for the entire period until maturity. Traditional debt securities have lower interest-rate risk because interest payments can be reinvested at current interest rates; if rates rise, the interest payments can be reinvested at those higher rates.

96. In certain circumstances the lack of interest reinvestment is highly desirable. Pension plan administrators often prefer to invest some funds in a security with a guaranteed return over the life of the investment. This is a particular concern for organizations that issue guaranteed investment contracts (GICs), whereby the organization may be contractually obligated to provide a certain rate of return to its contract holders. With a traditional debt security the pension administrator must reinvest interest payments. If interest rates decline, the administrator may be unable to achieve the desired return.

97. In the past zero-coupon bonds were packaged by a financial institution, so an administrative cost was added to the cost of the principal and interest strips. Zero-coupon bonds were also somewhat less liquid than other U.S. Treasury securities. Currently zero-coupon bonds are so common that they are regularly quoted in financial pages.

Interest-Only (I/O) Strips

98. As described in the immediately preceding paragraphs, an I/O strip is a repackaged security consisting of the interest coupons that have been stripped from a fixed income security. Treasury strips are the I/O strips from U.S. Treasury notes or bonds. Because there is no final principal payment, I/O Treasury strips have low interest-rate risk relative to other debt issues. Because they are repackaged Treasuries, I/O strips essentially have no risk of default.

99. I/O strips from mortgage-backed securities (see Section IV. A. 4.) have greater risk than I/O Treasury strips because of the possibility that the mortgages will be repaid prior to maturity.

Original Issue Discount Bonds (OIDs)

100. OIDs are bonds issued at a deep discount (often without interest payments), usually by municipalities. They contain all of the interest-rate risk of a zero-coupon Treasury as well as the credit risk of the issuing institution.

IV. A. 4. Securitized Debt Issues

Pass-Through Certificates (Pass-Throughs or Participation Certificates (PCs))

101. A pass-through or PC is a financial instrument consisting of a bundle of mortgages (or other monetary assets) that have been purchased by a financial institution, then packaged and resold as undivided interests; each interest is for a prorata share of the entire bundle. For example, a bundle of $10 million of 30-year 10% mortgages may be sold as 1,000 undivided interests of $10,000 each. The financial institution receives payments of

mortgage interest and principal; the receipts, less servicing fees, are remitted to the interest holders in proportion to their share of the bundle of mortgages. A holder of one interest would receive 1/1000 of the principal payments and 1/1000 of the interest payments.

102. Terms for a FHA/VA pass-through consist of an interest rate, an amortized repayment schedule for principal and interest, and servicing fees. Prepayments by individuals who are transferred, who purchase a different home, or who refinance their loan must also be considered. Although prepayments are less predictable than regular principal and interest payments, with a large number of mortgages it is possible to estimate prepayments with reasonable accuracy unless low interest rates result in significant refinancing. By using estimated prepayments, together with scheduled repayments of principal and interest, it is possible to compute an estimated return (internal rate of return, or IRR) for a pass-through certificate.

103. When interest rates declined in 1984 certain mortgage pools experienced prepayments of 50%. Because the prepayments to investors could be reinvested only at considerably lower interest rates, investors incurred significant opportunity losses. In 1986 many financial institutions held large amounts of mortgage obligations and suffered major losses because they borrowed short term and lent long term.

104. The quoted yield on a pass-through is the IRR of the cash inflows (interest and principal, including estimated prepayment of principal) and the cash outflows (current market price of the pass-through). The realized yield depends on the actual prepayments of principal if the security is purchased at either a premium or a discount from par.

105. The realized yield on a pass-through that is trading at a premium will be less than the quoted yield if actual prepayments are more rapid than assumed. Conversely, the realized yield will be greater than the quoted yield if prepayments are slower.

106. The realized yield on a pass-through that is trading at a discount will be greater than the quoted yield if actual prepayments are more rapid than assumed. Conversely, the realized yield will be less than the quoted yield if actual prepayments are slower.

Collateralized Mortgage Obligations (CMOs)

107. CMOs are an extension of pass-through certificates. As in the case of pass-throughs, CMOs are a sale of rights to the principal and interest payments from a bundle of mortgage obligations. The difference is that CMOs have been divided into classes (tranches). Each class, or tranche, receives a prorata share of the interest payment, but the first tranche receives all of the principal payments. When the first tranche has been retired, interest payments continue to be made so that each remaining tranche receives a prorata share of interest payments, but the second tranche now receives all principal payments.

108. The final tranche receives a stream of payments that is closer to payments from a zero-coupon bond than from a traditional bond, while the first tranche receives a stream of payments similar to those from a short-term bond. In some cases CMOs include a class Z, or zero, tranche. A class Z receives neither interest nor principal until all prior classes have been retired.

109. CMOs and similar securitized debt issues can be difficult to analyze because the borrower has the option to repay the loan early (prepayment option). Such debt issues originally consisted of only a few tranches; valuing the separate classes was complex but not beyond the normal capabilities of many corporate investment professionals.

110. More recent CMO issues often contain more than 20 tranches. Tranches scheduled to be retired late in the life of a CMO issue will be repaid early only if earlier tranches are repaid early. Early repayment of a later tranche will occur if there is a very large decline in interest rates (resulting in more prepayments), if there is a significant and relatively permanent decline in interest rates, if interest rates vary significantly, or it they frequently decline below the interest rate of the CMO issue.

111. CMOs can be analyzed using variants of the Black-Scholes option pricing model (see IV. D., and Cox and Rubinstein, 1985). Essentially, the analysis involves linking a series of options, because options to prepay later tranches can be exercised only if the options to prepay earlier tranches are exercised. Option-adjusted spread (OAS) models are now available for a few thousand dollars, and some can be run on personal computers. While OAS models simplify the analysis, the problem is further complicated because the Black-Scholes model (and OAS models) requires a knowledge of the variance of interest rates. The variance must be estimated using a record of past interest rate volatility, combined with other economic data.

112. Sophisticated simulation models to evaluate complex CMOs can easily require 20 minutes of CPU time on a supercomputer. Because of this complexity, analyzing the later tranches of complex CMOs is probably beyond the normal capability of all but the largest or most sophisticated organizations in the country.

113. Liquidity. Illiquidity and lack of pricing information are serious concerns for most mortgage-backed obligations. Because these debt issues are complex to analyze and may be illiquid and because a market price is often unavailable, many of these debt issues are suitable only for very large institutional investors. However, the market for these instruments is growing and becoming more liquid.

Credit Card Pass-Through Certificates (CARDs, Certificates for Amortizing Revolving Debt)

114. CARDS are similar to CMOs in that many individual credit card accounts

(accounts receivable) are grouped, then the rights to the interest and principal payments from individual accounts are "passed through" to investors in proportion to their interest in the pool of receivables.

115. The primary differences between a CARD and a CMO are: (1) a CARD is unsecured debt; there is no collateral other than each individual cardholder's promise to pay. (2) To enhance the credit rating of a particular CARD issue, the cash flow of the pool of specified credit card accounts exceeds the projected net amount (after expected defaults and servicing costs) needed to fund payments to investors.

116. CARD issues are of two types. One type is the sale of a debt issue backed by existing credit card receivables; as customers repay their credit card debt the interest and principal are passed through to investors in the CARD issue. The second type of issue begins to repay principal after some stated length of time; the debt issue is backed by revolving credit card debt. As card holders pay for previous purchases, new credit card purchases are used to replace the old collateral.

Certificates of Automobile Receivables (CARs)

117. CARs are pass-through certificates backed by automobile receivables. They are similar to credit card-backed receivables except that automobile loans are not revolving lines of credit.

118. <u>Liquidity.</u> As in the case of some CARDs, CARs may be illiquid investments and little information may be available concerning their market price. The market for CARs is growing, however, and the market is becoming more liquid, particularly for CARs from larger issuers.

IV.B. Futures And Forwards

IV. B. 1. Futures Contracts

119. A future, or futures contract, is a standardized exchange traded obligation to buy (accept delivery of) or sell (deliver) an asset at a future date at a fixed price. Standardized terms include the delivery date, the quantity or dollar amount of the contract, and, in the case of commodity futures, the quality of the product to be delivered. Futures contracts exist for a wide variety of commodities, stock market indices, foreign currencies, and debt instruments.

120. Unlike options contracts, where the purchaser has a right but not an obligation to buy or sell an asset, a futures contract entails a firm obligation to make a transaction. The specified asset must be exchanged on the specified delivery date, or else the contract must be settled by making a cash payment equal to the change in the value of the asset.

121. Certain futures contracts, such as futures on indexes, must always be

settled by making a cash payment. Most other futures contracts, even those for commodities, are settled by making an offsetting futures transaction rather than by actually delivering, or accepting delivery, of the underlying asset. The purchaser of a futures contract usually sells the contract before the delivery date, while the seller of a futures contract typically buys an identical contract before the delivery date.

122. Futures contracts require an "initial margin" deposit equal to some percent of the contract value. The margin deposit, payable in either cash or U.S. Government securities, is required of both the buyer and the seller.

123. Futures contracts involve daily cash settlements; they are "marked-to-market" at the end of each trading day. At the end of a trading day brokerage firms remit to the futures exchange an amount equal to the net decrease in the value of all futures contracts held by their clients, or, if the value of those futures contracts increases, the brokerage firm receives an amount equal to the value of the increase.

124. At the end of each trading day brokerage firms credit each of their accounts for the increase in value of their futures contracts or debit those accounts for the decrease in value of their futures contracts. This process is referred to as "daily cash settlement." At the end of each day brokerage firms compute a "maintenance margin" for each account: the margin that is required at the end of a particular day. Maintenance margin is typically lower than the initial margin. If the amount in a customer's account is below the maintenance margin then the customer receives a "margin call." The customer must either deposit an amount equal to the difference between the account balance and the maintenance margin or else a futures contract, or contracts, will be sold from the customer's account.

Stock Index Futures

125. The purchaser of a stock index future receives the value of that index on the contract delivery date. As an example, an investor purchases a June S&P 100 index future for 350; the index then rises to 380 on the June delivery date. On the delivery date the purchaser of the futures contract would receive $15,000, determined as follows: conceptually the purchaser pays $350 times a multiplier specified by the exchange (500 in the case of S&P 100 futures), or $175,000, and receives $380 x 500, or $190,000, for a net gain of $15,000.

126. There are two primary differences between purchasing a stock index futures contract and purchasing the individual stocks that make up the index: (1) the futures contract does not pay dividends, and (2) no cash payment is required to purchase a futures contract, only an interest-bearing margin deposit to ensure that a customer will be able to complete the transaction on the delivery date.

127. Because the relationship between a futures contract and the index itself is so direct, there is a simple way to determine the value of an index futures

contract, using four variables: (1) the current value of the index, (2) the interest rate for government securities that mature near the delivery date, (3) the expected present value of dividends that would be earned by owning the stocks in the index, and (4) the delivery date.

128. An investor who purchases all stocks in an index in proportion to their weight in that index will earn the change in value of the stocks (or, equivalently, the index) plus the dividend rate multiplied by the amount invested. By investing the same funds in risk-free U.S. Treasury securities and purchasing a futures contract for the index, that investor could earn the risk-free interest rate (Rf) multiplied by the investment, plus the difference between the cost of a futures contract and the value of the index on the delivery date:

(1) Purchase stocks:
     Investment x (1 + dividend rate)
   +   Ending value of index
   −   Current value of index (Spot)
(2) Buy index futures contract and T-bills:
     Investment x (1 + Rf)
   +   Ending value of index
   −   Market price, futures contract (Future)

129. Because the dividend rate earned on stocks (alternative 1) is almost always lower than the risk-free rate (alternative 2), and because both alternatives pay the ending value of the index, an investor would choose alternative (2) (buy an index future rather than the stocks themselves) unless a futures contract (Future) sells for more than the index (Spot) itself.

130. The following symbols will be used in the formulas that follow:

Future   Current price of a futures contract.

Spot   The current (spot) price of an asset (the asset underlying a particular futures contract).

Rf   The risk-free interest rate, in practical terms, the rate on Treasury securities that mature on or near the delivery date of the futures contract.

Pv Div   The present value of expected dividends during a particular period. For example, if a futures contract for the S&P 100 index expires in six months, Pv Div would be the present value of the dividends paid by all stocks in the index during the next six months.

t   Time until expiration of a futures contract in years. For example, if a futures contract expires in six months, $t = .5$.

131. A formula can be developed to establish an arbitrage relationship between the two investment options. An investor can obtain the ending value of the index under the second option by purchasing a futures contract. The current cost is less than the futures price because payment is not required

until the delivery date. The current payment is shown in the lefthand side of equation (3). Under the second alternative an investor can receive the ending value of the index by purchasing the stocks themselves. Unlike option (1), an immediate payment is required, but the actual price paid is the value of the stocks themselves (or the spot price), less the present value of the dividends, as shown on the righthand side of equation (3). Thus, arbitrageurs can be expected to ensure that the price of index futures contracts are determined by the following formula:

$$(3) \quad \frac{Future_t}{(1 + Rf)} = Spot - Pv\ Div$$

or,

$$(4) \quad Future_t = (Spot - Pv\ Div) \times (1 + Rf)$$

Foreign Exchange Futures

132. Analysis for a futures contract for a foreign currency is nearly identical to the analysis for an index futures contract but is slightly more straightforward. Consider two new symbols:

R$ The risk-free interest rate for U.S. investments. In the previous section R$ was represented by Rf, but because this section discusses other currencies, Rf is replaced by R$.

Ry   The risk-free interest rate for investments in Japan (the Japanese yen).

Suppose that a U.S. investor is deciding whether to purchase a futures contract for Japanese yen or to purchase the yen and invest them in a Japanese bank. The equivalent to formula (1), above, is:

$$(5) \quad \frac{Future_t}{(1 + R\$)} = Spot - (Pv\ interest\ on\ yen)$$

But because the Pv of the interest on the yen is:

$$(6) \quad Pv\ interest\ on\ yen) = \frac{RY \times Spot}{1 + RY}$$

equation (5) becomes

(7) Future = spot   x $(1 + R\$) / (1 + RY))$

133. The premium or discount on a foreign exchange contract is determined by the difference in expected inflation rates between two countries. Except for differences too small or too difficult to be arbitraged away, interest rates are basically the same throughout the world, after adjustment for expected inflation in each country (foreign exchange effects). (When exchange restrictions exist, the differences that cannot be arbitraged away may be significant. In addition, interest rates for a particular firm may

vary in different parts of the world because of a lack of information about the credit risk for that firm in some countries.)

Commodities Futures

134. Commodities futures are slightly more complex than index or foreign exchange futures because a physical good is involved. In equation (8) that follows, the left side is equivalent to equations (3) and (5) from above. However, if an investor were to purchase the commodities themselves the cost would include the spot price of the commodity, plus the present value of holding costs (storage, insurance, etc.). Those costs would be reduced by a benefit that is not present by purchasing the futures contract: the value of having the commodities readily available, sometimes referred to as convenience yield (conv yield).

The formula becomes:

(8) $\dfrac{\text{Future}}{t}$ = Spot + PV holding costs – PV conv yld $(1 + Rf)$

Or,

(9) Future = $(\text{Spot} + \text{PV}(\text{hold} - \text{conv})) \times (1 + Rf)^t$

Interest Rate Futures

135. Interest rate futures are contracts to acquire fixed income securities that will be issued at a future date or that are presently outstanding. Interest rate futures are available for Treasury issues and for certain other highly liquid debt issues. Active markets exist for futures contracts on 90-day Treasury bills (actually 91 days), on 90-day certificates-of-deposit, and on 90-day Eurodollars. Active markets also exist for futures contracts on certain issues of U.S. Treasury bonds, U.S. Treasury notes, and GNMA certificates.

136. Futures contracts on U.S. Treasury bonds call for delivery at a future date of a Treasury bond with at least 15 years remaining until maturity (or until the earliest call date) as of the delivery date. Futures contracts on Treasury notes call for delivery at a future date of a Treasury note with no less than 6 1/2 years and no more than 10 years remaining until maturity as of the delivery date. Arbitrage relationships for futures contracts for Treasury bonds and notes are complicated because the seller of a futures contract has the opportunity to deliver any of numerous Treasury issues. GNMA futures contracts are somewhat more complicated and are not discussed in this document. For further information on pricing of futures contracts on long-term fixed-rate financial instruments, see Schwarz, Financial Futures, 1986.

137. An arbitrage price for 90-day Treasury bills futures contracts (and other futures contracts on short-term fixed-rate financial instruments) can be

computed by considering the relationship between (1) a purchased futures contract and (2) an equivalent investment consisting of a loan at the short-term interest rate for the period ending on the delivery date of the futures contract, plus a purchased Treasury security that matures on or near the maturity date of the debt issue associated with the futures contract. For example, consider a futures contract for a 90-day Treasury bill to be issued in 90 days (with a maturity date of 91 days after the issue date). By purchasing a Treasury security that matures in 181 days and by borrowing for 90 days, an investor constructs an investment that has the same effect as purchasing the futures contract. If the price relationships are different, then an opportunity exists for arbitrage profits.

IV. B. 2. Forwards

138. A forward contract is conceptually identical to a futures contract except that forwards are not traded on exchanges. That results in three practical differences. First, forward contracts are not standardized. They can be for any amount and can mature at any date. Because the exchange-traded futures contracts rarely extend beyond one year, forward contracts must normally be used for any long-term arrangements.

139. A second practical difference is that execution of a futures contract is guaranteed by an exchange, a guarantee that is partially assured through the practice of daily cash settlement, or marking to market. Forward contracts, of necessity, are backed by the creditworthiness of the two counterparties entering a forward contract. If one of the two counterparties has too great a credit risk, it may be necessary to back the contract with collateral. It may also be necessary to enter into an arrangement similar to the exchange-based practice of marking to market. Thus, a forward contract may entail added considerations when compared to a futures contract.

140. The final difference is that forward contracts are considerably less liquid than exchange-traded futures contracts. Because there is no standardized market there may be few practical alternatives, other than a reverse transaction between counterparties.

IV. C. Swaps

141. Swaps are arrangements whereby one party agrees to exchange (swap) a specified payment to a second party in exchange for a different specified payment (although typically the parties agree to set off payments, with one party paying the other party net). The two parties to the agreement are referred to as counterparties. The exchanges are typically for different interest payments (coupon or interest-rate swaps), for payments in differ-

ent currencies (currency or foreign exchange swaps), or for exchanges of both a different currency and the interest payments associated with those currencies (cross-currency swaps).

Coupon or Interest-Rate Swaps

142. Interest-rate swaps enable organizations to effectively convert one type of interest payment into a second type. For example, a fixed-rate interest payment may be converted to a floating-rate interest payment, or a floating-rate interest payment that varies with the T-bill rate can be converted to a floating-rate interest payment that varies with the LIBOR rate.

143. Interest-rate swaps are the exchange of interest payments based upon a stated principal amount (the "notional" principal). When the stated principal is for the same currency, there is no exchange of principal. Most interest-rate swaps are exchanges of a fixed-rate interest payment for a floating-rate interest payment. The fixed-rate payment is made by the fixed-rate payer and the variable-rate payment is made by the variable-rate payer. However, exchanges of one floating-rate payment for a different floating-rate payment (e.g., LIBOR for T-Bill) are also common. Interest-rate swaps involve the risk of the creditworthiness of the second party to a swap.

144. Common Swap Terms. The following are common swap terms that will be used in this section:

Fixed-rate payer. Pays the fixed-rate interest payment and receives the floating-rate interest payment. Has bought a swap. Has established the equivalent of a long-term liability and a floating-rate investment (asset).

Floating-rate payer. Pays the floating-rate interest payment and receives the fixed-rate interest payment. Has sold a swap. Has established the equivalent of a floating-rate liability and a long-term investment (asset).

Flat, or LIBOR Flat. The floating-rate payment is typically based on the current yield of the London Interbank Offer Rate (LIBOR). LIBOR flat indicates that the floating-rate interest payment will be equal to the LIBOR rate. LIBOR plus .5 means that the floating-rate payment will be equal to the LIBOR plus 50 basis points, or .5 percentage points. The day count for calculating interim interest payments for the LIBOR is actual/360, or the actual number of days since the last interest payment, divided by 360.

Treasury Yield Curve. The fixed-rate interest payment is frequently established by the rate on Treasury issues that mature on or near the expiration date of the swap. If a swap dealer were to quote a seven-year swap as Treasury yield curve plus 2 versus the three-month LIBOR flat, the floating interest payment would be at the three-month LIBOR rate on the date of each payment date (in most cases semiannually). The fixed rate payment would be the yield on Treasury securities that mature on the expiration date of the swap plus 2, as quoted on the date that the swap begins. Although each side of the swap computes their interest payment, only the difference between the two payments is exchanged.

Fixed Rate-Floating Rate Swaps

145. In a fixed-for-floating swap two counterparties agree to swap fixed-rate for variable-rate interest payments for a stated period based on a notional principal amount. For example, a six-year agreement based on a $10,000,000 notional principal may call for a 10% fixed interest payment, payable semiannually, in exchange for a semiannual interest payment equal to the three-month LIBOR rate. This swap is referred to as a 10% fixed versus the three-month LIBOR flat.

146. Fixed-for-floating coupon swaps originated because organizations with good credit ratings found that they had a comparative advantage over lesser credit risks when borrowing medium-term (3-5 years) or longer at fixed rates of interest. In addition, financial institutions, which frequently have high credit ratings, generally have more of a preference for floating-rate debt, because many of their assets are invested in floating-rate investments. Because of the comparative advantage, a swap contract is, ideally, not a zero-sum game. Both counterparties may find that a swap arrangement offers them a lower cost loan.

147. A good credit risk may find that it is able to borrow fixed-rate funds for five years at 10.5% and variable-rate funds at the six-month LIBOR + 1/2 (LIBOR + 1/2). A lesser credit risk may be able to borrow fixed rate at 11.5% or variable rate at LIBOR + 3/4. The good credit risk firm is able to borrow fixed rate at 100 basis points less than the lesser credit risk but only 25 basis points less for variable-rate funds. If the good credit risk firm prefers variable-rate funds and the lesser credit risk prefers fixed-rate funds, there is an obvious opportunity to reduce the joint cost of the loan by 75 basis points:

	Fixed-rate	Floating-rate
Alternative 1		
Good credit borrows floating		LIBOR + .50%
Lesser credit borrows fixed:	11.5%	
Alternative 2		
Good credit borrows fixed	10.5%	
Lesser credit borrows floating:		LIBOR + .75%
Savings for alternative two:	+ 1.0%	– .25%

148. In a simple swap firms may agree to a swap whereby the good credit risk borrows fixed at 10.5% and the lesser credit risk borrows at LIBOR plus 3/4. Concurrently, the firms agree to swap interest payments. The lesser credit risk may agree to swap 10.9% fixed for LIBOR + .45%:

	Good-credit	Lesser-credit
Payment to lender	− 10.5%	− LIBOR + .75%
Swap receipt	+ 10.9%	+ LIBOR + .45%
Difference	+ .4%	.30%
Swap payment	LIBOR + .45%	10.90%
Net cost	LIBOR + .05%	11.20%
Alternative of borrowing direct	LIBOR + .50%	11.50
Savings	.45%	30%

149. Although arbitrage opportunities continually arise in finance, it is rare for such opportunities to persist. In evaluating swaps, it is essential to consider differences between the swap being offered and other alternatives. For example, fixed-rate loans commonly include a call feature enabling the borrower to prepay a loan; interest-rate swaps normally contain no such prepayment option. Thus, an apparent savings may be a result of failure to consider the value of a prepayment feature. As another example, a swap may entail greater credit risk than other alternatives because the counter-party to a swap is in financial difficulty.

Plain Vanilla Swaps

150. A basic swap is often referred to as a generic or a plain vanilla swap (although many swaps are now tailored to the needs of individual parties). The fixed payment in a generic swap is made either semiannually or annually and is computed using a 30-day/360-day year day-count. The floating payment is based on a common index (e.g., LIBOR, T-bills, Fed Funds, or Prime) and is quoted flat (i.e., LIBOR + 0%). The payment frequency is the term of the floating index (six-month LIBOR would be paid semiannually). The reset frequency (how often the floating rate is recomputed) is the term of the floating index, except for Treasury bills, where the index is reset weekly and for Prime or Fed Funds, where the index is reset daily. Actual days/360-day year is used except for the day-count unless the floating rate is based on Treasury bills, in which case actual days/365-day year is used for the day-count.

Mismatches

151. The terms of a generic swap may be altered, but any changes obviously affect the economics of the transaction. Certain changes to the basic terms are referred to as mismatches.

152. Day-Count Mismatch. A swap may use a day-count that differs from the normal day-count.

153. Reset-Frequency Mismatch. The reset frequency of a swap may not agree with the maturity of the floating-rate index. For example, the floating-rate

may be recomputed quarterly even though the rate is based on the six-month LIBOR.

154. Payment-Frequency Mismatch. A floating-rate payment may be based on the three-month LIBOR, but payments may be required only semiannually. In this case the fixed-rate payer loses the benefit of quarterly compounding.

Reverse Swaps

155. A swap may be reversed or canceled by an agreement between the original counterparties to a swap whereby one party makes a payment to the other counterparty and the swap is canceled (reversed). A swap may also be reversed by entering into a second and offsetting swap with a different counterparty. In the case of a reverse with a different counterparty an organization is now exposed to the risk that either or both of two parties will be unable to complete the agreement in the event of financial difficulties.

Currency Swaps

156. A currency swap is an exchange of two currencies at the current exchange rate (e.g., U.S. dollars for Japanese yen at a rate of 150 yen/$), combined with an agreement to reexchange those currencies at a specified future date. The agreement may also call for periodic payments between the two counterparties based upon the interest rate differential between the two countries whose currencies are being swapped.

157. A swap agreement might call for the immediate exchange of $10 million for 1.5 billion yen. Two years later the two payments would be swapped at the same exchange rate. As described in section IV.B.1.b., an immediate swap of currencies at the existing exchange rate, combined with an agreement to reexchange those currencies at the same exchange rate at a later date, is a fair exchange only if the two countries have interest rates that are approximately equal. To compensate for differing interest rates, currency swaps may also include periodic payments from the party initially exchanging the weaker currency (currency from the country with the higher interest rates). These periodic payments are designed to compensate for lost interest.

158. In effect, a currency swap is an immediate exchange of currencies, combined with a series of forward trades during the life of a swap and a final forward trade at maturity. While a currency swap is identical to a foreign currency future in effect, they differ in two respects. First, a swap contract is typically for periods of longer than one year, while futures contracts are rarely available for periods in excess of one year. Second, differential payments may be made at intermediate periods with a swap contract but only at delivery date for a futures contract.

159. Cross-Currency Swaps. A cross-currency swap is a coupon or interest

swap in different currencies. For example, a German firm may have a small subsidiary in the United States while a U.S. firm may have a small subsidiary in Germany. Each firm may wish to have its subsidiary borrow in the host country but may find that the subsidiaries are at a comparative disadvantage in obtaining funds because they are not well known. In such a situation, the U.S. parent may borrow in the United States, the German parent may borrow in Germany, and the two firms may then agree to swap dollars for marks at the current exchange rate, swap interest payments on the two loans, then reverse the initial swap of dollars for marks at the expiration of the loan period at the exchange rate as of the date of execution of the swap.

160. In some cases a firm may prefer to obtain financing for subsidiaries in several countries but may decide that it is less expensive to issue debt in its home country. It is possible to construct elaborate swaps to cover such situations. When several swaps are combined to produce a desired result, the parties are said to "cocktail" swaps.

IV. D. Options

161. Options contracts are available for most assets for which futures contracts are available. Options contracts are similar to futures contracts except that the purchaser of an options contract has the right, but not the obligation, to enter into a specified financial transaction. The owner of a call option will benefit from favorable price movements in the asset underlying the option but will not suffer as a result of unfavorable price movements, other than the loss of part or all of the option premium. The reverse is true for the holder of a put option. In addition, the owner of an option may execute that contract at any time up to the expiration date. (A so-called American option may be executed at any time up to the expiration date. European options may be exercised only at expiration. Asian options, which are average rate options, are also available.) In contrast, futures contracts may be executed only at the delivery date (equivalent to option expiration date).

162. An option is defined, or described, by five factors: (1) the underlying asset, such as an option to purchase tangible items (e.g., IBM stock, bushels of wheat, or a given number of yen) or an option to receive an intangible (e.g., the value of an index); (2) the type of option, such as a call (option to buy at a stated price) or a put (option to sell at a stated price); (3) the expiration date of the option, such as May (which would normally mean the third Friday in May for U.S. exchange-traded options); (4) the strike price, which is the price at which an item may be purchased (for a call option) or sold (for a put option); and (5) the quantity, such as 100 shares of stock.

163. Call Options. Call options give the purchaser the right, but not the

obligation, to make a purchase at a specified price. At expiration date if the price of the underlying asset (such as IBM stock) is greater than the strike price, the owner of the option receives the difference, multiplied by the quantity, from the writer of the option. If the price of IBM were 120 on the expiration date, the holder of an IBM 115 call option would receive $ 500 (100 shares x [$120 - $115]) from the writer of the option. Thus, the holder has the potential for unlimited gain and the writer the potential for unlimited loss.

164. Put Options. Put options give the purchaser the right, but not the obligation, to make a sale at a specified price. At expiration date if the price of the underlying asset is less than the strike price, the owner receives the difference between the strike price and the actual price, multiplied by the quantity. If the price of IBM were 105 on expiration date, the owner of an IBM 115 call option contract would receive $1,000 from the option writer when the option is on 100 shares. The holder of a put option has the potential of gaining the strike price multiplied by the quantity if the value of the underlying asset were to fall to zero.

165. Covered Written Options. An investor who owns an asset, such as IBM stock, and who then writes a call option on that stock is said to have written a covered call option. Similarly, if an investor has sold an asset short, and has then written a put option on that asset, the investor is said to have written a covered put option. If the price of the asset increases above the strike price the writer of a call option suffers a loss on the option, but that loss is exactly offset by the gain on the underlying asset that the investor owns.

166. Some investors write deep out-of-the-money call options (options with a strike price well above the current price of an asset, such as a 130 IBM call when the price of IBM is 115) as a way to increase the earnings on a portfolio. Because there is little chance that an out-of-the-money option will pay off, the system may seem like a simple way to make money.

167. In fact, although there is only a slight chance that deep out-of-the-money options will pay off, they sometimes do, and on average the loss is more than enough to offset the many small gains; in effect the writer is borrowing money from the purchaser of the option at an interest cost that is comparable to similar debt. Because the actual price of options is usually quite close to their theoretical price, on average this combined strategy, before commissions and other trading costs, earns the purchaser of an option nothing more than the return to an investment of comparable risk.

168. Because commissions and trading costs are often high, (principally because the spread between bid and ask is often large) options are sometimes an unattractive investment.

169. Uncovered Options. The writer of a call option who does not own the underlying asset or the writer of a put option who has not sold short the

underlying asset is said to have written an uncovered or a naked option. As in the case of writers of deep out-of-the-money covered call options, in many cases writers of deep out-of-the-money naked options believed they had found a method to earn abnormally high returns. In particular, prior to the sharp market decline of October 19, 1987, many investors routinely wrote uncovered put options on the S&P 100 index. When the market declined those investors suffered severe losses that in many cases far exceeded their earlier gains.

170. Value of an Option. The price or value of an option might seem to depend upon the expected future value of the underlying asset. As in the case of futures contracts, however, the value of an option can be determined by mathematics. In the case of options, the mathematical formulas are variations of the Black-Scholes options pricing model. While the formulas are considerably more complicated than those for futures contracts and beyond the scope of this statement, they are relatively simple to apply. Programs are widely available for use with popular calculators and spreadsheet programs (Cox and Rubinstein, 1985).

171. The theoretical value of an option depends on five factors: (1) the current price of the underlying asset, (2) the time until expiration of the option, (3) the volatility in price of the underlying asset, (4) the strike price of the option, and (5) the interest rate on risk-free fixed-income securities (typically T-bills) expiring at about the same time as the option contract. A final variable, the present value of any expected dividends or interest, is needed to determine the value of an option on common stocks or interest-bearing securities. In practice, the theoretical value of an option, as determined by Black-Scholes type models, is frequently very close to the actual option price.

172. Liquidity. Liquidity may be a serious problem for some options contracts. The number of shares of common stock traded on the New York Stock Exchange is usually similar to the equivalent shares of stock traded on the options exchanges (option contracts traded, multiplied by 100, because each contract is for 100 shares of stock). This fact is a highly misleading indication of option liquidity. A stock listed on an options exchange may have 20 separate options issues. For example, a stock selling for 50 may have options at the prices of 40, 45, 50, 55, and 60. If options contracts at each of those prices are available for two months for both put and call options, 20 separate options are associated with the stock. Thus, the trading volume in any particular options issue should be considerably lower than the trading volume in the associated common stock.

173. There are two other liquidity problems. First, in many cases there is considerably more trading in deep out-of-the-money options than in other options. Second, proportionately far more option trading occurs in highly visible stocks. For example, the trading volume in IBM stock is often 2% of the total of the NYSE volume. On a typical day IBM options may

account for 7% or 8% of the total volume in common stock options. Disproportionate trading also occurs in the options for other highly visible stocks, such as Apple Computer.

174. Customized options are also available from various sources, including banks, brokerage firms, and investment banks. Such nonexchange-traded options are usually highly illiquid.

175. Large Price Spread. When there is low trading volume in a particular options issue, the spread between the bid and the ask price is typically high. For example, the spread in price for an option selling in the $3.00 range may exceed $.50 for an illiquid option. The cost of such options can be considerably higher than the theoretical cost simply because of the cost of trading at the spread. This can be a problem with any thinly traded financial instrument.

176. Trading Volume. A sizeable trade in illiquid options will probably affect the price significantly. For example, 50 contracts a day may be a normal trading volume for a particular stock option. If an investor were to place a buy order for 50 contracts at the market when the market is 3 bid and 3 1/4 asked, it is likely that the trade will be made at a price that is well above 3 1/4. As in the case of a large price spread (see preceding paragraph), this can be a problem with other thinly traded financial instruments.

177. Unfair Markets. There have been numerous charges that certain options markets are operated in an unfair manner. For example, if the market for a particular option issue is 3 bid and 3 1/4 asked, it is reasonable to assume that if an investor were to place an order for two contracts at the market, the order would be executed at 3 1/4, or possibly at 3 1/8, if the investor is fortunate. Because of normal price fluctuations in the market, some trades might be executed at higher prices and some at lower prices (this may also be true for other financial instruments).

178. By observing a quote machine (Quotron or others) as orders are placed and executed, it is possible to determine whether or not an investor receives a fair price in the options markets. In practice, with a bid of 3 and an ask of 3 1/4 and in a reasonably active options issue, market orders to buy two or three contracts would rarely be executed at a price below 3 1/4, and some orders would be executed at a price above 3 1/4. Trades executed outside of the bid-ask range could result from an illiquid market or an unfair market.

179. Because of the problems of illiquidity, and possibly with unfair markets, it is important that anyone who regularly uses options be aware that there may be significant costs, in addition to broker fees, associated with trading in options contracts. Such trading should be monitored by someone using a quote machine showing the bid and asked prices.

180. While the above discussion has generally been in terms of common stock

options, options contracts also exist for foreign exchange rates, debt instruments, and commodities. The analysis and the risks for such options are similar to those for common stock options.

IV. E. Equities and Securities with Equity Features

181. Common stock is the most common form of equity security, and for most firms it is still the only type of equity security issued. Other types of equity securities are used on occasion.

182. Multiple Classes of Equity. In order to maintain voting control within a family or within a group of executives, some firms have multiple classes of equity securities. One class typically has supervoting rights so that it can control the election of directors. For example, A-class stock with one voting right per share may be sold to the general public. B-class stock with 100 voting rights per share may be retained or sold to a restricted group of shareholders. The super-voting right shares may also contain restrictions on the right of sale, so that majority voting remains within the group if several members of the group wish to sell their shares or even if some members become dissatisfied with the way the firm is managed.

183. Mezzanine Financing. In the case of new company financing, a financial institution or venture capital group may provide equity financing for a firm, with the written provision that the equity be converted into debt or be put back into the company at a future date or under certain conditions. Such financing is considered below the debt section of the balance sheet but above the pure equity section, so is considered mezzanine financing.

184. Mezzanine financing is currently in limited (but increasing) use. It can be complex to analyze because various events can trigger many types of payouts. Such securities can best be analyzed through the use of contingent claims analysis (Trigeorgis and Mason, 1987).

185. Warrants. A warrant gives the holder the right to purchase stock in a corporation. Many debt issues include as a package a bond and a warrant, and some preferred stock issues include a warrant. Investment bankers also sometimes receive warrants in exchange for underwriting services. Warrants are similar to options but are somewhat more complex because of the many possible ways to structure a warrant.

186. Warrants often contain a provision that they may be exercised only after a waiting period of several years. Another difference is that warrants actually cause dilution because the number of shares is increased whenever a warrant is exercised. In contrast, with exchange-traded common stock options, all transactions involve the corporation whose stock is being optioned. Neither of these problems is severe, but the standard option valuation programs written for calculators and personal computers may not properly value warrants unless the programs are modified.

IV. F. Caps, Floors, and Collars

187. A cap is a limitation on the maximum interest rate that a borrower will be required to pay during the period of a loan. The cap may be either a limitation on a specific loan or a financial instrument that effectively limits the interest rate that its purchaser will pay on a separate fixed-rate instrument.

188. Cap on a Particular Instrument. A floating-rate loan with a 10% cap limits the maximum interest rate that the borrower will pay to 10%. Similarly, a floating-rate loan with a 6% floor guarantees the lender that the minimum interest rate that the lender receives will be 6%. A collar is a combination of a cap and a floor; a collar with a 10% cap and a 6% floor guarantees that the borrower pays no more than 10% interest expense while the lender receives no less than 6%. Many debt issues are sold with interest rate caps. However, individual caps, floors, and collars are private agreements, often entered into between a corporation and a financial institution.

189. Interest Rate Caps as Financial Instruments. There is also a small private market for interest rate caps. For example, a corporation may prefer floating-rate debt. By issuing a capped debt issue (at 10%, for example) and at the same time separately selling a 10% interest rate cap, a firm is issuing the equivalent of floating-rate debt. If the interest rate is below 10% the firm pays the floating interest rate to its lenders. If the interest rate is above 10% it pays 10% to its lenders but pays the difference between the floating rate and 10% to the purchaser of the interest rate cap. In some cases corporations find that the equivalent floating interest rate is less for a capped debt issue combined with sale of a cap than for a straight floating-rate debt issue.

190. An interest rate cap calls for a payment at specified intervals, usually at the payment frequency of the debt issue. For example, a capped corporate bond pays interest semiannually. An interest rate cap for such an issue would normally call for a semiannual payment to the owner of the cap. For example, the interest rate on a debt issue may be prime plus 2 as of June 15 and December 15, capped at 14%. If on June 15 prime plus 2 is equal to 16, and if the cap is for $10 million, the cap holder would receive $100,000 for the six-month period ending June 30 ($10 million x 2% x 1/2 year).

191. Series of European Options. A cap is equivalent to a series of call options. Consider a five-year cap that calls for semiannual payments to the owner of the call if floating rates exceed the cap. This is equivalent to 10 options, one of which expires at each semiannual period.

192. Although a cap is nothing more than a series of options, the Black-Scholes model that is widely used to value stock options and index options must be modified before it is used to value caps, floors, or collars. First, the

call-type feature in caps, floors, and collars can be executed only at interest payment dates; this makes them like European options instead of like American options. A second problem is that the Black-Scholes model uses a particular distribution of price changes, or returns, that is not valid for interest rates (a log-normal distribution). Neither of these may pose serious problems in valuing caps, collars, and floors, but anyone purchasing or selling such instruments should be aware that valuation may be complex.

PART V: HEDGING

193. Hedging is the process of protecting, or insuring, against a change in the price of an asset, liability, or future transaction. In the past hedging was accomplished through the use of options, futures, and forwards. Newer financial instruments, such as swaps, caps, collars, and floors are now available, so that the choices are far more numerous than in the past.

V. A. Hedging Assets, Liabilities, and Expected Future Transactions

194. <u>Hedging a Long Asset Position.</u> One of the earliest uses of hedging was to protect against a price decline in a commodity or other asset that a firm or individual owned. Such a position can be hedged by purchasing a put option, giving the holder the right, but not the obligation, to sell the asset at the strike price of the put option on or before the option expiration date. If the price of the asset declines below the strike price the holder is completely protected against any decline below that strike price (except for the risk of default by the option writer in the case of over-the-counter options, or for the unlikely risk of default of the clearing house for exchange traded options). If the strike price was below the spot price of the asset at the time the put option was purchased and the price of the asset declines, the holder will suffer a loss, up to the difference between the spot and strike price. The owner of the asset benefits from any increase in price. The cost of such protection is the premium paid to acquire the option.

195. A long asset position can also be hedged by selling a futures contract for the asset that is owned. When an owned asset is combined with a written futures (or forward) contract, the owner of the combined position is immune to price changes, either favorable or unfavorable. The firm will, in effect, sell the asset at the spot price as of the date the futures or forward contract is purchased, less normal transaction costs and plus or minus the premium or discount on the contract.

196. <u>Hedging a Commitment, or Expected Need.</u> In many cases a firm expects

to acquire an asset or is committed to acquire an asset at some time in the future, and desires to protect against price increases. A purchased call option will protect the holder against any price increases above the strike price. If the strike price is above the current cash price, the holder of the call option is protected only against price increases above the strike price. The holder of the call option benefits if the asset price declines. The cost for such protection is the premium paid to acquire the option.

197. A firm can also hedge against price increases on an asset it plans or is committed to acquire by purchasing a futures or forward contract. A plan or commitment to acquire an asset, combined with a purchased futures or forward contract, makes the holder immune to price changes. In effect, the firm will pay the spot price at the time the futures or forward contract is acquired, less normal transaction costs and plus or minus the premium or discount on the contract.

198. Hedging a Future Payment or Expected Future Payment of Funds in a Foreign Currency. When a firm plans to make a future payment in a foreign currency, it can protect itself against changes in exchange rates by: (1) purchasing a call option on that foreign currency or (2) purchasing a futures or forward contract on that currency. A call option protects against increases in the cost of the foreign currency, while the futures or forward contract makes the holder of the combined position immune to changes in the exchange rate.

199. Hedging the Future Receipt or Expected Future Receipt of Funds in a Foreign Currency. A firm can protect against changes in exchange rates when it plans to receive a future payment in a foreign currency by: (1) purchasing a put option on that foreign currency or (2) selling a futures or forward contract on that currency. A put option protects against declines in the value of the foreign currency below the strike price, while the futures or forward contract makes the holder of the combined position immune to changes in the exchange rate.

200. Hedging the Need or Expected Need to Borrow in the Future. As in the case of assets and foreign currencies, liabilities can be hedged through options, futures, forwards, and forward rate agreements. Many so-called hedges against interest-rate changes provide less exact hedges than those for physical assets or for foreign currencies. That is because many hedging instruments are for debt that is similar to, but not identical to, the debt that a firm expects to acquire. A firm may expect to borrow intermediate term fixed rate. Interest rate futures contracts are available for intermediate term fixed-rate Treasury securities but not for corporate borrowings. Although the difference between corporate and Treasury borrowing rates is stable, there have been times when that difference changed more than expected. Thus, hedging corporate borrowings with futures contracts on Treasury debt will most likely not be an exact hedge.

201. Borrowings can also be hedged through a forward rate agreement (FRA),

and such an agreement can provide an exact hedge, although FRAs are typically based on the T-bill or LIBOR rates. In a forward rate agreement two counterparties agree to pay (accept) the discounted present value of the gain or loss incurred as a result of changes in some interest rate, multiplied by the notional principal.

V. B. Hedging with Options, Futures, and Forwards

202. Hedging with Options. When used as a hedge, options provide insurance against unfavorable price movements. Purchased call options provide insurance against unfavorable price increases; purchased put options provide insurance against unfavorable price declines.

203. Because options give the holder the right, but not the obligation, to exercise the option, they protect the holder against unfavorable price movements but allow the holder to benefit from favorable price movements. Thus, they provide insurance but at a cost. That cost is considered the option premium, and the premium (option cost) increases as the amount of protection increases and as the time increases. For example, when the S&P 100 is 350, a purchased S&P 100 360 call option provides protection only against price increases above 360 so is less expensive than an S&P 100 350 call option, which provides protection against price increases above 350. Similarly, a September S&P 100 360 call option is less expensive than an October S&P 100 360 call option because the October option provides protection for a longer period.

204. Hedging with Futures and Forwards. When used as hedges, futures and forwards make the holder of the hedge immune to price changes. They are, in effect, an exchange of risks between one party who is long in an asset position and a second party who is short in that same asset. As described in section IV. B., arbitrage relationships cause futures contracts to be described by relationships that do not depend on the expected future price of the asset. So long as markets are not thin, the cost of a futures contract is simply the broker's commission, which is typically low. In practice, most futures contracts with reasonably active markets do sell for near their theoretical prices.

205. Comparison of Options and Futures-Forward Contracts. As discussed in the preceding paragraphs of this section, options contracts sell at a cost that reflects the cost of insurance, while a futures contract is simply an exchange of risk between two parties, so the cost is usually minimal. The difference between options and futures can be understood best by considering a synthetic futures contract.

206. A synthetic purchased forward contract can be developed by purchasing a call option and by writing a put option with identical strike prices and expiration dates for the call and put options (a synthetic written forward contract can be developed by purchasing a put option and by writing a

call option). The cost of the combined position is simply the cost of the brokerage commissions and the cost of the spread between the bid and ask price for each of the two options. The holder of the combined position (purchased call and written put) is, in effect, purchasing insurance against the possibility that prices will increase and selling insurance against the possibility that prices will decline. Thus, the combined position can be analyzed in the same manner as a futures or forward contract in Section IV. B.

PART VI: INTERNAL CONTROL OF FINANCIAL INSTRUMENTS

207. There are at least six basic steps involving internal control of financial instruments. (1) Establish a set of objectives, such as hedging a commitment to purchase commodities or maintaining an investment portfolio that is invested a particular way. (2) Evaluate the desirability of the purchase or sale (issue) of a financial instrument in relation to other financial instruments (or combinations of instruments) that could meet the same needs. This phase includes both an evaluation of the direct financial aspects of the proposed transaction (performed by a treasury, finance, or investment department) and a concurrent evaluation of tax and accounting aspects of the proposed transaction (performed in conjunction with the accounting department). (3) Monitor the actual purchase or sale to ensure that the actual price is identical, or close to, the expected price. (4) Monitor the firm's situation and the financial instruments that it owns or has issued, to ensure the firm's objectives are being met. (5) Ensure that transactions are properly accounted for under GAAP. (6) Ensure that there is a proper segmentation of duties.

208. <u>Objectives.</u> To control financial instruments it is essential to establish a formal set of objectives. A firm that uses large quantities of commodities may establish policy that expected usage will be hedged for at least 40% of expected usage at all times and at no more than 75%. The policy may call for weekly or monthly meetings to establish a more narrow target or for weekly meetings to establish an exact target.

209. A firm may establish general or specific objectives for its pension fund, such as a range of between 50% and 60% invested in equity securities, between 30% and 40% in fixed-income securities, and 20% in real estate at all times. The policy may call for at least half of the equities portfolio to be invested in an index fund, at least half of the fixed-income portfolio to be invested in Treasury securities, and at least half of the fixed-income portfolio to be invested in issues that mature in less than two years.

210. A firm may establish objectives for the amount of debt that is subject to floating interest rates and to the amount of its assets that are subject to foreign exchange risk.

211. Evaluating Individual Instruments Prior to Purchase or Sale. In the case of more complex financial instruments, such as options, futures, swaps, and caps, many organizations do not have the expertise necessary to evaluate them. Although these instruments may seem complex, in most cases they can be evaluated with well-developed and reliable methods. Unless a firm uses quantitative methods to make at least a rough approximation of the value of a financial instrument, there is a possibility that it will not receive a fair price from the transaction.

212. In some cases, such as complex swap arrangements or certain securitized transactions with numerous tranches, a firm probably should not undertake the transaction without outside assistance.

213. Monitoring the Actual Transaction. In some cases firms do not receive a fair price from a financial transaction. In the case of options or thinly traded stocks it is essential that someone monitor the actual transactions, because a market order may cause significant price movements.

214. In the case of fixed-income securities a firm should call several brokers to ensure that a quoted market price is reasonable.

215. Monitoring the Situation. Once a firm has established a set of objectives it is imperative to monitor or audit its financial position. Monitoring is a continual process that must be done on a current basis. This task is often difficult for a firm because its accounting department may lack the expertise needed to evaluate complex financial instruments.

216. Three situations are of particular concern. First, hedging is often a combination of mathematics and experience. In many cases an exact hedge is unavailable. It is imperative that someone evaluate what purport to be inexact hedges to determine whether they are in fact inexact hedges or simply speculation.

217. The second situation of primary concern is thinly traded instruments or instruments for which a market price is not readily available. To monitor a firm's financial situation properly it is necessary to be able to estimate the value of its various assets and liabilities. Some instruments can be valued only imprecisely, for example, obscure tranches of a securitized debt issue, certain warrants or debt issues from unsuccessful leveraged buyout firms, or equity securities of thinly traded corporations.

218. The third problem is that financial instruments are becoming extremely complex. Investments such as multiple-tranche asset-backed securities are extremely difficult to evaluate. Few organizations are capable of analyzing such instruments. In addition, many debt instruments contain extremely complex covenants, conversion provisions, and other restrictions, so that although a particular organization may have personnel who are competent to evaluate the instrument, the cost may be so great that the organization would be better off investing in traditional debt instruments.

219. Accounting in Accordance with GAAP. The accounting rules for financial

instruments are changing rapidly. To avoid unexpected financial reporting results, a firm should consider reviewing GAAP requirements with its public accounting firm prior to major investments in unfamiliar financial instruments.

220. Separation of Duties. Any system of internal control should be based on a clearly defined separation of duties. As an example, a firm should segregate its trading activities from its accounting for trading. Similarly, custody of the securities or assets being traded should be separated from both accounting and trading.

221. As discussed, it is important that both the treasury and accounting departments be capable of analyzing the instrument and of evaluating whether it is being used properly (as a hedge, for example). Once a firm decides to use a financial instrument it is important to monitor the trade executions (particularly with thin markets, where orders may be executed outside of the bid-ask spread) and to review trade confirmations for possible errors. In addition, the accounting department should be capable of analyzing the accounting and tax implications of any instrument that the organization uses. This task is particularly difficult because the rules are sometimes conflicting and because in many cases rules for financial instruments are not well established.

222. Formal Policy. Beyond a certain size, an organization should have a formal policy; the larger and more complex the organization, the more detailed and comprehensive the policy. Typical items covered in a written policy are:

Personnel
a. List of members of the investment committee.
b. Schedule of when the committee should meet and of what should be covered in the meeting.
c. Approval and review process.
d. Periodic internal (external) reporting requirements.

Investments
a. Objectives with regard to safety of principal.
b. Limitations on illiquid investments.
c. Acceptable issuers.
d. Acceptable instruments.
e. Acceptable credit ratings by various ratings services (e.g., Moody's, Standard & Poor's, Duff & Phelps, and Keefe's Bank Watch).
f. Maturity range for individual instruments and for the average of all instruments.
g. Exposure limits.
h. Position limits.

Hedging

    a. Range to be hedged (e.g., hedge between 50-60% of future receipts denominated in foreign currencies; hedge between 50-75% of commodities expected to be acquired within one year).

    b. Method of hedging (e.g., hedge expected payments in foreign currencies with futures or forwards contracts; hedge future receipts denominated in foreign currencies with near-the-money options; hedge expected commodity purchases with deep out-of-the-money options).

GLOSSARY

ACU

Asian Currency Unit. Euro-dollars deposited in Far East financial centers.

Agencies

Debt securities of federal agencies such as the FHLMC.

AIBD

Association of International Bond Dealers

All-in costs

All-inclusive financing costs. (1) All costs associated with a particular issue of debt or equity; e.g., the all-in financing cost of home mortgages through sale of a pool of many different mortgages is normally lower than the cost of financing the loans on a one-by-one basis. The increase in administrative costs associated with a pool is offset by the reduced risk associated with a pool and by the greater supply of lenders. (2) Rate of return on the fixed-interest rate side of a fixed for floating rate swap.

All-or-nothing underwriting

A security issue that will be canceled if the underwriter is unable to resell the entire issue at an agreed-upon minimum price (cf best-efforts underwriting).

American depository receipt (ADR)

Certificate representing an interest in the shares of a corporation based in a country other than the United States. The actual shares are held in trust by a bank.

American option

An option that may be exercised at any time up to the expiration date (cf European option, which may be exercised only on the expiration date).

Americus trust

Arrangement whereby equity securities are placed in trust and rights to dividends (primes) and appreciation (scores) are sold separately.

Amortization

The repayment of debt through installment payments.

Annuity

An investment producing equal cash payments for a specified number of periods.

Arbitrage

The purchase of an asset in one market and simultaneous sale in another to profit from price discrepancies for an identical security or product. The term now is loosely applied to trading in similar securities (cf index arbitrage) or to trading where an investor believes that he or she has superior information about a firm that may be acquired (cf risk arbitrage).

Assignment

The sale of a swap contract. Such a sale must be approved by the remaining counterparty (cf swap contracts).

At-the-money

An option whose exercise (strike) price is equal to the current price of the underlying security (cf near-the-money).

Auction-rate preferred

A variation of floating-rate preferred stock whose distinguishing feature is a method of establishing the rate: the dividend is reset every 49 days in an auction.

BA

Banker's acceptance.

Baby bonds

Bonds paid to the holder of a bond in lieu of interest (cf multiplier bonds).

Back-to-back loans

Two parties in two countries make loans to one another. The loans are for an equal amount at the time the loan was made and fall due on the same date but are denominated in the currency of the lender. Unless the exchange rate between the two countries is the same on the loan date as on the payment date, one party will have a gain and the other an equivalent loss.

Banker's acceptance

A written demand accepted by a bank to pay a given sum at a future date (cf trade acceptance).

Basis

The difference in yields or market prices between two financial instruments; e.g., the difference in yield between short-term and intermediate-term corporate bonds or the difference between the current price of the S&P 100 index and the futures price of that index.

Basis point

.01 percentage point. Typically the change in yield for a particular financial instrument or the difference in interest yields between two financial instruments.

Bearer security

A security for which the primary evidence of ownership is possession of the security.

Bearish vertical spread

A combination of two call options, one written with a low striking price and one purchased with a high striking price. If the underlying security declines in price the investment is profitable; otherwise there is a loss.

Best-efforts underwriting

Underwriters do not commit themselves to selling a security issue but promise to use their best efforts (cf all-or-nothing underwriting).

Black-Scholes (B-S) option pricing model

A mathematical model used to compute the theoretical value of an option. The model uses five factors to determine the option value: (1) the risk-free interest rate (Treasury bill rate); (2) the time to expiration of the option; (3) the striking price of the option; (4) the current price of the underlying security; and (5) the volatility (standard deviation) of the underlying security. Another factor must be considered for stock options: (6) the present value of expected dividends. To adjust the model for interest-bearing securities, the present value of expected interest payments is substituted for the present value of expected dividend payments.

The model does not use an estimate of the future value of the underlying security. In practice, the B-S model, or variations of it, provide excellent estimates of the actual price of options listed on major exchanges.

Block

A large quantity of securities, typically 10,000 or more shares of common stock.

Bond anticipation note (BAN)

Short-term debt instruments issued by states or municipalities that will be repaid through the proceeds of an anticipated bond issue.

BONUS

Borrowers' options for notes and underwriting facilities, a borrowing facility that permits a firm to issue either Euronotes or U.S. domestic debt.

Book-entry securities

Securities whose purchase and sale is recorded in a book, or register. That record is the official record of an investor's ownership, because no certificate of ownership is issued.

Bottom straddle-bottom vertical combination

A combination of a purchased call and a purchased put designed to limit the maximum loss but not the maximum profit.

Bridge financing

Originally short-term loans to provide temporary financing until permanent financing was arranged. Occasionally the bridge financing is in the form of equity.

Broker

One who brings buyers and sellers together. Unlike a dealer, a broker, when acting in the capacity of a broker, does not buy or sell for his or her own account, (cf dealer).

Bull FRN

Reverse FRN.

Bull-bear bonds

Bonds whose repayment of principal is linked to the price of a second financial instrument. The bonds consist of two tranches, or series. In one, the principal repayment increases with the price of the second instrument. In the other, principal repayment decreases with the price of the second instrument.

Bulldog bonds

A bond issue made in London, denominated in British pounds issued, and made by a non-U.K. borrower (cf Samurai bonds, Yankee bonds).

Bullet payment

A large final payment to repay a bond (in contrast to payment in equal installments).

Bullish vertical spread

A combination of two call options, one written with a high striking price and one purchased with a low striking price. If the underlying security increases in price the investment is profitable; otherwise there is a loss.

Bunds

German Treasury securities.

Bunny bonds

Multiplier bonds.

Butterfly spread

A combination of four purchased call options (butterfly call spread) or of four purchased put options (butterfly put spread), all with the same expiration date on the same underlying security but with different striking prices. A butterfly call spread earns a small profit if, at the time of expiration, the price of the underlying financial instrument is close to its price when the options were purchased; otherwise, there is a small loss. A butterfly put spread loses a small amount if the price at the time of expiration is close to the price at time of purchase; otherwise there is a small loss.

Call option

An option to purchase an asset at a stated exercise price (the striking price), on or before a specified date.

Call premium

(1) The difference between the price at which a firm may call (redeem)

its bonds and the face value of those bonds. (2) The market price of a call option.

Cap

(1) A limitation on the maximum interest rate that a borrower will be required to pay during the period of a loan. (2) A financial instrument that effectively provides an interest rate cap.

Capped floating rate note

A floating rate note with an upper limit on the borrower's interest rate.

CAPS

Convertible adjustable preferred stock, which is convertible every quarter into shares of common stock or into cash, at the issuer's discretion.

CAR

Certificates of Automobile Receivables. Pass-through securities backed by automobile receivables.

CARD

Certificates for Amortizing Revolving Debt. Pass-through securities backed by credit card receivables.

Cash and carry

The simultaneous purchase of a security and sale of a futures contract. The balance is financed with a loan or a repo.

Cash settlement

(1) A settlement provision on some options and futures contracts calling for a cash payment rather than delivery of the underlying financial instrument; the difference between the security price and the striking price of an in-the-money option is paid to the option holder. (2) Payment for an equity security on the trade date, as opposed to "regular way" settlement in five working days.

CATS

Certificates of Accrual on Treasury Securities. A U.S. Treasury bond that has been reissued by Salomon Brothers as a series of zero coupon bonds (cf TIGRs).

CBOE

Chicago Board Options Exchange.

CBT or CBOT

Chicago Board of Trade.

CD

Certificate of Deposit. A certificate providing evidence of an interest-bearing time deposit.

CEDEL

Euroclear. Centralized clearing system for Eurobonds.

Cheapest-to-deliver

Selection of commodities that will be the least expensive to deliver on the delivery date of a futures contract.

Clearinghouse

A corporation set up by an exchange to clear trades for exchange members (e.g., for securities, options, or commodities).

CLEO

Collateralized lease equipment obligations. Securities backed by lease equipment receivables.

Closed-end mortgage

A mortgage against which no additional debt may be incurred (in contrast with an open-end mortgage).

CME

Chicago Mercantile Exchange.

CMO

Collateralized mortgage obligation.

Collar

A floating interest rate loan that has both an upper and a lower limit to the interest rate (i.e., a cap and a floor).

Collateral

Assets pledged as security for a loan.

Collateral trust bonds

Bonds secured by equity securities owned by the borrower.

Collateralized mortgage obligations

CMO. Mortgage-backed bonds repaid in installments. A CMO typically consists of several tranches (classes) that are retired in a specified order.

Commercial paper

Unsecured notes issued by firms (typically large corporations) that mature within nine months. The face value of the paper represents both principal and interest.

Committed facility

A legal commitment made by a bank to make a loan to a customer.

Consol

A perpetual bond issued by the British government; interest is paid in perpetuity, but there is no repayment of principal.

Convergence

Price movement of a futures or forward contract toward the cash price.

Conversion ratio

The exchange ratio of the number of shares of common stock for which convertible securities may be exchanged (e.g., 2:1 or 5:2).

Convertible security

A fixed-income security or a preferred stock that includes an option to exchange that security for a stated number of shares of another security, possibly at a stated cost (typically an option to convert that security into a specified number of shares of an equity security).

Corporate bond equivalent

Annual yield computed on a basis equivalent to the yield on coupon securities (payment made semiannually); i.e., the corporate bond equivalent for T-bills, which are noninterest-bearing (discount) securities.

Coupon

(1) Coupon attached to a bearer bond that must be surrendered in exchange for a semiannual interest payment. (2) The interest payment on debt.

Coupon stripping

The process of producing a zero-coupon bond from an interest-bearing bond. It may be accomplished by physically separating the coupons from a bond, then selling the coupons and the bearer bond separately, or by selling the rights to the funds from the coupons and the bond, which are held by a trustee.

Cover

Eliminate a short position by buying the securities sold short.

Covered option writing

The process of selling call options on a security owned by the investor or of selling put options on a security that has been sold short by the investor.

Credit scoring

A system of assigning scores to firms on the basis of their likelihood of default.

Cross-default clause

A clause in a loan agreement stating that a firm is in default on a particular loan if it is in default on any other loan.

Currency swap

An arrangement between two parties to exchange payments with one another at a future date at an exchange rate specified at inception.

Currency warrant

Options (usually detachable) included with a security issue giving the holder rights to purchase foreign currency at a fixed price.

Dealer

A dealer acts as a principal in a trade. When acting in that capacity, the dealer buys or sells for his or her own account (cf broker).

Debenture

Unsecured bond.

Defeasance

A borrower irrevocably sets aside cash or U.S. Government securities sufficient to repay both the interest and principal of a debt. Both the debt and the offsetting cash or securities are removed from the borrower's balance sheet.

Delayed rate setting

Arrangement whereby a buyer obtains funds through a fixed-rate debt issue, but, through a side arrangement with an investment bank, a payment will be made to or by the borrower. The payment equals the discounted present value of the interest differential between the rate on the date of the debt issue and the rate of a future date (cf forward rate agreement).

Delta

The estimated change in price of an option, divided by the price of the underlying asset. An option whose price changes by $1 as the price of the underlying assets changes by $4 has a delta of .25. Deep out-of-the-money options have a delta of near 0 while deep in-the-money options have a delta near 1. Near-the-money options have a value closer to .5, but the value depends heavily on the time until expiration.

Depository institution

An institution, such as a bank, savings and loan association, or credit union, that accepts cash deposits for customers.

Depository Trust Company

DTC. The DTC and its related organization, the National Securities Clearing Corporation (NSCC), operate a book entry system for maintaining and transferring ownership in corporate stocks and bonds. The DTC and NSCC also maintain a book entry system for Treasury securities, most agency securities, most commercial paper, and for many municipal bond issues.

Derivatives

Financial instruments such as customized options that have been derived from more basic financial instruments. Derivatives include convertible bonds, swaps, and warrants. Unlike traditional financial instruments, the value of a derivative is partially determined by the credit risk of the financial institution issuing the derivative.

DI

Depository institution.

Discount securities

Noninterest-bearing debt securities, such as T-bills, that are issued at a discount and redeemed at face value on maturity.

Dividend strips

Rights to all future dividends paid on an issue of preferred stock through some future date, such as the first call date (cf interest strips).

DK

Don't know, or DKed. When one party to a securities trade lacks knowledge about a trade, the trade is said to be DKed. Such lack of knowledge is usually due to incomplete or conflicting instructions regarding the buyer, the seller, or the method of payment.

Drop lock

The clause in a floating rate instrument whereby the interest rate becomes fixed if the floating rate drops to a specified rate.

DTC

Depository Trust Company.

Dual currency bonds

Bonds whose principal is repaid in one currency and whose interest payments are made in a second currency.

Duration

A measure of the discounted, weighted average time to receipt of payments of a debt instrument. For example, if there are two equal annual payments remaining to a debt issue, the weighted average time to receipt is one and one-half years. If the amounts to be received are first discounted at some discount rate, then the discounted second payment will be smaller than the second payment, and the discounted weighted average time to receipt will be less than one and one-half years.

Dutch auction

An auction in which the lowest price necessary to sell the entire issue is the price charged to all bidders who bid that price or more.

Dutch auction preferred

Money market preferred stock (MMP). Preferred stock whose dividend is periodically reset through dutch auction (typically every 49 days, to satisfy the 45-day Internal Revenue Service holding period for the dividends-received deduction for corporate investors).

ECU

European Currency Unit.

Equivalent bond yield

Corporate bond equivalent.

Eurobond

A bond issued in a European country and payable in a currency foreign to that of the host country (e.g., U.S. dollar, yen, or deutsche mark) and sold simultaneously in a number of countries throughout the world. Most Eurobond syndicates are formed by London branches of underwriters.

Eurocurrency deposits

Deposits made in a bank in Europe in a foreign currency. Dollars and marks deposited in London are referred to as Eurodollars and Euromarks, respectively.

Euroclear

(CEDEL) Centralized clearing system for Eurobonds.

Eurocurrency

Money deposited in banks away from their home country.

Eurodollar

Deposit of dollars into an account denominated in U.S. dollars in foreign (non-U.S.) banks, in foreign branches of U.S. banks, or in international banking facilities (branches of domestic or United States banks that are located in the United States and that are designated as international banking facilities, or IBFs).

European currency unit

(ECU) A currency unit whose value changes with the weighted average change in value of a basket of European currencies.

European option

An option that can be exercised only on its expiration date.

Exdividend date

Date on or after which a purchaser of stock is not entitled to the next dividend. The exdividend date is five business days before the date of record.

Exercise price

The price at which an option may be exercised. For a put option, the price at which the underlying asset may be sold. For a call option, the price at which the asset may be purchased (strike price).

Expiration date

The date on which an option expires.

Extendable bond

A bond whose maturity may be extended. The extension clause may give that option to the borrower or to the lender.

Federal funds

Funds, primarily bank reserves, held by Federal Reserve banks. Banks with excess reserves may loan the excess to other banks, typically overnight. The rate on these loans is known as the federal funds rate.

Federal funds rate

The interest rate at which banks borrow or lend federal funds.

Federal Home Loan Mortgage Corporation (FHLMC)

Publicly held corporation that buys conventional mortgages from mortgage lenders and packages them into FHLMC participation certificates (PCs). PCs are sold to mortgage buyers or are swapped for original mortgages. Also called Freddie Mac.

Federal National Mortgage Association (FNMA)

Corporation owned by private shareholders but chartered by the U.S. Government. FNMA funds the purchase of mortgages through the sale of debentures, short-term notes, and pools of mortgages that may be federally insured or uninsured (conventional). Also called Fannie Mae.

Financial leverage

Gearing. The ratio of debt to debt plus equity.

Flat

The market interest rate for a fixed income security (i.e., the three-month T-bill flat is the interest rate for three-month T-bills).

Flip-flop note

A note that gives the holder an option to switch between two different types of debt.

Floating-rate note

A note whose interest payment is determined by a short-term interest rate (such as the prime rate or the U.S. Treasury bill rate).

Floating-rate preferred

Preferred stock whose dividend rate is reset quarterly and pegged to the lowest of selected yields on U.S. Treasury obligations.

Floor

An option whereby one counterparty promises that the second counterparty will receive a minimum interest rate over a given period.

Forfeiting

The purchase at a discount of payment promises issued by importers (promissory notes or bills of exchange).

Forward

An agreement to purchase (accept delivery of) or sell (deliver) a given asset at some future date (cf future).

Forward cover

The purchase or sale of a forward foreign currency in order to offset a known future cash flow in the currency.

Forward exchange rate

The current market rate at which one currency may be exchanged for another at some specified future date (cf spot exchange rate).

Forward interest rate

The fixed interest rate on a loan to be made at some future date.

Forward rate agreement

FRA. An agreement between two counterparties to protect themselves against changes in interest rates. The parties fix a date, an interest rate, and a nominal principal amount. The parties agree to pay (accept) the discounted present value of the gain or loss incurred as a result of changes in interest rates multiplied by the stated amount (cf delayed rate setting).

FRA

Forward rate agreement.

FRN

Floating rate note.

Funded debt

Debt maturing in more than one year.

Future

Futures contract. An exchange-traded contract to buy a commodity or a financial instrument on a future date at a fixed price. Purchasers must post a margin, which varies daily, because the contracts are marked-to-market each day (cf forward).

Geisha bond

Shogun bond.

General obligation bond

Municipal bond backed by the full faith and credit of the municipality, to be repaid through general revenue or borrowing receipts.

Global note facility

Bonus.

Government National Mortgage Association (GNMA)

A government-owned corporation that guarantees privately issued securities backed by pools of federally insured mortgages. Most commonly, monthly interest payments and the amortization and prepayments of principal are "passed through" to the investor. GNMA obligations are backed by the full faith and credit of the U.S. Government. Also called Ginnie Mae.

Governments
> Debt issues of the United States Government. Governments include debt issued by the Treasury Department (Treasuries) and by agencies of the U.S. Government (agencies).

Grey market
> The purchase and sale of Eurobonds prior to the time that their issue price is set.

Guaranteed bond
> A bond whose interest and principal payments are guaranteed by a firm other than the issuer.

Haircut
> The difference between the amount of collateral given and the funds borrowed. Typically a term used in repurchase agreements.

Hedge
> Buying one asset and selling another so as to protect against risk, or purchasing a financial instrument such as an option or future, to protect against the financial risk associated with an existing asset or liability or with an anticipated transaction.

Hedge ratio
> The number of shares, or the amount of other assets being hedged, to buy for each option or future contract that is written or bought in order to create a safe position.

Horizontal spread
> The simultaneous purchase and sale of two options that are identical except for their expiration date.

ICON
> Indexed Currency Option Note.

IMM
> International Monetary Market. Financial futures market within the Chicago Mercantile Exchange.

Immunization
> Combination of an asset and a liability that are subject to offsetting changes in their value.

Implied volatility
> The volatility of an asset (such as IBM stock, the S&P 100 index, or corn) implied by the Black-Scholes option pricing model when the current market price of the asset is used in the model. Because all variables in the model are known, except for the volatility, by knowing the price of the option it is possible to determine the stock volatility implied in the price of an option. A major change in implied volatility may indicate that some

investors believe that a major event such as a takeover is likely to occur (cf volatility).

Income bonds
Bonds on which interest is paid only if earned. Missed interest payments are usually cumulative and sometimes compounded.

Increasing rate debt
Often issued in a leveraged buyout when a loan is made in anticipation of the sale of parts of the firm to retire debt. The interest rate is increased at specified dates.

Indenture
A written agreement establishing the terms of a bond issue.

Index arbitrage
Non-risk arbitrage whereby an arbitrageur purchases (sells) an index futures contract and simultaneously sells (purchases) the stocks in that index (or a representative sample of those stocks). Also referred to as program trading.

Indexed bonds
Bonds whose interest payments vary with an index such as the consumer price index or with a commodity such as oil. Such bonds typically carry a guaranteed rate and a contingent rate, with the contingent payment sometimes separable from the debt instrument.

Industrial development bonds
Bonds issued by a state or local government to finance buildings that are to be leased to privately owned businesses. The objective is to attract employers to a region through tax-exempt financing.

In-the-money
An option contract that would require a payment to the holder if it were exercised immediately. A call option is in the money when its exercise price is below the price of the underlying asset; a put option is in the money when its exercise price is above the price of the underlying asset.

Interest rate cap
Protection against increases in the interest rate on floating-rate debt. The agreement may call for a maximum interest rate in any one payment period or may require that the borrower pay only a portion (e.g., 50%) of the difference between the average floating interest rate and some limit or ceiling.

Interest rate swap
A financial transaction whereby two parties agree to pay each other the equivalent of interest payments on a notional principal. The three basic types of interest rate swaps are: (1) coupon swaps, when one party pays a fixed interest rate and the other a floating rate, both in the same currency;

(2) basis swaps, when both parties pay floating interest rates in the same country, but payments are determined by different indices; and (3) cross-currency swaps, when interest rates are computed on principal amounts denominated in two different currencies (the rates may be either fixed or floating).

Inverse floaters
Reverse FRN.

Inverted yield curve
Abnormal situation in which short-term interest rates are higher than long-term rates.

Investment grade bonds
Bonds rated Baa or above by Moody's rating service, or BBB or above by Standard & Poor's rating service.

I/O strip
Interest only strip (cf PO strip, zero coupon bonds).

ISDA
International Swap Dealers Association. An organization that has created standard contracts for interest rate swaps to reduce legal and administrative costs associated with swaps.

Junior debt
Subordinated debt (i.e., other debt has first claim to the borrower's assets in the event of default).

Junk bond
A high-yield bond rated below investment grade because of the degree of risk (cf investment grade bond).

Letter of credit
Letter from a bank stating that it has established a credit in favor of a customer. Payments to a particular party, normally a supplier of the bank's customer, are guaranteed up to a stated amount during a specified period.

Lettered security
A security not registered with the SEC and that cannot be sold through public markets.

LIBOR
London Interbank Offered Rate. The interest rate at which major international banks in London offer to loan funds to each other (LIBID is the London Interbank bid rate, while LIMEAN is the mean of the bid and the offer).

Liquidity premium
The additional return for investing in an asset that is not readily convertible into cash without affecting the market price.

Lockup CD

A CD issued with the understanding that the buyer will not trade the instrument. The issuing bank may prohibit the buyer from taking possession to ensure compliance with the agreement.

Long position

To own an asset, such as common stock, a call option, or a put option (cf short position).

LYON

Liquid Yield Option Note. LYONs or convertible LYONs typically are floating-rate debt issues that are convertible into common stock of the issuing corporation.

Margin

Cash or securities that are deposited with a financial institution to ensure that an investor will honor a financial commitment. Examples include a margin of 50% for equity securities that have been purchased or sold short and a margin on options that may range from 20% to 30% of the value of the underlying asset. Repurchase agreements often require that the borrower deliver securities in excess of the amount borrowed; the excess represents the margin.

Mark to market

A procedure whereby the value of financial assets such as a futures contract, a written option position, or an equity position purchased on margin is reestablished based on current values each day. If the position has suffered a loss, the investor will be required to post additional margin or else the position will be sold.

Market risk

The risk that all securities are subject to as a result of changes in the general economy. Examples include changes in oil prices, interest rates, or exchange rates.

Mezzanine

Balance sheet classification below the liability section but above shareholder's equity. Mezzanine financing includes mandatorily redeemable preferred stock and putable common stock typically issued during a leveraged buyout.

Minimax bond

A floating rate note whose interest rate payments are limited by a narrow collar. That is, the interest rate cannot raise above some limit nor fall below a second limit.

Mismatch bond

A floating-rate note whose interest rate is set more frequently than the rollover period (e.g., a note whose interest rate is reset quarterly based on the three-year Treasury rate has a three-month reset rate but a three-year rollover period).

Mortgage-backed bonds
Bonds whose underlying collateral is a pool of mortgages (cf collateralized mortgage obligations, pay-through bonds).

Mortgage bond
Bond secured by a mortgage on property, plant, or equipment.

Multiplier bonds
Bonds that provide holders the option of taking interest payments in the form of additional multiplier bonds. Also known as bunny bonds.

Naked option
Uncovered option.

National Securities Clearing Corporation
NSCC (cf Depository Trust Company).

NIF
Note issuance facility.

Nonrefundable debt
Debt that may not be called prior to maturity. Refundable debt can be called to replace it with lower cost financing.

Note-issuance facility
NIF. A facility that permits borrowers to issue short-term paper (typically three to six months maturity) in their own names. Typically a group of underwriting banks guarantees the availability of funds, up to a limit, by purchasing any unsold notes on the rollover date or by offering standby credit.

Notional principal
Notional amount. A hypothetical amount on which payments are determined in an interest rate swap; this notional principal is neither paid nor received.

Off-balance sheet financing
Financing that is not shown as a liability on a firm's balance sheet.

OID debt
Original issue discount debt.

Operating leverage
Fixed operating costs, which cause a firm's profits to vary more with changes in sales activity.

Option
The right, without the obligation, to purchase or to sell a specified underlying asset (cf put option, call option, underlying asset).

Original issue discount debt
(OID debt) Debt initially offered at less than face value.

Out-of-the-money
An option that would not require a payment to the holder if it were exercised. A call option is out-of-the-money if its exercise price is above the current price of the underlying asset; a put option is out-of-the-money if its exercise price is below the current price of the underlying asset.

Over-collateralize
To increase the credit rating of an asset-backed security by collateralizing that security with more than one dollar of collateral for each dollar of security.

Overnight repo rate
The interest rate paid on overnight repurchase agreement transactions (cf repurchase agreement).

Participation certificates
See Federal Home Loan Mortgage Corporation.

Partly paid bonds
Debt securities that require the buyer to pay a portion of the total price on the issue date and additional amounts at predetermined future dates.

Pass-through certificates
Notes or bonds backed by packages of assets such as mortgages or credit card receipts. These instruments require that interest, amortized principal, and any prepayments of principal be "passed through" to the holders of the instrument (cf Federal National Mortgage Association, CARs, CARDs).

Perpetuity
An investment paying a level series of payments in perpetuity. There is no payment of principal (cf consol).

PO strip
Principal strip (cf I/O strip, zero-coupon bond).

Poison put
A debt covenant allowing the debt holder to put his debt back to the issuer in the event of a hostile takeover.

Portfolio insurance
Hedging strategy designed to protect a portfolio of common stocks from declines in the market while permitting the portfolio to benefit from most increases in the market. The strategy is implemented whenever some stock index such as the S&P 500 declines below some level, and normally consists of selling stock index futures or purchasing stock index put options. Such portfolio insurance has a cost and usually cannot be imple-

mented during a rapid market decline such as the October 1987 stock crash.

Positive yield curve

Normal situation where long-term interest rates are above short-term yield rates (cf inverted yield curve, yield curve).

Premium

(1) The price paid for an option contract. (2) The amount by which a bond price exceeds its par or face value.

Primes

Rights to dividend payments from equity securities that have been put into trust for separate sale of dividend rights (primes) and appreciation rights (scores) (cf Americus Trust, scores).

Principal

(1) The face amount of a security. (2) The basis for an interest calculation.

Putable common stock

Common stock, normally issued during a leveraged buyout, that can be put back to the issuer during certain circumstances.

Put option

An option to sell an asset at a specified price on or before a stated exercise date.

Recourse

In a recourse loan the purchaser of the financial instrument has recourse against the general credit of the original issuer of the debt in the event of default. For example, a firm may sell its receivables to a second party with recourse. The second party may then resell those receivables to a third party. In the event that the receivables are uncollected, the third party has recourse against the first party.

Refunding

To replace existing debt with a new issue of debt.

Registered bonds

Book-entry bonds. See Book-entry securities.

Reinvestment risk

The risk that an investor will be unable to reinvest the cash flows from an investment at as favorable a yield as was being earned from the original investment.

Repo

Repurchase agreement.

Repurchase agreement

Buy-back, Repo, RP. The purchase of securities from a securities dealer with an agreement that the dealer will repurchase those securities at a later date at a prearranged price.

Residual
The last tranche or class of an asset-backed pass-through security issue.

Revenue anticipation notes (RAN)
A short-term debt issue to be repaid from anticipated revenues such as real estate or sales taxes.

Revenue bonds
A municipal bond whose interest and principal will be paid from the revenues generated by a project to be funded with the proceeds of the revenue bond. Examples include hospitals and toll roads.

Reverse FRN
Bull FRN, inverse floaters. Floating rate note whose interest rate rises as some general interest rate (e.g., Treasury bill rates) decreases, and vice versa.

Reverse swap
A financial transaction to offset the effect of an existing swap.

Revolving underwriting facility
RUF. An issuance facility for short-term Euronotes (cf note issuance facility).

Risk arbitrage
The practice of purchasing common stock in companies where a takeover is expected or has been announced. The purchaser anticipates either that the takeover will be made at a price higher than the current price of the stock or that the takeover will not go through, so the stock can be sold short. Not arbitrage in its traditional meaning of profiting from small discrepancies in the prices of identical assets in different markets.

Rollforward
To purchase a new option in order to replace an option that is about to expire.

RP
Repurchase agreement.

RUF
Revolving underwriting facility.

Samurai bond
A yen bond issued in Tokyo by a non-Japanese borrower (cf Bulldog bond, Yankee bond).

Scores
Appreciation rights to an equity security (cf primes, Americus Trust).

Secured debt

Debt that, in the event of default to the borrower, has the first claim to some or all of the borrower's assets.

Securitization

The process of converting receivables and other assets that are not readily marketable into securities that can be placed and traded in capital markets. The objective of securitization is to raise funds at a lower cost than the cost of general obligation borrowings, or to achieve some other perceived advantage such as off-balance sheet financing.

Securitized assets

Assets used in a securitization transaction. Typically these assets are accounts receivable, single family mortgages, auto loans, credit card receivables, and similar assets.

Securitized loan

A loan wherein the investor looks to the underlying asset, rather than the general rating of the firm, for repayment of debt. Factoring when accounts receivable are used as collateral was the original form of a securitized loan.

Self-liquidating loan

A loan to finance current assets such as inventory or receivables. The sale of those assets will be used to liquidate the loan.

Senior debt

Debt that, in the event of default, must be repaid before subordinated debt is repaid.

Serial bonds

Bonds that mature in successive years.

Series bonds

Bonds that may be issued in several series by the same underwriter.

Shelf registration

A securities registration option that permits an issue of securities to be preregistered, then issued in whole or in part at a later date.

Shogun bond

A dollar bond issued in Japan by a non-Japanese borrower. Sometimes referred to as a Geisha bond.

Short against the box

A short sale of securities that are identical to securities owned. The transaction has the temporary effect of a sale while permitting the investor to defer taxes until the securities are actually delivered.

Short sale

Sale of security that an investor does not own (cf naked position, written option).

Sinker

Sinking fund.

Sinking fund

Fund that is established to retire debt.

Spot

Spot rate, or spot market. The cash price at which a commodity, index, or other asset can currently be purchased.

Spot exchange

The current exchange rate between two rate currencies.

Spread

(1) The difference between the bid and the asked price for an asset. (2) The difference between the price at which an underwriter buys an issue from a firm and the price at which the security is sold (underwriter's spread). (3) The difference between yields of two financial instruments.

Standby agreement

The agreement in a rights issue that an underwriter will purchase any securities that are not purchased by the public.

Standby commitment

A bank commitment to lend up to a stated amount of funds during a specified period, but only in the event of some contingency, such as a construction firm that can obtain standby financing only if it is unable to obtain a permanent mortgage loan.

Step-down bond

A bond whose coupon is decreased over time.

Step-up bond

A bond whose coupon is increased over time.

Stop-out price

The lowest price (highest yield) accepted in a Treasury auction for a new issue.

Straddle

The combination of a purchased put option and a purchased call option with the same exercise price and exercise date. Such a combination is profitable if there is a wide swing (either up or down) in the price of the underlying asset.

Strike price

The exercise price of an option.

Stripped bond

A bond that has been subdivided into a series of zero-coupon bonds (P/O, or principal only securities) and a series of interest payments (I/O, or interest only securities). Various other combinations are also possible.

STRIPS

Separate trading of registered principal of securities. The Federal Reserve, at the request of a bondholder, will separate a security issue into its individual coupon components and its principal payment. The pieces may be traded separately (cf CATS, TIGRs).

Subordinated debt

Junior debt. Debt that, in the event of default, is repaid only after more senior debt is repaid.

Super poison put

A debt covenant that permits a debt holder to put the debt to the issuer in a variety of circumstances, including a hostile takeover or actions by management that will significantly reduce the credit rating of the debt issue. Also referred to as event-risk covenants. These covenants can include agreements to increase (or decrease) a security's yield upon the occurrence of certain events.

Sushi bond

A Eurobond issued by a Japanese firm.

Swap

An arrangement whereby two parties agree to exchange amounts on different terms (e.g., in different currencies or at interest rates determined by different factors, such as a fixed-rate payment and a floating-rate payment).

Swap option

An option to enter into a swap agreement.

Swingline facility

A borrowing facility that provides temporary financing while a borrower replaces U.S. commercial paper with Eurocommercial paper or while a borrower is awaiting the receipt of funds from a new issue from an NIF.

Synthetic instrument

A combination of financial instruments that have the characteristics of a second instrument. For example, a purchased S&P 100 call option and a written S&P 100 put option with the same strike price and expiration date combine to form a synthetic S&P 100 future contract. The combination is not identical to a S&P 100 future contract, because the put option can be exercised early without the permission of the writer of that option.

Tax anticipation notes

TANs. Notes issued by municipalities in anticipation of future tax receipts.

TED spread

The difference between the prices of three-month Treasury bills and Eurodollar futures.

TIGRs

Treasury instrument growth receipts. U.S. Treasury bond reissued by Merrill Lynch as a series of zero-coupon bonds (cf CATS).

Top straddle-top vertical combination

A combination of a written call and a written put that limits the maximum profit but not the maximum loss.

Tranches

Segments of a financial arrangement or financial instrument. Classes of similar debt instruments.

Treasuries

Debt instruments issued by the U.S. Treasury.

Trust deed

The agreement between the bond trustee and the borrower describing the terms of the bond.

Uncovered option

An option that is held on its own; i.e., a written option that is not offset by a position in the underlying asset. Naked option.

Underlying asset

(1) Asset to be delivered upon execution of an option or a futures contract (e.g., IBM stock is the underlying asset for an IBM stock option). (2) Asset pledged as security under a borrowing arrangement that gives value to a guarantee.

Underpricing

An issue of securities that sells for less than the market value established shortly after the initial offering.

Underwriter

A firm that purchases an issue of securities from a firm, then resells them to the public.

Undivided interest

Each security holder has a proportionate interest in each cash flow generated by a pool of assets. In contrast, some pools of assets, such as collateralized mortgage obligations, are divided so that some classes of security holders receive certain cash flows (e.g., payments of principal) sooner than other classes.

Unfunded debt
    Debt maturing in less than one year (cf funded debt).

Volatility
    The variability of an asset, such as General Electric stock or soybeans, typically measured by the standard deviation of the market price of the asset.

Voluntary termination (swap market)
    Agreed-upon cancellation of a swap contract, usually involving a lumpsum payment from one party to the other.

Warrant
    Long-term call option to purchase common stock from the firm itself.

When issued
    The practice of trading securities after the auction date but before the settlement date.

WI
    When issued.

Yankee bond
    U.S. dollar-denominated bond issued in the United States by a non-U.S. borrower.

Yield curve
    Curve showing the relationship between the interest rate on a debt issue and the term until maturity of that issue (cf positive yield curve).

Yield to maturity
    The internal rate of return on a bond. The effective rate of interest after considering the reinvestment of interest payments.

Zero-coupon bond
    A bond that pays no interest. A zero-coupon bond can be issued as such or can be created by separating an interest-bearing bond into an interest-only security and a principal-only security (the zero-coupon bond).

BIBLIOGRAPHY

General

Arthur Andersen & Co., *Accounting for Securitized Transactions by Sellers/Issuers.* Arthur Andersen & Co., Chicago (September 1989).

Arthur Young, *Financial Instruments.* Newsletters of various dates in 1988 and 1989. Ernst & Young, New York.

Brealey, Richard A. and Stewart C. Myers, *Principles of Corporate Finance, Third Edition.* McGraw-Hill, New York (1988).

Coopers & Lybrand, *Guide to Financial Instruments.* Coopers & Lybrand, New York (1990).

Financial Accounting Standards Board, *Description of FASB Project on Financial Instruments and Off-Balance Sheet Financing.* FASB, Stamford, CT (June 1986).

Kay, Robert S. and D. Gerald Searfoss, *Handbook of Accounting and Auditing, Second Edition.* Warren, Gorham & Lamont, Boston (1989).

Price Waterhouse, *Hedging: Foreign Exchange and Interest Rate Risk Management: Implementation Guide.* Price Waterhouse, New York.

Rollins, T., D. Stout, and D. O'Mara, "The New Financial Instruments." *Management Accounting* (March 1990), pp. 35-41.

Smith, C. W. and C. W. Smithson, *The Handbook of Financial Engineering.* Harper & Row, New York (1990).

Stewart, John E. and Benjamin S. Neuhausen, "Financial Instruments and Transactions: The CPA's Newest Challenge." *Journal of Accountancy* (August 1986), pp. 102-111.

Stigum, Marcia, *The Money Market, Third Edition.* Dow-Jones Irwin, Homewood, IL (1990).

Walmsley, Julian, *The New Financial Instruments.* John Wiley & Sons, New York (1988).

Caps

Salomon Brothers, Inc., *Interest Rate Caps and Floors: Tools for Asset/Liability Management.* Salomon Brothers, Inc., New York (May 1986).

Contingent Claims Analysis

HBS Case Services, *Contingent Claims Analysis.* 286-114, Harvard Business School, Boston (1986).

Trigeorgis, Lenos and Scott P. Mason, "Valuing Managerial Flexibility." *Midland Corporate Finance Journal* (Spring 1987), pp. 14-21.

Futures

Arthur Andersen & Co., *Accounting for Interest Rate Futures.* Arthur Andersen & Co., Chicago (1985).

Schwarz, Edward W., Joanne M. Hill, and Thomas Schneeweis, *Financial Futures: Fundamentals, Strategies, and Applications.* Dow-Jones Irwin, Homewood, IL (1986).

Hedging

Stewart, John E., "The Challenges of Hedge Accounting." *Journal of Accountancy* (November 1989), pp. 48-60.

Options

AICPA Issues Paper, "Accounting for Options." American Institute of Certified Public Accountants, New York (1986).

Arthur Andersen & Co., *Accounting for Options.* Arthur Andersen & Co., Chicago (1986).

Cox, John C. and Mark Rubinstein, *Options Markets.* Prentice-Hall, Englewood Cliffs, NJ (1985).

HBS Case Services, *Introduction to Options.* 286-104, Harvard Business School, Boston (1986).

HBS Case Services, *Options Pricing.* 286-112, Harvard Business School, Boston (1986).

The Options Clearing Corporation, *Characteristics and Risks of Standardized Options.* The Options Clearing Corporation, Washington, D.C. (1987).

Securitized Debt

Arthur Andersen & Co., *Accounting for Securitized Transactions by Sellers/Issuers.* Arthur Andersen & Co., Chicago (September 1989).

Fabozzi, Frank J., *The Handbook of Mortgage Backed Securities.* Probus Publishing Company, Chicago (1988).

Goldman Sachs, *Asset Securitization-Credit Card Backed Securities: an Introduction.* Goldman Sachs, New York (January 1987).

HBS Case Services, *A Note on the Pricing of Mortgage-Backed Securities.* 287-060, Harvard Business School, Boston (1987).

Pavel, Christine A., *Securitization.* Probus Publishing Company, Chicago (1989).

Smith, Donald J. and F. Mark D'Annolfo, "Collateralized Mortgage Obligations: an Introduction." *Real Estate Review* (Vol. 16, Num. 1, Spring 1987), pp. 30-42.

Zweig, Philip L., *The Asset Securitization Handbook.* Dow Jones-Irwin, Homewood, IL (1989).

Swaps

Arnold, Tanya S., "How to Do Interest Rate Swaps." *Harvard Business Review* (September-October 1984), pp. 96-101.

Field, Peter, "Swaps Make the World Go Round." *Corporate Finance* (May 1986), pp. 55-58.

HBS Case Services, *Foreign Currency Swaps*. 286-073, Harvard Business School, Boston (1986).

Salomon Brothers, Inc., *The Interest Rate Swap Market: Yield Mathematics, Terminology and Conventions*. Salomon Brothers, Inc., New York (June 1985).

Wishon, Keith and Lorin S. Chevalier, "Interest Rate Swaps— Your Rate or Mine?" *Journal of Accountancy* (September 1985), pp. 6-84.

Accounting

Financial Accounting Standards Board, *Emerging Issues Task Force Consensus*, numerous issues. Financial Accounting Standards Board, Norwalk, CT.

_____, *Statement of Financial Accounting Standards No. 5: Accounting for Contingencies (amended)*. Financial Accounting Standards Board, Stamford, CT (1975).

_____, *Statement of Financial Accounting Standards No. 12: Accounting for Certain Marketable Securities*. Financial Accounting Standards Board, Stamford, CT (1980).

_____, *Statement of Financial Accounting Standards No. 52: Foreign Currency Translation*. Financial Accounting Standards Board, Stamford, CT (1981).

_____, *Statement of Financial Accounting Standards No. 64: Extinguishment of Debt Made to Satisfy Sinking-Fund Requirements*. Financial Accounting Standards Board, Stamford, CT (1982).

_____, *Statement of Financial Accounting Standards No. 76: Extinguishment of Debt*. Financial Accounting Standards Board, Stamford, CT (1983).

_____, *Statement of Financial Accounting Standards No. 77: Reporting by Transferors for Transfers of Receivables with Recourse*. Financial Accounting Standards Board, Stamford, CT (1983).

_____, *Statement of Financial Accounting Standards No. 78: Classifications of Obligations That Are Callable by the Creditor*. Financial Accounting Standards Board, Stamford, CT (1983).

_____, *Statement of Financial Accounting Standards No. 80: Accounting for Futures Contracts*. Financial Accounting Standards Board, Stamford, CT (1984).

_____, *Statement of Financial Accounting Standards No. 84: Induced Conversions of Convertible Debt*. Financial Accounting Standards Board, Stamford, CT (1985).

_____, *Statement of Financial Accounting Standards No. 105: Disclosure of Information About Financial Instruments with Off-Balance-Sheet Risk and Financial Instruments with Concentrations of Credit Risk*. Financial Accounting Standards Board, Norwalk, CT (1990).

_____, *FASB Technical Bulletins: No. 84-4, In-Substance Defeasance of Debt*. Financial Accounting Standards Board, Stamford, CT (1984).

_____, *FASB Technical Bulletins: No. 85-2, Accounting for Collateralized Mortgage Obligations*. Financial Accounting Standards Board, Stamford, CT (1985).

Taxes

Internal Revenue Service, *Technical and Miscellaneous Revenue Act of 1988 (TAMRA)*. Internal Revenue Service (1988).

Internal Revenue Service, *Revenue Announcement 89-21*. Internal Revenue Service (1989).

Other

Most investment banks and large brokerage firms offer publications that describe the mechanics of various financial instruments. Most large accounting firms offer publications that describe various accounting and tax regulations concerning financial instruments.

Statements on Management Accounting

Statement Number 4N
September 7, 1990

PRACTICES AND TECHNIQUES

Management of Working Capital: Cash Resources

In accordance with the charge to the Management Accounting Practices (MAP) Committee to issue statements on management accounting principles and practices, Statements on Management Accounting are promulgated to reflect official positions of the National Association of Accountants (NAA). The work of the MAP Committee is based on a framework for management accounting, whose principal categories are:

1. Objectives
2. Terminology
3. Concepts
4. Practices and Techniques
5. Management of Accounting Activities

Statements on Management Accounting

Statement Number 4N
September 7, 1990

Practices and Techniques:
Management of Working Capital: Cash Resources

National Association of Accountants, Inc.

Acknowledgments

The National Association of Accountants is grateful to all who contributed to the publication of Statement 4N, "Management of Financial Working Capital: Cash Resources." Appreciation is extended to members of NAA's Management Accounting Practices Committee and its Subcommittee on SMA Promulgation. Special thanks go to Professor Ned C. Hill, Marriott School of Management, Brigham Young University, for his research and writing associated with the project, and to SMA Subcommittee member Thomas E. Huff for his valuable contributions and general oversight.

INTRODUCTION

1. Effective working capital management is important for all businesses. This Statement has been prepared to help financial and management accountants understand the key issues involving financial working capital so that they will be able to manage it more effectively.

2. Investment in working capital is usually defined as the difference between a firm's short-term assets and its short-term liabilities. To facilitate understanding of working capital management, components of working capital related to line functions (i.e. receivables, inventories, and payables) will be discussed in a forthcoming SMA. This Statement addresses financial working capital, which falls under the management of a firm's treasury function.

STATEMENT SCOPE

3. The management of financial working capital entails managing cash receipts and disbursements and also the management of the short-term investment and borrowing portfolios. To familiarize managers with financial instruments, SMA 4M, UNDERSTANDING FINANCIAL INSTRUMENTS, is strongly recommended; it provides a comprehensive discussion of instruments essential for effective management of financial working capital.

4. To manage financial working capital effectively, the manager must: i) understand the cash management system; ii) be able to estimate the costs and/or benefits of alternative strategies; and iii) rely upon the appropriate method of evaluation.

5. Because cash inflows and outflows are not synchronized, a firm needs to maintain access to cash either from its own liquidity portfolio, or from back-up liquidity. The liquidity portfolio consists of cash balances in banks and securities, whereas back-up liquidity refers to bank credit lines or other short-term borrowing arrangements for periods when the normal store of liquidity is insufficient.

6. A representative cash management system consists of the following:

    a. collection system - brings cash into the firm.

    b. disbursement system - makes payments with cash.

    c. concentration system - moves cash from deposit banks to the concentration bank.

    d. disbursement funding system - moves funds from the concentration bank to the disbursement banks.

    e. banking relations and compensation issues.

    f. cash forecasting system.

7. Exhibit 1 illustrates the major relationships of a representative cash management system.

EXHIBIT 1
Major Relationships of a Cash Management System

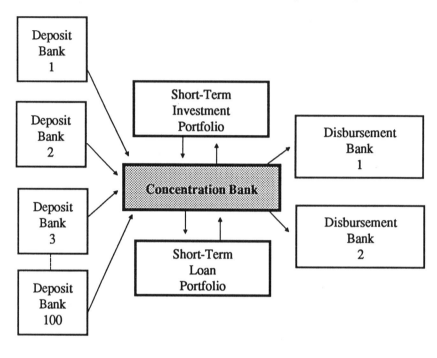

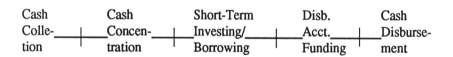

Cash Collection	Cash Concentration	Short-Term Investing/ Borrowing	Disb. Acct. Funding	Cash Disbursement

For this example, cash is received into 100 different deposit banks and pooled into one concentration bank. Cash is disbursed by 2 disbursement banks. When cash balances build up at the concentration bank, the cash is either used to invest in short-term securities or to pay off short-term debt. When there is a cash short-fall in the concentration bank, cash is pumped in from the sale of short-term securities or from increasing short-term loans.

METHOD OF EVALUATION

8. In general, conceptual objectives underlying financial working capital management include:
   - Speed cash inflows.
   - Slow cash outflows.
   - Minimize idle cash.
   - Minimize administrative costs connected with cash flows.
   - Maintain good relations with customers and suppliers.
   - Minimize the cost of providing backup liquidity.
   - Maximize the value of information provided to management.

9. It is important to recognize that working capital represents an investment analogous to the acquisition of equipment or building a facility. As such, to determine whether a given expenditure is warranted, the present value of the incremental benefits (discounted at an appropriate rate) should exceed the present value of incremental costs.

10. When implementing any strategy regarding one component of financial working capital, all differential cash flows related to the strategy must be considered. For example, when a firm offers more liberal credit terms, its receivables may increase, thereby forcing the firm to sell short-term securities, reduce cash balances, and/or increase short-term funding from banks before ultimately generating incremental cash flows. Alternatively, reduction of idle cash may be possible only through an increase in transactions costs. Clearly tradeoffs exist over a broad spectrum of control variables; assessing the value of the strategy using discounted cash flow analysis offers a powerful analytical framework.

11. One point of concern in the evaluation is the relative need to work with a discounted cash flow framework. While the short-term nature of a working capital outlay may limit the materiality of the discount calculation, it is important to recognize the limits of the simplification. Where the commitment duration is very short and timing of the benefit coincides with the expenditure, the need to discount is reduced. On the other hand, where the outlay is long term and there is a delay between the expenditure and its related benefit, proper discounting is critical.

12. Notwithstanding the desire to have financial working capital investments justified financially, the strategic implications of the decision must be considered. For example many firms have installed sophisticated electronic data interchange (EDI) systems. In turn potential suppliers are required to have EDI capability as a pre-condition of business. While a supplier could perhaps assess the decision to invest in EDI capability using traditional financial techniques, the decision has strategic implications which may dominate the quantitative analysis.

CASH BALANCE AND BANK FEES

13. Cash is stored in deposit accounts in commercial banks. It may be stored in time deposits, including certificates of deposit (CDs), or demand deposits. Time deposits earn interest, but current law prohibits banks from paying corporations interest on demand deposits. Hence, one of the primary objectives of financial working capital management is to reduce cash kept in demand deposits and move it as quickly as possible into accounts or investments that earn interest.

14. Demand deposits arise from two sources: transaction balances or compensating balances. Compensating balances may be maintained to compensate banks for various services rendered. Though demand deposits may not receive interest, banks may give "earnings credits" based on the level of these compensating balances. The compensating balance is the average available balance (see para. 15) minus the reserve requirement imposed by the Federal Reserve. The remainder is termed the free balance. An earnings credit rate is then applied to the free balance to determine the credits earned that can offset bank charges (see para. 17). Exhibit 2, Part B provides an example of a balance analysis.

EXHIBIT 2
Account Analysis Example

A. Service Charges for November

Item	Number	Each	Total
Deposits	286	$0.14	$40
Wire transfers	20	$7.50	$150
Coin and currency	10	$5.00	$50
Account maintenance	10	$30.00	$300
Checks presented	2000	$0.08	$160
TOTAL CHARGES			$700

B. Balance Analysis

Average ledger balance		$262,857
Check float		−$128,286
Average available balance		$134,571
Reserve requirement	12.00%	−$ 16,149
Available balance		$118,422
Earnings credits	8.11%/12	$800
EXCESS EARNINGS CREDITS		$100

15. Banks maintain two kinds of demand deposit balances; ledger and available. A ledger balance records the accounting transaction, but not necessarily a value change since the check has not yet cleared. An available balance, however, records all transactions for which value has actually changed hands — for example, checks which have had time to clear the

drawee bank. An availability delay is the length of time it takes a check to clear the drawee bank and thus be recorded in the available balance. Available balances may be transferred to another bank or used as compensating balances.

16. The cash balance reflected in a company's ledger is called the company book balance. Due to delays in processing checks and deposits, book balances may overstate or understate the amount of cash actually available in the company's bank accounts. Consequently cash should be managed on the basis of bank balances (as opposed to book balances). Book balances can provide useful information however regarding outstanding checks and other short-term planning data.

17. Bank charges arise from services the bank provides to the firm, such as deposit processing, credit voucher handling, checks paid, account maintenance, wire transfers, and return item processing. Many banks provide their customers with an account analysis, which summarizes monthly bank charges and analyzes balances the firm has maintained during the reporting period. Please see Exhibit 2 for a simplified example of account analysis.

18. Bank charges can be paid through compensating balances, fees, or a combination of these forms of payment. Recent trends have seen corporations moving away from balance compensation toward fee compensation. Factors favoring fee compensation include:

- The reserve requirement and low earnings credit rate mean that the firm may do better by investing, earning interest, and paying the bank by fees.
- Fees can be put in a budget and compared with other services the corporation receives.
- Excess balances may be absorbed by the bank. In contrast, fees are not usually overpaid.

Factors favoring balance compensation include:

- In order to benefit by removing balances and paying by fees, the balances must indeed be removable. In some accounts, however, it is impossible to completely remove all balances each day.
- Some bankers may view the firm's relationship with the bank more favorably if balances are used for compensation.
- Compared to short-term investments, bank balances are more readily accessible than short-term securities when the firm needs cash quickly.
- Some banks levy a surcharge if they are to be paid in fees.
- Balances may obscure certain true costs and give the cash manager a negotiating position to obtain services without being subjected to normal budgeting constraints.

Each account must be evaluated to determine which form of payment method is less costly.

MANAGING THE COLLECTION SYSTEM

19. A firm's collection system consists of a set of banks, company processing centers, and procedures to collect incoming cash. A collection system affects the timing of components of cash inflows. In designing the collection system, firms try to:

   - Speed the inflow of cash by reducing mail time, processing time, and availability time. This total time delay is referred to as <u>collection float</u> and is illustrated in Exhibit 3:

EXHIBIT 3
Cash Flow Timeline for a Paper-based Collection System

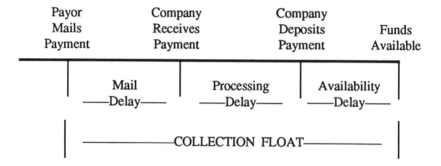

   - Reduce costs of operating the collection system.
   - Increase effectiveness of information processed.

   There are, of course, trade-offs between these three elements. Speeding the inflow of cash may require high operating costs. Reducing operating costs may result in poorer information needed to process accounts receivable.

20. To achieve these goals, firms must consider the optimal number and location of collection points. In general, with more collection points, mail time will be shorter providing better availability. Mitigating these benefits are higher processing costs of additional collection points. Typically when collection points are close to customers, near major airports, or near Federal Reserve banks, shorter mail and availability times are attainable. But operating collection points in large cities may require higher operating costs.

   Some firms may choose to operate their collection system through a lockbox service provided by a bank. The bank picks up the mail, processes the deposit and transfers information to the company. Other firms use electronic payment systems such as automated clearing house (ACH) systems or wire transfers to collect from customers. Electronic systems bypass mail and manual processing and can guarantee availability on the payment date.

21. It is important to capture information from the check or return document that will enable the accounts receivable department to credit the appropriate customer's account with payment. Some firms have their own personnel process the checks; however this may delay collection float. Other firms use a lockbox for processing checks but send a photocopy to accounts receivable personnel. Other firms capture electronic information from the check and accompanying documents and transmit these data to the accounts receivable department.

22. Cost of collection systems include primarily time value costs, processing costs, and administrative costs. The cost of float represents an opportunity cost because the cash is unavailable for use during the time the payments are tied up in collection float. The annual opportunity cost of collection float is measured by multiplying the average daily cash flow by the average float days by the firm's annual opportunity cost. Appendix A illustrates the calculation of the cost of float.

MANAGING THE CONCENTRATION SYSTEM

23. A concentration bank receives deposits from field banks and/or lock box banks in the firm's collection system, transfers funds to the firm's disbursement banks, and serves as the focal point for short-term credit and investment transactions. To perform the latter function, cash balances in the concentration bank are monitored. When the level exceeds desired levels, cash is used to buy short-term investments or used to pay down credit lines. When the level becomes too low, the firm sells short-term investments or draws on bank credit lines.

24. Funds can be transferred from field banks and/or lockbox banks to the concentration bank by wire transfer, a depository transfer check (DTC), or an ACH transfer. A wire transfer results in same-day availability of funds, but a high expense. With a DTC, availability of funds is governed by the concentration bank's availability schedule. With ACH transfers, availability is always the business day following transfer initiation.

25. A concentration system involves costs of excess balances, transfer costs, administrative costs, and control costs.

   • Demand deposit balances become excess balances when the average available balance in an account is above that required for compensation of the account.

   • Transfer costs include bank charges for services such as wire transfers, ACHs, DTCs, and for receiving and reporting information.

   • Administrative costs include costs of managing the concentration system.

- Control costs include possible theft or fraud losses and the costs to minimize them.

Administrative and control costs are very difficult to quantify but should nevertheless be considered in evaluating concentration system costs.

As with most financial working capital issues, incremental costs of concentration system must be judged against the expected value of benefits provided in order to minimize overall cost.

MANAGING THE DISBURSEMENT SYSTEM

26. Disbursement systems include the banks, the payment mechanism, and procedures that the firm uses to facilitate the movement of cash from the firm's centralized cash pool to disbursement banks and then on to suppliers. The problem of moving cash from the concentration bank to disbursement banks is called the disbursement account <u>funding</u> problem. The problem of moving cash from disbursement banks to payees is the disbursement bank <u>assignment</u> problem.

27. Disbursement control may be centralized or decentralized. A primary advantage of decentralized control is that by allowing field managers more autonomy, payees may receive faster availability of checks and can resolve disputes more readily. However centralized systems in which only two or three disbursement banks serve the entire firm can operate with lower overall bank balances than a system of many local disbursement accounts. Moreover, compliance with company policy on cash discounts and payments to suppliers is enhanced; in decentralized systems, field managers may become excessively aggressive leading to delayed payment and strained vendor relations.

28. Costs of the disbursement system include time value costs, excess balances, transaction costs, payee relations, and costs of information and control. Exhibit 4 shows elements of the disbursement timeline including mail, payee processing, and clearing times.

EXHIBIT 4
Disbursement System Timeline

	Mail	Vendor Processing	Clearing
Mail Check			Check Clears

A dollar value for this component of the objective function is computed by multiplying dollar flow per calendar day times the length of the timeline times the cost of capital. The following example illustrates the approach. This component also includes the costs associated with missing cash discounts. Costs of maintaining good payee relations, providing timely information about the disbursement system, and maintaining adequate control are difficult to quantify, but should be considered in any assessment of the disbursement system.

DISBURSEMENT CONSIDERATIONS

ISSUE: Through the use of a remote disbursement program, a business can slow the clearance of its payments by one day. Assuming a monthly disbursement volume of $10,000, a cost of capital of 12%, and a monthly service charge of $250 for the arrangement, should the strategy be pursued?

SOLUTION: By slowing the clearing of funds, the business can earn an monthly investment return of $100 (($10,000/365) x (365/12) x .12), which is below the offsetting monthly fee of $250. Therefore, the program should be rejected.

29. Commercial banks and others offer various services to help firms reduce disbursement costs. Examples are reconciliation services, stop payment services, zero-balance accounts, automatic investment services, and controlled disbursing accounts.

30. Zero-balance account (ZBAs) allow firms to reduce excess balances when they maintain several accounts at one bank. Exhibit 5 illustrates this advantage. ZBAs also lower administrative costs by furnishing separate accounting for each ZBA and by providing automatic funding of disbursing accounts. In addition, ZBAs can facilitate decentralization by providing local check-writing authority while maintaining funding control at headquarters.

EXHIBIT 5
Zero Balance Account

Three regular accounts:

| Payroll | Vendor | Refunds |
| Account | Account | Account |

Note: Each has a buffer balance to prevent overdrafts.

Three zero balance accounts tied to a master account:

Master Account

Payroll   Vendor   Refunds

Note: The separate accounts have a zero balance. Any checks clearing against them are funded by the master account at the end of the day.

▓▓▓▓▓▓▓ = Buffer needed in account

31. Banks that offer automatic investment services reduce excess balances in disbursement accounts at the end of the day by investing in overnight accounts. Controlled disbursing accounts allow firms to transfer funds from the concentration bank to cover an entire day's disbursements early in the day. The firm can then invest the balance in its concentration bank in securities. When this transfer and investment occur early in the day, the firm obtains the best rates on its investment.

32. Control over all phases of the disbursement system is essential to insure that disbursements are made only by authorized persons for authorized purposes. Sometimes it may be necessary to halt a disbursement in the middle of the timeline as new information or disputes emerge.

MANAGING THE SHORT-TERM INVESTMENT PORTFOLIO

33. The short-term security portfolio is held to provide a temporary store of cash. Therefore, securities held should be liquid. In choosing short-term securities, managers should consider the safety of the principal, marketability, price stability, maturity, and after tax-yield.

34. A security that is marketable can be sold in a large volume very quickly without a substantial price concession. The existence of a large, active secondary market is necessary for a security to have high marketability. To avoid the price instability that comes with longer term securities, portfolio managers generally confine their investments to securities with a maturity of less than one year. Short-term investments are often chosen so that the investment matures on a date that the firm forecasts it will need cash.

35. The yield of a security is usually of secondary importance to its liquidity. There is an inverse relationship between liquidity and yield. The more liquid a security, the lower its yield. There is a positive relationship between yield and risk. The higher the risk, in general, the higher the expected yield.

36. Short-term investment securities include U.S. Treasury securities, federal

agency securities, negotiable certificates of deposit, bankers acceptances, commercial paper, repurchase agreements, and money market preferred stock. Important attributes of each of these investments is described in Appendix B. See also SMA 4M, UNDERSTANDING FINANCIAL IN-STRUMENTS for an expanded discussion of many of the newer financial instruments and their uses. Exhibit 6 illustrates the after-tax approach to evaluation.

EXHIBIT 6
Investment Considerations

ISSUE: A business with a 40% marginal tax rate has an excess balance of $1000 for which it seeks an appropriate investment over a period of three months. Among the alternatives are the following:

- A time deposit paying an 8% return.
- A 90-day Treasury bill selling for $98.00.
- A ten-year Treasury bond having a rate of 9%, a current price of $101.00, a future price of $100.00, and a transaction cost of $5.00 at the time of sale.
- Auction rate preferred stock yielding 6.8%; transactions costs will be $12.

Recommended Approach:

A) Restate Returns. The returns of the various instruments must be restated on a consistent basis, net of any transactions costs and net of any taxes.

In this regard, the Treasury bill has a pre-tax yield equal to 8.16% [(100–98)/98 * 360/90]. After tax this is 4.90% [8.16 x (1–.4)].

The Treasury bond, on the other hand, pays 9% less the capital loss of 1% [(100–101)/101] and a transactions cost of 0.5% (5/1000) for a total of 7.5%, or 4.5% after tax.

The preferred yields only 6.8%; however, the company may exclude 70% of its dividend income from taxation. Its after-tax yield is as follows:

Taxable income:	$(68 - 12) \times .3$	$= 16.80$
Tax:	$16.8 \times .4$	$= 6.72$
After-tax return =	$\left(\dfrac{68 - 12 - 6.72}{1000}\right)$	$= .0493$
	or 4.93%	

B) Evaluate other considerations. In addition to the yield data computed above, the manager must assess other considerations including safety and liquidity before committing the firm's resources.

MANAGING SHORT-TERM BORROWING

37. Most short-term borrowing consists of bank loans and the sale of commercial paper. Bank borrowing consists of several different types of credit arrangements including lines of credit and term loans.

38. Single payment loans are granted for a specific financial purpose with a definite beginning and ending time. The note can be either a discount note or an add-on note. On a discount note the amount of cash advanced under the loan agreement is the face value of the loan less the amount of interest for the period covered. The interest rate is fixed at the time the note is originated. For an add-on note the full principal amount is received when the note is initiated. The interest is added to the principal to determine the cash flow at maturity. The interest rate can be fixed or variable.

39. A credit line is an agreement for a firm to borrow up to a specified limit during a particular time period. Although technically in force for a set time period, usually a year, most credit lines represent an on-going relationship with the bank, and are renewed at maturity. The line of credit provides a very flexible source of short-term financing. The borrower has access to a large amount of credit but pays interest only on the actual borrowing. Borrowing under a credit line takes place through specific short-term notes ranging from overnight to as long as 90 days or more. Actual borrowing is usually through a sequence of short-term notes made under the terms and conditions of the credit line. Many borrowers roll over the notes at maturity and keep the credit line in force for years, thus effectively using the credit line as a longer term source of funding. Credit lines also provide a back-up source of cash to pay off maturing commercial paper. Most organizations issuing commercial paper maintain an unused credit line in an amount sufficient to back up their commercial paper. When negotiating for a line of credit, smaller companies may find it necessary to pledge inventory and receivables, and if necessary provide personal pledges from owners in order to secure the lines.

40. Corporations pay banks in various ways for credit lines. A commitment fee is often assessed on the amount of the line, e.g. 1/4% of the line. It may alternatively be based on the unused portion of the credit line. The second element is the interest rate paid on borrowings against the line. Virtually all credit lines carry a variable interest rate. Banks may also require the firm to keep compensating balances for the credit line.

41. Other forms of short-term borrowing include revolving credit lines and term loans. A revolving credit agreement is similar to a line of credit, but is usually established for more than one year. A term-loan has a fixed maturity, usually of an intermediate range of two to seven years. The total amount of the loan is forwarded to the borrower when the loan is made and is repaid in periodic installments over the life of the loan.

42. In choosing between different loan alternatives, the financial manager compares features such as terms, maturity, security required, and covenants

on the loans. One of the most important features is the effective interest rate of the loan. This effective rate must be calculated consistently across loans so a valid comparison can be made. Appendix C shows how to calculate the effective interest rate for different forms of short-term borrowing.

43. Foreign Currency: In today's increasingly global economy, a business does not have to be the size of a Fortune 500 firm to be involved in the transnational movement of funds. Of the transactions that are normally emphasized, revenue and income translations are the most common. However, the risk encountered in the repatriation of cash generated abroad is enormous and varies considerably across countries and currencies. In view of volatility of foreign currency exchange rates and the continuing move toward offshore manufacturing/material sourcing, the need to manage working capital balances (exposure) is increased since an uncovered working capital exposure may risk global competitiveness of the product.

44. There are three basic ways to manage currency risk. Each exposure may be individually covered at the point of creation through the use of options or forward contracts. On the other hand, the use of currency basket or portfolio hedges can be more efficient if there is a counteracting movement in the relevant currencies. Finally, one may leave the position open, and, through speculation on currency movements, hope to generate a higher return.

RECOMMENDATIONS

45. As the intensity of competition increases, firms need to review the entire operation of their financial working capital management program. The cost of inefficiencies and non-value adding activities, while perhaps minor individually, may significantly reduce overall corporate wealth when considered collectively.

46. From a strategic perspective, appropriate issues include:

- Is our use of available technology to manage cash receipts, disbursements and provide liquidity consistent with our vision of where the company is headed?

- From a global perspective, are we making the best use of available financial instruments and arrangements? What does it cost to upgrade our systems? Do we know and manage our risk exposures?

- Are our personnel appropriately recruited, trained and supervised to manage in an environment where cross-border working capital management is increasingly common?

47. From an operational perspective, the complexity of options facing the manager of financial working capital requires that a systematic and consistent approach to evaluating policy variables be established. For these issues, the NAA recommends that cash receipts and disbursement be conceptualized along the cash flow time line and where possible evaluated with a method that incorporates time value of money concepts.

APPENDIX A
The Cost of Float

Assume a firm's annual sales are $365 million ($1,000,000 per day on average). Assume that average mail time is 4 calendar days from customer to the firm headquarters where all checks are processed. Also assume that the firm takes one day to process checks and that the average availability time is 2 days. The firm's cost of capital is 12%. How much does this investment in financial working capital cost the firm?

$$\begin{aligned} \text{Opportunity cost} &= \text{(Average daily} \quad \text{x} \quad \text{(Average} \quad \text{x} \quad \text{(Capital} \\ \text{of float} &\quad \text{cash flow)} \qquad\qquad \text{float time)} \quad \text{Cost)} \\ &= (\$1,000,000) \times (4 + 1 + 2) \times (.12) \\ &= \$7,000,000 \times .12 \\ &= \$840,000/\text{year}. \end{aligned}$$

By not collecting cash for 7 days on average, the firm actually has $7,000,000 tied up in an investment in the collection system. With a cost of capital of 12%, the firm's opportunity cost is $840,000 per year. If the firm could accelerate collections by reducing the mail time by 2 days, processing time by one day, and availability time by one day, then the opportunity costs would fall to:

$$\begin{aligned} \text{Opportunity cost} &= (\$1,000,000) \times (2 + 0 + 1) \times (.12) \\ &= \$360,000/\text{year}. \end{aligned}$$

This would result in an annual savings of $480,000. Of course, this amount would have to be compared with the cost of collecting checks faster to see if the decision is a good one.

APPENDIX B
Short-Term Investments

U.S. Treasury securities are direct obligations of the U.S. Treasury and are backed by the full faith and credit of the United States government. They are considered free of default risk. Treasury securities are also considered low risk because they have excellent marketability. They are very actively traded in secondary markets in large volumes at very narrow spreads. Common U.S. Treasury securities are Treasury bills, having a maturity at issue of a year or less. These securities are sold at a discount and do not bear interest as such. Treasury notes bear interest semiannually and are issued with a maturity of between 1 and 10 years. Treasury bonds are longer term (10 years or more) securities that are usually not purchased for short-term portfolios except when the bonds are close to maturity.

Federal agency securities are interest-bearing securities generally issued and redeemed at face value. These securities are generally not backed by the full faith and credit of the U.S. government, although many consider it inconceivable that the U.S. government would let one of these agencies default on its obligations. Agency issues are usually smaller and not quite as marketable as government securities.

Negotiable certificates of deposit (CDs) are bank deposits that can be traded in the money markets. Most CDs have a maturity between 1 and 3 months but they can be for several years. They are generally sold at face value and have a denomination of $1 million. CDs are not guaranteed by the Federal Deposit Insurance Corporation for amounts over $100,000. Therefore, investors should be careful to investigate the financial condition of the issuing bank. CDs of larger banks are quite marketable.

Bankers acceptance (BAs) are essentially time drafts that arise out of financing for commercial trade, frequently on international transactions, involving a letter of credit which has been "accepted" by a bank. They come in a wide variety of maturities and denominations. Liquidity of BAs is provided by dealers who make an active secondary market in these securities. BAs are backed by the issuing bank and usually the letter of credit that stands behind the transaction.

Commercial paper is an unsecured short-term loan to a corporation. Although commercial paper is negotiable, there is not an active secondary market for most paper so it is held until maturity by the purchaser. Because of the weak secondary market, the yield on commercial paper is higher than on otherwise similar securities with a greater marketability. The maturity on commercial paper can be from 1 day to 270 days. To help potential investors determine the level of risk in commercial paper, most firms' paper is rated by Moody's Investors Service, Standard and Poor's Corporation, or Fitch Investor Service.

A repurchase agreement is the purchase of a security from another party, frequently a bank or a security dealer, who agrees to buy it back at a specified time and at a specified price. U.S. Treasury securities are often used as the underlying security to be repurchased. The rate for these investments tends to be slightly less than that on Treasury securities. While overnight repurchase agreements are most common, longer maturity agreements are available. Risk is generally thought to be small since a government security is behind the transaction. Firms often have the security transferred to a third party for safekeeping to insure that securities are available for sale if the issuer defaults.

Eurodollar deposits are dollar-denominated deposits held in banks outside the United States, although not necessarily in Europe. Most Eurodollar deposits are time deposits, and suffer from the same illiquidity as a domestic time deposit. Eurodollar CDs are dollar-denominated CDs issued by London banks or branches of other foreign banks in London. Eurodollar CDs are more liquid than Eurodollar time deposits. The original maturity can be from overnight to several years. However, most have original maturities of 6 months or less. An active secondary market is maintained. Higher yields (than on domestic CDs) are available because of the added risk associated with deposits outside the United States and absence of strict reserve requirements imposed by the Federal Reserve Bank. Eurodollar securities may be purchased through most large banks in the U.S.

Auction rate preferred stock is equity which is usually purchased by other corporations that invest in short-term debt instruments. To keep price from fluctuating, the dividend rate is reset regularly—usually every seven weeks. Unless the auction process fails, investors get a chance to sell the stock if they don't like the rate. A major advantage of these securities for income tax purposes is the 70% dividend exclusion allowance provided on the dividend income.

APPENDIX C
Effective Interest Rate

Add-on Interest. A single payment add-on interest loan has the simplest effective interest rate calculation. To calculate the effective rate, first determine the total payment to be made at maturity, MP. This consists of principal plus interest plus any loan fees paid at maturity. Second, determine the net proceeds of the loan, PR. These proceeds are the amount of cash the borrower carries away from the lender. This is the principal amount of the loan less any fees paid at origination. The effective rate, i, is determined as follows:

$$\text{Effective Interest Rate} \quad = \quad i = \frac{MP - PR}{PR} \times \frac{365}{t}.$$

Assume the treasurer has a 60-day, single payment add-on loan for $500,000 from Metropolitan Bank. The loan has an interest rate of 12% per annum (assume Metropolitan uses a 360-day year) and a loan origination fee of $500, which is paid in advance. The effective annual rate is found by computing the amount due at maturity ($500,000 x .12 x 60/360 = $10,000 in addition to the $500,000 principal) minus the amount received initially ($500,000 minus the $500 fee). This amount is divided by the initial amount and annualized by multiplying by 365 over the term of the loan:

$$i = \frac{510,000 - 499,500}{499,500} \times \frac{365}{60} = 12.79\%.$$

Thus, the quoted rate is 12% but the actual effective rate is 12.79%. This is due to the initial fee payment and the difference between 365 and 360 days.

Discount Loans. The procedure for calculating the effective rate on a discount loan is the same as on the add-on loan: determine the cash flow paid at maturity, subtract the cash flow proceeds received at origination, divide by the proceeds, and adjust to an annualized basis. The interest should be subtracted in advance.

The treasurer receives a quote from another bank for a rate of 11.5% with no obligation fee on a discount loan of $500,000 for 60 days. If the bank is using a 360-day year to specify the interest, the amount to be received from the bank initially is $500,000 - [$500,000 x .115 x 60/360] = $490,416.67. The effective interest is then computed in a manner similar to the previous example:

$$i = \frac{500,000 - 490,416.67}{490,416.67} \times \frac{365}{60} = 11.89\%.$$

16

Line of Credit. Determining an effective annual rate for a credit line arrangement is more difficult because of the different forms of compensation possible. The approach, however, uses the same concept as above. Suppose the treasurer has a credit line for $1,000,000 and expects to draw on average $500,000 against the line. Assume a commitment fee of 1/4%, a compensating balance of 5% of the line, and an interest rate of 12%. The effective rate is computed by using the net proceeds from the loan (after subtracting the compensating balance) as the denominator ($500,000 – .05 x $1,000,000) = $450,000. The numerator includes interest payments and commitment fees:

$$i = \frac{(.12 \times \$500,000 + .0025 \times \$1,000,000)}{(\$500,000 - .05 \times \$1,000,000)} = 13.89\%.$$

Thus, the quoted rate is 12% but the actual effective rate is almost 2 percent higher because of the commitment fee, compensating balance, and size of the line relative to the loan.

REFERENCES

Altman, Edward I. (ed.), *Handbook of Corporate Finance*, John Wiley and Sons, New York (1986).

Brandon, Margaret B., "Contemporary Disbursing Practices and Products: A Survey," *Journal of Cash Management* (March 1982) pp. 26-39.

Ferguson, Daniel M. and Maier, Steven F., "Disbursement System Design for the 1980s," *Journal of Cash Management* (November 1982) pp. 56-69.

Handbook of Securities of the United States Government and Federal Agencies, and Related Money Market Instruments, 31st Edition. New York: First Boston Corporation, 1984.

Hill, Ned C. and Ferguson, Daniel M., "Cash Flow Timeline Management: The Next Frontier of Cash Management," *Journal of Cash Management*, May/June 1985, pp. 12-22.

Hill, Ned C. and Sartoris, William L., *Short-Term Financial Management*, MacMillan, New York (1988).

Stigum, Marcia. *The Money Market: Myth, Reality, and Practice, 2nd Ed.* Homewood, Ill.: Dow Jones-Irwin, 1983.

Vander Weide, James and Maier, Steven F., *Managing Corporate Liquidity: An Introduction to Working Capital Management*, Wiley, New York (1985).

Statements on Management Accounting

Statement Number 40
January 15, 1991

PRACTICES AND TECHNIQUES

The Accounting Classification of Real Estate Occupancy Costs

In accordance with the charge to the Management Accounting Practices (MAP) Committee to issue statements on management accounting principles and practices, Statements on Management Accounting are promulgated to reflect official positions of the National Association of Accountants (NAA). The work of the MAP Committee is based on a framework for management accounting, whose principal categories are:

1. Objectives
2. Terminology
3. Concepts
4. Practices and Techniques
5. Management of Accounting Activities

Statements on Management Accounting

Statement Number 40
January 15, 1991

Practices and Techniques:
The Accounting Classification of Real Estate Occupancy Costs

National Association of Accountants, Inc.

Acknowledgments

Representatives of the Industrial Development Research Foundation made the National Association of Accountants aware of significant problems that confront those who wish to compare costs of real estate occupancy. To address the level of divergent practice by providing guidelines intended to promote greater uniformity in accounting treatment, the NAA has joined the IDRF in sponsoring research leading to a Statement on Management Accounting.

The NAA is grateful to all who contributed toward publication of SMA 4 O, "The Accounting Classification of Real Estate Occupancy Costs." Special thanks go to Allen Toman, KPMG Peat Marwick, for his research and writing associated with this project.

The NAA is very appreciative of the high level of cooperation and support provided by members and staff of the Industrial Development Research Foundation. In particular, we wish to recognize the Real Estate Asset Management Subcommittee of the IDRF's Research Committee, chaired by Michael Bell, of La Salle Partners, and including Ken Hallawell, CC&F Management Co.; David Jarman, Contel Corp; Edward Matisoff, GTE Inc.; Dr. Hugh Nourse, University of Georgia; Henrik Petersen, American Express Co.; and Joseph Rooney, Xerox Corp. Joel Parker, IDRF director of research, provided outstanding staff support and coordination among the various parties.

The NAA is, as always, grateful to the chairmen and members of its Management Accounting Practices Committee and the Subcommittee on SMA Promulgation for their individual contributions, collaboration, and general oversight.

Introduction

1. This Statement is intended to help management accountants address problems involving the determination of the appropriate occupancy costs and/or the assignment of these costs to specific accounts associated with the use of real estate assets by business units. Occupancy costs can be further divided into two basic categories: costs of operation and costs of providing the fixed assets.

2. This Statement addresses the identification, classification, and treatment of costs of fixed assets that are owned or leased by the company and used by business units of that company. The occupancy costs for owner-occupied buildings will be similar to those incurred in space leased from others.

3. Proper determination and assignment of these costs is of concern to operating executives as well as management accountants as these costs often are substantial and have a significant impact on business unit profitability and the valuation of assets.

4. Determining and assigning occupancy costs have been a source of numerous problems to accountants and business analysts. These problems are evidenced by the multiple methods employed by various firms for assigning these costs, the lack of generally accepted definitions for classifying various costs, and the lack of internal company policies for measuring and assigning these costs. Practices for determining what is an occupancy cost and for classifying those costs are subject to wide variation in the industry for basic real estate-related cost items, such as utilities, treatment of depreciation, repairs and maintenance, as well as for less clearly real estate-related cost items such as employee cafeteria services, central office administrative costs, and management fees.

5. This Statement suggests the basic categories and the types of costs that should be assigned to various categories in order to provide a consistent presentation of the costs associated with the occupancy of real estate assets. Occupancy costs for business units occupying company-owned real estate assets or leased real estate should reflect costs that would be

   a. charged by a typical owner to an unrelated party with a commercial lease that provides for tenants to pay a portion of certain operating costs in addition to base lease payments; and

   b. reasonably anticipated to be incurred by an unrelated company engaged in a similar business operation.

   Exhibit 1 provides four general tests to aid in the determination of whether a specific cost should be classified as an occupancy cost. A positive answer to each of the questions would indicate that the cost is an occupancy cost.

Statement of Scope

6. A company provides for its physical space requirements through two basic methods: leasing from a third party or owning the space and making it available to its business units. The alternative methods of obtaining the use of space may have substantial impacts on the short-term and long-term financial positions of a company. The development and use of a set of basic categories and general definitions can provide basic information that is necessary for intercompany and intracompany comparison and evaluation.

7. There are three general types of cost construction to which cost of occupancy is relevant: full costs, responsibility costs, and differential costs (a detailed discussion of these appears in SMA Number 4B Allocation of Service and Administrative Costs, June 13, 1985). However, this Statement is concerned with the components of occupancy costs, not their determination. This Statement pertains to the preparation of internal reports; however, it may equally be used as a guide for preparing information for external reporting purposes.

8. The measurements of full cost, responsibility cost, and differential cost are all relevant to the determination of occupancy costs. For purposes of this discussion, it is assumed that a full cost methodology is most appropriate for determining occupancy costs. Occupancy costs should reflect economic reality tempered by the difficulties in establishing exhaustive guidelines that capture all situations.

Definitions

9. Occupancy Cost is the total cost incurred by a company to provide space for the operation of its business units. Occupancy costs can be divided into the costs of operation and costs of providing and maintaining the fixed asset.

   a. Costs of operation include those items associated with the day-to-day operation of a facility: utilities, management, cleaning, repairs, etc.

   b. Costs of providing the fixed asset include those items associated with construction, ownership, and the long-term integrity of the physical structure. Such items include: capital costs, capital improvements, property taxes, insurance and depreciation charges.

   (Note: Certain costs of providing a fixed asset may be viewed as either capital or operating expenses, depending on the magnitude of the expense. For example, a company may expense minor capital additions or improvements.)

10. Occupancy Cost is usually measured on a per square foot basis (cost per square foot) based either on gross or useable square footage occupied by and/or allocated to the business unit. Cost per square foot equals the total occupancy costs assigned to a business unit divided by the square footage occupied by or allocated to that business unit.

The most common methods for defining square footage measures are those developed by the Building Owners & Managers Association (BOMA). An alternate set of definitions, used widely in New York City, are those of the New York Board of Real Estate (NYBRE). While other methods of definition exist, these are the two most common measures. For purposes of this Statement, the particular definition of measure is not at issue; rather the Statement's focus is on the classification of items that are included as occupancy costs.

Occupancy Cost—Categories

The following is a list of items considered appropriate for calculation of overall occupancy costs, together with their definitions.

11. Rental or Leasing Expense: This includes all payments to third parties directly related to the use of real estate facilities by a business unit.

12. Administration: This includes all costs directly associated with managing the operations of the building on a day-to-day basis.

    a. Compensation (salaries, wages, and benefits) of administrative personnel, such as the building manager and staff, attributable to the day-to-day operations of the building.

    b. General expenses incurred to manage the facility, such as supplies, furniture (expensed amounts), telephone, temporary help, postage, and licenses.

    c. Management fees, if the building is managed by a third party, or management fees assessed by a central company operating group for services relating to day-to-day management.

    d. Professional fees, provided by a third party or as part of building management, pertaining directly to operations, such as legal, accounting, bookkeeping, and data processing.

13. Cleaning: This includes all costs directly associated with cleaning the building on a day-to-day basis.

    a. Compensation for cleaning personnel.

    b. Service contracts and periodic cleaning expenses, including trash removal.

    c. General cleaning expenses, such as supplies, equipment replacement (expensed amounts), maintenance, and employee uniforms.

14. Repairs and Maintenance: This includes repairs and maintenance undertaken as a normal part of operations. It does not include capital improvements or replacement of structural components of fixed assets. For example, normal roof maintenance and repairs would be included in this category, but replacement or upgrade of a roof would not, because it is capitalized and the expenses are reflected in depreciation expense over its life.

a. Employee compensation for repair and maintenance personnel.

b. Service contracts and periodic service expenses, such as elevator, fire and life safety, windows, roof electrical, plumbing and heat, ventilation and air-conditioning.

c. General repair and maintenance expenses, such as supplies, equipment replacement (expensed amounts), and maintenance.

15. Utilities: This includes all utilities directly related to occupancy by the business unit of the facility, such as electricity, gas, sewer, water, and steam.

16. Roadways, Parking and Grounds: This includes roads, parking (surfaces or structures), and grounds that are integral to the use of the facility and that would be provided to a typical user.

a. Employee compensation for roadway, parking, and grounds personnel.

b. Service contracts and periodic service expenses for such items as lawn mowing, snow plowing, minor repairs (as contrasted with resurfacing) of parking lots or roadways, reseeding, and planting.

c. General roadway, parking, and grounds expenses, such as supplies, equipment replacement (expensed amounts), and maintenance.

17. Security: This includes all expenses associated with providing normal security for a typical user. Costs of additional security measures should be classified as a business unit expense rather than as a cost of occupancy. (Examples of abnormal security costs would be guards in high value retail stores, such as jewelry stores; data processing facilities requiring specialized security; or security for military contracts.)

a. Employee compensation for the provision of security relating to normal usage of the facility by a business unit.

b. Service contracts and periodic service expenses for security relating to the safe and prudent operation of the facility, not primarily related to the nature of the line of business.

c. General security expenses, such as supplies, equipment replacement (expensed amounts), and maintenance.

18. Insurance: This includes insurance expense relating directly to operations and to protection of facilities for use by a typical user. This includes general liability insurance as well as insurance on specific equipment required for normal building maintenance or operation, such as boilers. This also includes fire insurance on the building and the contents to the extent that these reflect costs associated with a typical user. Insurance specific to the type of business or business operations, such as disease research or other high risk uses, business interruption, and product liability, should be considered business unit costs rather than occupancy costs.

19. Taxes: This includes business and property taxes, real and personal, relating directly to the operation and provision of facilities for use by business units. These include occupancy taxes, use taxes, and other taxes directly related

to the existence and availability of the facility. Personal property taxes on items required for operation or administration of the facility should be included. Where feasible, specific personal property used by the business unit for the conduct of its business should be charged to the business unit rather than included as an occupancy cost.

20. Depreciation: Depreciation expense is an occupancy cost because it reflects the allocation of the cost of the asset over its useful life. Depreciation of fixed assets (building and improvements) as well as depreciation of equipment directly relating to the administration or operation of the building are examples of items that fall into this category. Only depreciation expense actually recorded on the books of the company should be reflected as part of this cost. (Also see paragraph 23.)

Depreciation associated with furniture and equipment used by business units in the course of business should not be included as a cost of occupancy.

Replacement reserves for capital improvements should not be considered an occupancy cost. When capital items are replaced, their cost will be reflected as depreciation expense. Similarly, capital improvements should be reflected as an occupancy cost through depreciation expense rather than directly.

21. Capital Cost: This includes the normal costs of the capital used to provide the business unit with useable space. These include interest expense on borrowed funds and/or cost of capital on internal funds provided for building constructing, equipping, and improving space (See SMA 4A Cost of Capital, November 1, 1984).

In the case of a capital (financing) lease, the interest cost is readily identifiable, as is depreciation. In an operating lease, the capital costs are included in the lease or rent expense. If a company owns its own real estate, capital costs may have to be imputed if specifically identifiable funds were not used to build or acquire the property.

Companies should exercise care when comparing occupancy costs internally between its own business units, particularly if return on investment (ROI) is used to measure business unit performance.

Capital costs not directly relating to either the provision of the physical facilities or equipment required to operate and maintain the facility are not occupancy costs. Among the items that, in general, should not be considered occupancy costs are capital costs for

a. Equipment such as copiers, computers, loading equipment, etc. used in day-to-day business operations.

b. Uses relating primarily to business operations or marketing, not for providing space for those operations. Provision of raw space for a company museum or show room is an occupancy cost; special finishes and equipment are not.

c. Uses relating to employee relations or amenities. For example, the capital costs incurred to provide space for an employee cafeteria or gymnasium are occupancy costs; however, costs of equipping and operating these spaces are business unit expenses.

Uses and Limitations of Costs of Occupancy Measurement

22. The general purpose of accounting separately for occupancy costs versus other business unit costs is to provide a basis for

    a. Comparing costs of occupancy for business units within an industry as well as across industries;

    b. Measuring business unit performance exclusive of occupancy cost variances; and

    c. Measuring underlying real estate values, as contrasted with specific business unit performance.

23. Quantification of occupancy costs is not, by itself, a sufficient basis for comparison among companies or a measure of underlying real estate values. There are differences among businesses and industries in the key variables that affect occupancy costs. Among the key variables that would need to be examined, and perhaps normalized, in order to make these comparisons are

    a. Cost of capital (debt and equity) at the time of acquisition or construction, and during a given operating period. This will vary for different companies.

    b. The capital structure (debt versus equity) used in determining the capital cost basis. This will be a key determinant for the cost of capital.

    c. Acquisition or construction costs. These vary over time and directly influence the initial resource requirements and the base for determining the cost of capital.

    d. Depreciation. Real estate assets acquired or placed in service at different dates may reflect variations in the period and method for determining this cost item. Additionally, depreciation using historical cost could be different if depreciation methods differ, i.e. straight line or accelerated. Some companies also measure such costs using an "equivalent lease rate" for internal comparisons among business units.

    e. Age of each real estate asset; i.e., when it was acquired or placed in service. This will affect such items as: the depreciable basis; the level of capital improvements that may be required; and, current maintenance cost requirements.

    f. Level of maintenance and service provided to space users, including preventive maintenance programs.

Summary of Recommendations

24. There are significant variations in current practices in the measurement of cost of occupancy. Many categorization and measurement practices are too broad, resulting in attribution of costs that should be attributed to business units rather than to occupancy costs.

25. A generally agreed set of categories and definitions of occupancy costs will simplify cost classifications and will provide a means for

    a. comparison of costs of occupancy within companies or among companies,

    b. comparison of business unit performance,

    c. determination of underlying real estate asset values.

26. Therefore, the following recommendations are made:

    a. Costs of occupancy for business units occupying company-owned real estate assets should reflect costs that would be

    • charged to an unrelated user by a typical owner; and

    • reasonably anticipated to be incurred by any unrelated company or business unit engaged in a similar business operation.

    b. Classification of costs of occupancy should be standardized and policies developed following the guidelines suggested in the Definitions section of this document.

    c. Determination of whether a particular cost should be included within a category should be based on

    • the direct relation the cost item bears to providing, operating, or maintaining the facilities.

    • industry guidelines, such as those of BOMA or NYREB, with explicit modifications to reflect the companies' specific circumstances.

    d. In establishing cost of occupancy guidelines and definitions, the underlying goals should be to make it possible for managers and analysts to determine

    • whether a particular cost is properly attributable to costs of occupancy or to other operating expenses of the business or the business unit;

    • how costs of occupancy compare among companies with similar space requirements; and

    • the adjustments required to measure underlying asset value.

27. Each company should assign specific accounts and subaccounts within its own chart of accounts to occupancy costs. For illustrative purposes only, such a chart might appear as set forth in Exhibit 2.

    There are many other ways in which such a chart could be structured. Companies could consider:

    • Separate accounts for owned versus leased real estate facilities.

- Additional sub-accounts as desired.

- Using the trailing account identification code '00' for business units, geographical, or other responsibility breakdowns.

Exhibit 1: Suggested Tests for Identifying Occupancy Costs

Test 1: Does the cost directly reflect a cost of providing, maintaining, or using the real estate?

Test 2: Does the cost reflect a standard or typical amount or type of cost that would be charged, passed-through, or used as a basis for determining the lease rate for space leased by the company from an independent third party?

Test 3: Is the type of cost one that would be incurred by a typical user, or does it reflect special requirements of the business unit or the company?

For example, costs such as above-normal cleaning, airhandling, or security often reflect the requirements of the individual business and should be reflected as expenses of conducting business rather than as occupancy costs; costs such as operating employee cafeterias, providing day-care, or maintaining display facilities generally reflect business operating costs, not real estate occupancy costs.

Test 4: Is the type of cost one that the company would (or could) charge if it were to lease space to a typical unrelated firm?

Exhibit 2: Illustrative Chart of Accounts for Occupancy Costs

6000	**Occupancy Costs**
6100 00	**Rent/Lease Expense**
6200 00	**Administrative**
10	Compensation
20	General Expenses
30	Management Fees
40	Professional Fees
6300 00	**Cleaning**
10	Compensation
20	Service Contracts
30	General Cleaning Expenses
6400 00	**Repairs & Maintenance**
10	Compensation
20	Service Contracts
30	Supplies & Equipment
6500 00	**Utilities**
10	Electricity
20	Gas
30	Water & Sewer
40	Oil
6600 00	**Roadways & Grounds**
10	Compensation
20	Service Contracts
30	General Expenses
6700 00	**Security**
10	Compensation
20	Service Contracts
30	General Service Requirements
6800 00	**Insurance**
10	Fire
20	Liability
30	Operating Equipment: Boiler, Elevator, etc.
6900 00	**Taxes**
10	Property
20	Business
7000 00	**Depreciation**
7100 00	**Capital Costs**
10	Interest
20	Imputed Capital (memo only)

Statements on Management Accounting

Statement Number 5A
January 4, 1990

PRACTICES AND TECHNIQUES

Evaluating Controllership Effectiveness

In accordance with the charge to the Management Accounting Practices (MAP) Committee to issue statements on management accounting principles and practices, Statements on Management Accounting are promulgated to reflect official positions of the National Association of Accountants (NAA). The work of the MAP Committee is based on a framework for management accounting, whose principal categories are:

1. Objectives
2. Terminology
3. Concepts
4. Practices and Techniques
5. Management of Accounting Activities

Statements on Management Accounting

Statement Number 5A
January 4, 1990

Practices and Techniques:
Evaluating Controllership Effectiveness

National Association of Accountants, Inc.

Acknowledgments

The National Association of Accountants is grateful to all who contributed to the publication of Statement 5A, "Evaluating Controllership Effectiveness." Appreciation is extended to members of NAA's Management Accounting Practices Committee and its Subcommittee on SMA Promulgation. The NAA is especially thankful to Ralph G. Loretta and Randall C. Runk, both partners, Price Waterhouse, for their research and writing associated with this project. Those interested in pursuing in greater depth areas covered in this Statement may wish to refer to *The Price Waterhouse Guide to Financial Management*, written by Ralph G. Loretta and published by John Wiley and Sons, Inc., 1990.

NATIONAL ASSOCIATION OF ACCOUNTANTS
STATEMENT OF MANAGEMENT ACCOUNTING:
EVALUATING CONTROLLERSHIP EFFECTIVENESS

Table of Contents

INTRODUCTION

This statement is intended to help controllers measure and evaluate their performance. The National Association of Accountants (NAA) believes controllers need practical performance evaluation techniques to bring controller services in line with changing management expectations.

Management needs have continued to broaden the controller's role beyond the traditional responsibility for financial reporting, and internal control. In addition to accumulating, recording, and reporting financial information, controllers are expected to use their financial expertise and business skills as a decision support resource. Managers at all levels have increased demands for accurate, integrated, and pertinent financial and operating information delivered in a timely manner and in usable format. Because management still requires a sound control and reporting framework, controllers must balance independence, which is necessary to ensure the accuracy and integrity of financial information, with their necessary involvement in business decision making. Controllers must ensure that the financial function can respond effectively to management's changing expectations and needs. Tools for periodic self-evaluation can help meet this challenge.

STATEMENT OF SCOPE

To assist controllers in measuring and evaluating performance, this statement will briefly define standard controllership functions, identify key areas for evaluating each of these functions, recommend a methodology for structuring a self-assessment, and provide generic checklists to help controllers measure and evaluate their performance.

The methodology for conducting a self-assessment provides a focused review at two levels. At one level, the self-assessment examines specific controllership responsibilities and activities. Using service attribute checklists, the self-assessment defines the structure and features within the scope of the controllership services. Using performance indicator checklists, controllers summarize financial services quantitatively as a basis for evaluating the effectiveness of those activities for the organization. See Appendices A - E for the several checklists.

At a second level, the methodology directs attention to the control framework of the organization. Comprising the policies, organizational structure, and procedures that define the overall organization, as well as the controllership function, the control framework should permit the controllership function to execute effectively services that support an organization's essential activities. Evaluating the control framework enables the controller to detect flaws and thereby improve the delivery of financial services.

Controllership functions discussed in this statement may not all apply to any one organization. Controllers should use judgment in deciding which functions and evaluation techniques apply to their organizations. Since no organization is identical to another, individual company standards should be established for quantitative measures, and performance should be compared to these standards at least annually.

Although many controllers have responsibilities for management information systems activities and some treasury activities, they are beyond the scope of this document.

DEFINING CONTROLLERSHIP FUNCTIONS

Today's controllers fulfill dual, but complementary, roles in their organizations. They balance traditional financial services and internal control responsibilities with an expanding role as a decision support resource to management.

Transaction Processing and Controls

In their traditional financial services and internal control roles, controllers' objectives focus on maintaining effective transaction-processing systems. Controllers ensure that these systems process information effectively and with adequate controls to safeguard assets. In this role, controllers typically have responsibility for the following functions:

- General accounting, including internal and external financial accounting;
- Accounts payable;
- Payroll;
- Accounts receivable;
- Cash management; and
- Fixed asset management.

Decision Support

In today's operating environment, controllers must be a decision support resource. Controllership may be the only function, outside general management, that views the business as a whole. Companies lose a valuable point of view and reduce their business advantage if the controller is not involved in decision-making activities. Controllers fulfill their decision support role through a mix of planning, accounting, analysis, and reporting activities in the following functional areas:

- Planning,
- Capital budgeting,
- Operational budgeting and expenditure control,
- Cost accounting and cost management,
- Financial analysis,

- Acquisitions and divestitures,
- Special projects, and
- Tax services and accounting.

EVALUATING CONTROLLERSHIP FUNCTIONS

Evaluating the controllership function should be based on a strong understanding of controllership services and on quantifiable performance indicators. This section outlines key areas to be considered when evaluating the controllership function. It also introduces service attribute and performance indicator checklists as important tools for conducting a self-assessment.

Transaction Processing and Controls

Service attribute checklists summarize and define the structure and activities within the broad scope of controllership services. They provide a basis for identifying service gaps and redundancies, as well as recommending expansion and/or reduction of existing services. Service attribute checklists are included as Appendix A, Service Attributes for Transaction Processing.

Performance indicator checklists enable the controller to quantify key elements of available financial services. Used alone or as a basis for comparison among operating units or within an industry, these performance indicators allow the controller to target improvement efforts and to specify improvement objectives using quantifiable performance measures. Performance indicator checklists are included as Appendix B, Performance Indicators for Transaction Processing.

General Accounting

The general accounting function includes supervision of general ledger accounting, financial reporting, budget control reporting, and cash control.

Evaluation of the general accounting function should cover the processes for summarizing and recording all financial transactions that affect an organization; summarizing and reporting the impact of actual financial transactions on operations and financial position; reporting actual versus budgeted financial transactions; and performing key tasks related to proper control of cash receipts and bank account reconciliation.

Evaluation of the general accounting function should include

- Categorization of data (chart of accounts),
- Data accumulation and storage,
- Journal entry processing,
- Interfaces with subsidiary systems,
- Closing procedures,
- Reporting - internal and external,

- Cash control,
- Bank account reconciliation, and
- Accounting controls.

Accounts Payable

The accounts payable function governs activities related to the receipt, recording, and payment of goods and services used by the organization.

Evaluation of the accounts payable function should include analyses of invoice and check processing, general ledger interfaces, and vendor inquiry. All systems that support this function should be examined for appropriate levels of controls.

The nature and extent of linkages with purchasing, treasury, general accounting, and other financial information systems should also be examined for adequacy. For example, the adequacy of controls surrounding requisitioning, vendor selection, and purchase order processing should be examined.

Evaluation of the accounts payable function should include

- Receiving,
- Reporting,
- Vouchering,
- Invoice processing,
- Disbursements, and
- Reporting.

Payroll

The payroll function is concerned with the control of payment and reporting of salaries and wages, payment and reporting of payroll taxes and withholdings, and procedures related to maintaining employee records.

Evaluation of the payroll function should include

- Time and attendance reporting;
- Payroll adjustment processing;
- Payroll deductions, net pay calculations, and employer liability policies;
- Payroll check production, distribution, and reconciliation;
- General ledger interface; and
- Funds sufficiency validation procedures.

Accounts Receivable

The accounts receivable function involves control of all procedures related to accepting and recording customers and orders, recording bills for goods and services rendered, and collecting and recording payments.

Evaluation of the accounts receivable function should include procedures and controls that relate to customer orders from the time of order entry through the collection of customer payments. Both automated and manual processes should be evaluated for accuracy and appropriateness. Linkages with the treasury department should be examined and communication flows evaluated.

Evaluation of the accounts receivable function should include

- Credit management,
- Invoice and credit memorandum processing,
- Customer master file maintenance procedures,
- Sales posting and cash application,
- Customer statement preparation,
- The monitoring of delinquent and uncollectible accounts, and
- Management and control reporting.

Cash Management

The cash management function is involved in those daily operations that permit an organization to meet near-term cash requirements, particularly cash receipt and disbursement activity.

Evaluation of the cash management function should encompass procedures to control both cash inflows and cash outflows. Methods used in collecting and monitoring cash inflows, disbursing and controlling cash outflows, and controlling intercompany transactions and transfers should be reviewed for adequacy. Automated systems for supporting cash management at the level required by the organization's cash transaction volume should also be evaluated.

The cash management function must respond to the results of business operations, including sales, purchases, capital expenditures, and cash investment. Bank services and relations should also be monitored as they may affect disbursement activity and control. Because of the operational nature of the cash management function and its reliance on the operations of the organization, an effective review must consider the constraints placed on cash management by other functional areas.

Evaluation of the cash management function should carefully consider

- Methods of cash collection,
- Methods of cash disbursement,
- Intercompany cash management and clearing control methods,
- Cash management systems,
- Cash flow forecasting methods, and
- Banking service and relations.

Fixed Asset Management

The fixed asset management function includes control of all procedures related to planning, controlling, and accounting for costs associated with the construction of buildings or the purchase of land, buildings, equipment, furniture, and other capital items used by the organization to conduct business. This function also includes responsibility for calculating and recording depreciation and gains or losses realized on the retirement of fixed assets.

Evaluation of the fixed asset management function should include review of procedures and controls for fixed asset acquisition, movement and transfer, adjustment, and retirement. Manual and automated systems should be evaluated wherever they affect the accuracy of records, tax data, or other management data (e.g., asset book value, insurance, and replacement cost data). Linkages with general accounts, financial planning, tax, and project accounting should be evaluated to ensure appropriate information flows. Approval and control procedures for movement or retirement of fixed assets should also be covered when evaluating this function.

Evaluation of the fixed asset management function should carefully consider

- Acquisition procedures,
- Property control,
- Accounting and tax analysis,
- Retirements, and
- Reporting.

Decision Support

An effectiveness review of the controllership's decision support role should consider each functional area linked to the organization's essential business activities. Since this role may be new for many controllers, the focus of this review should be on identifying service gaps and redundancies, as well as targeting services to be expanded or reduced. Tools for structuring and documenting this review are included as Appendix C, Service Attributes Checklist for Decision Support.

Planning

The planning function includes activities ranging from formulating planning procedures to providing management with the means to prepare rational action plans that anticipate financial consequences of current decisions.

Evaluation of the planning function should include careful consideration of both long-range (strategic) and short-term (operational) planning. An organization's long-range planning horizon must be sufficient to forecast the results of the strategies being implemented. These plans should address key issues such as company strengths and weaknesses, external threats and opportunities, and probability analyses for key assumptions. In contrast, short-term operating plans must reflect the goals and objectives of operating units and justify the resource requirements necessary to achieve the plan.

Planning procedures should be formalized and documented. Assumptions and variables should be clearly indicated so that plans may be revised based on internal or external changes. All plans must receive top management support and review to ensure consistency with the overriding strategies of the organization. Plans should be integrated in terms of key assumptions, objectives, and approaches used in development.

Evaluation of the planning function should carefully consider

- Long- and short-range planning procedures,
- Forecasting procedures,
- Plan preparation procedures,
- The extent of integration of various plans,
- The extent of plan integration with management and financial reporting systems,
- The level of detail for each type of plan, and
- The timeliness of plan preparation.

Capital Budgeting

The capital budgeting function is concerned with control over the execution of company plans, project and investment expenditures, and cash flow.

Evaluation of the capital budgeting function should consider the level of controller assistance to management in determining which assets to acquire. The evaluation should also include the appropriateness of descriptive and quantitative techniques used to analyze capital acquisition alternatives. A systematic approach to investment analysis gives management a meaningful basis for selecting the most attractive investment opportunities. The information required for this evaluation includes descriptions of the projects as well as estimates of their earning power based on descriptive and analytical techniques. These techniques may include discounted cash flows, internal rate of return, and cost-of-capital determination.

The approval and control process for capital expenditures, effective use of spendable resources, and development and control of performance standards for capital acquisitions should also be reviewed. Levels of approval over capital expenditures should be determined based on materiality. Optimal use of resources requires that capital plans encompass a sufficient planning horizon and be segmented to differentiate between required, discretionary, replacement, and expansion expenditures. The monitoring process includes status reporting for costs and completion dates.

Evaluation of the capital budgeting function should carefully consider

- The capital planning process,
- The asset evaluation process,
- The procedure for monitoring capital expenditures,
- Construction cost status reporting, and
- Post-acquisition performance monitoring.

Operational Budgeting and Expenditure Control

The budgeting and expenditure control function maintains adequate processes for monitoring managerial and operational performance. The annual budget is the key to controlling costs in accordance with company objectives.

Evaluation of the operational budgeting and expenditure control function should include a check that budgets are prepared in accordance with management directives and that they support corporate objectives and policies. Responsibility for expenditure control should be clearly defined to ensure accountability.

Annual budgets are as much a planning tool as a vehicle for control. They must be proactive and goal-oriented as well as consistent with overall corporate objectives so that they support the tactical side of corporate planning. Preparation procedures should be well-documented to ensure that all organizational units' plans are consistent with one another. A strict timetable for budget preparation allows various units of the organization to coordinate activities and assists in the development of a corporate budget.

The responsibility for budget preparation and subsequent expenditure control should be clearly defined to motivate individuals to meet corporate goals. Defined responsibility is the cornerstone for updating plans, monitoring trends, communicating results, and correcting problems in a timely manner.

Evaluation of the operational budgeting and expenditure control function should carefully consider

- The budget preparation process,
- Control of budget preparation,
- Integration among various budgets,
- Controls for expense processing,
- Controls for budget changes, and
- The budgetary reporting system.

Cost Accounting and Cost Management

The cost accounting and cost management function involves developing accurate product or service costs while recognizing the related production and organizational activities that affect those costs. This function supports product-pricing activities and provides important management reports that focus on cost drivers and quality measures.

Evaluation of the cost accounting and cost management function should consider how total product or service costs are calculated, updated, and used. The review should determine whether management understands the impact of related production and organizational activities on these costs. It should assess the extent that cost information is communicated and used to manage operations cost, to reduce product or service costs, and to price products and services.

Cost systems should effectively support product-pricing activities by providing accurate product costs. Inaccurate product costs can result in lost business due to overpricing or in retention of unprofitable businesses or product lines.

Cost systems should support operations performance measurement to ensure that essential business activities are adequately monitored. These performance measures can be financial and statistical and should include activities that affect product cost, quality, and delivery performance.

Effective cost management systems should provide concise management reports with data summarized appropriately for each management level. Management reporting should focus on cost drivers, delivery performance, and quality measures linked to the organization's essential business activities. Reporting formats should show accountability and force corrective action as needed.

Evaluation of the cost accounting and cost management function should consider

- The development of total product or service costs;
- Cost update procedures and cycles;
- The appropriateness of cost component calculations (fixed, variable, direct, indirect, internal transfer, overhead);
- The input into product-pricing activities;
- The impact on performance measurement;
- The quality and timeliness of cost reporting;
- The level of integration into other financial, operations, and manufacturing systems; and
- The effectiveness of inventory accounting and valuation methods.

Financial Analysis

The financial analysis function encompasses tasks performed as a follow-up to planning and budget preparation activities. Financial analyses are prepared retrospectively to evaluate past decisions and prospectively to forecast the impact of present or future actions.

Evaluation of the financial analysis function should determine how actual results and their implications are linked with plans as well as how variances are monitored as actual results are reported.

Management's ability to monitor the planning and budgeting functions is determined by the ability to compare actual results to original plans and to account for deviations. Financial analyses should also support product and service costing, profitability, and pricing analyses.

Evaluation of the financial analysis function should carefully consider

- Financial ratio analysis,
- The variance analysis process,
- The procedures for communicating and explaining variances, and
- The linkage between financial analysis and planning processes.

Acquisitions and Divestitures

The acquisitions and divestitures function includes identification and analysis of potential purchase or sale candidates.

Evaluation of this function should include a review of the acquisition and divestiture philosophy and the appropriateness of analyses used to evaluate acquisition or divestiture candidates.

The criteria used to identify and analyze potential candidates should be linked to strategic plans and be reviewed and updated as corporate and economic environments change. Candidate analyses should be based on a predefined structure and methodology so that alternatives are considered equally.

Evaluation of the acquisitions and divestitures function should review

- The criteria for analyzing acquisition and divestiture proposals,
- Information support systems for proposal evaluation,
- Methods for determining purchase or sale price,
- Techniques for considering the impact on financial performance,
- Post acquisition/divestiture review procedures, and
- Communication with the external investment community.

Special Projects

The special projects function supports projects not performed as part of an organization's routine activities. Examples include the review of dividend policy, the evaluation of manufacturing costs, and make/buy analyses.

Evaluation of the special projects function should investigate the process that determines how resources are committed to special projects as well as the procedures for channeling special project requests and coordinating these requests with other departments.

Mandatory channels for requesting special project assistance should be defined and budgets set with appropriate chargebacks to the requesting departments.

Evaluation of the special projects function should include

- Methods for channeling project requests,
- The degree of interdepartmental coordination,
- Processes for committing resources to a project, and
- Procedures for developing an appropriate organizational structure for special projects.

Tax Accounting and Services

The scope of and responsibility for tax services in organizations varies by tax reporting and recordkeeping requirements, and by the technical depth and organizational structure of the tax group. Most organizations cannot meet their tax requirements in a cost-effective manner without a responsible, permanent group. An effectively organized and experienced tax group can contribute significantly to controllership effectiveness and, more importantly, to the overall profitability of an organization. Major ongoing contributions of the tax group include

- Optimizing the effective tax rate,
- Preparing all tax returns and administering compliance,
- Ensuring integrity between book and tax records,
- Advising the organization on ways to maximize tax benefits arising from current and future operations,
- Developing a corporate tax policy for all items of taxes and for all aspects of company operations, and
- Reviewing tax provisions for financial reporting.

Tax-reporting relationships are shaped by the size of the tax group, scope of responsibilities, and staff experience. The tax group may report to the controller, treasurer, general counsel, or chief financial officer. The scope of the effectiveness review will vary by organization, based on the level of support for major tax activities routinely obtained from outside tax specialists. Other considerations, such as the existence of foreign operations, will also shape the responsibilities and the scope of the effectiveness review. An effectiveness review of the tax function should consider

- The tax environment;
- Tax policy, procedure, and compliance; and
- Tax planning.

The tax environment defines the scope and level of activity of the overall tax function. Evaluating the tax environment considers the tax requirements of the organization as well as the technical capabilities and organizational structure of the permanent tax group. Understanding the tax environment includes recognizing the role of outside specialists to meet tax requirements. Evaluating the environment should also reveal whether tax goals and opportunities are achieved effectively.

Tax policy provides the broad framework that defines tax responsibilities, information needs, and the approach used to meet tax planning and compliance needs. Policy directly influences the attitudes of personnel involved in tax functions. It defines tax priorities and the necessary qualifications to meet requirements.

Tax procedures ensure consistent performance of activities to achieve planning and compliance requirements. Clearly defined and well-documented procedures will compare the actual against the recommended conduct of tax activities. Failure to follow established procedures may reduce tax effectiveness and produce problems that include failure to realize full tax benefits, optimize tax rates, and comply with regulatory requirements.

Organizations comply with tax requirements by accurate and timely preparation of returns and reports based upon tax-related accounts. Compliance includes ensuring that requirements for tax-related transactions are met. It should also include the analysis of accounts into which these transactions flow. Tax compliance dictates that managerial and operational activities conform to relevant statutes and regulations of federal, state, local, and foreign taxing authorities.

Tax planning plays an important role in the financial function's contribution to profit. Tax planning must be integrated into daily operations and into merger, acquisition, and reorganization plans and strategy. For example, the timing of dividend payments and the availability and use of tax credits can affect business-planning decisions.

Tax planning should also be an element of pension and benefit planning. It can ensure the proper installation of employee benefit plans that will maximize tax benefits to the corporation and its employees.

WORKING WITH THE INTERNAL AUDIT FUNCTION

Organizations depend on an effective internal audit function as an essential managerial control. Regardless of formal reporting relationships, the controller is linked with the internal auditing function to ensure that adequate protection exists for an organization's assets. Internal audit achieves this mission by evaluating systems and methods of internal control using financial and operational audits.

Management objectives and needs should define the scope of internal audit activities. Financial auditing evaluates and verifies the flow and accuracy of accounting information. Because key operational controls must also exist, internal audit services include auditing operational practices, systems, and controls. These audits extend beyond financial services into other functional areas, such as production, information services, and marketing. To the extent that an organization uses computer-based systems and controls, internal audit evaluates those systems as part of financial and operational reviews.

Results of these audits give the controller and general management a better understanding of the adequacy of key controls and can provide detailed assessments of the

- Accuracy and reliability of financial and operating information;
- Levels of compliance with policies, procedures, and outside regulations; and
- Operational efficiencies of the systems under review.

Evaluating Internal Audit

An effectiveness review of the internal audit function should focus on four key elements:

12   *Evaluating Controllership Effectiveness*

- The scope of internal audit activities,
- Audit planning,
- Audit performance, and
- Organizational independence.

Focusing on these areas provides an evaluation of the internal audit function based on its organizational position and status. The evaluation can compare actual internal audit performance against management expectations. It may highlight gaps between an organization's control systems and the technical expertise and resources available to evaluate them.

Scope of Internal Audit Activities

The internal audit scope establishes the role played by the internal audit department in an organization. The scope delineates the responsibilities and purpose of internal audit activities. It tells an organization where auditing emphasis will be placed. The scope reflects underlying management commitment to internal audit studies and probable support for findings and recommendations.

The objectives of evaluating the scope of internal audit activities include determining that

- An approved policy statement describes the purpose, responsibilities, and source of authority for internal audit activities;
- Activities emphasize the evaluation of control systems to ensure data integrity and to assess operational efficiencies;
- The internal audit department reviews and tests computer-based systems and addresses broader data security issues;
- The internal audit scope clearly defines responsibilities for verifying compliance with policies, procedures, and regulations;
- The scope of operational audits is clearly defined and consistent with management objectives; and
- Internal audit access to upper management and the audit committee is explicitly stated.

Organizations realistically define the internal audit scope when staffing levels, depth, and technical expertise reasonably match the complexity of existing control systems. How effectively the internal audit department achieves stated objectives may signal that the internal audit scope should be redefined or staffing deficiencies corrected. In addition, the frequency and degree to which changes in audit activities occur should cause management to reassess expectations of internal audit's role within the organization.

Many organizations use the internal audit staff for special projects beyond a previously established audit scope. Internal audit effectiveness may be impaired if these projects compete for staff or disrupt audit schedules. Since internal audit departments may draw from other financial and functional areas for staffing needs, objectivity may be compromised if auditors evaluate activities that they previously performed. (The section on organizational independence beginning on page 16 will discuss these issues further.)

Organizations of all sizes use computers as part of their internal control systems. The internal audit scope should encompass computer-based systems when an organization relies upon them to generate and store key financial and operational information. Internal audit staff who evaluate computer-based systems should have sufficient technical knowledge of those systems. Audit scope should address data security, computer installation effectiveness, and disaster recovery planning. The scope should be broad enough that internal audit can recommend ways to improve controls over computer-based systems before they are installed. Tools for structuring and documenting this review are included as Appendix D - Service Attributes for Internal Audit Activities.

Audit Planning

A comprehensive audit plan lays the foundation for an effective internal audit department. The audit plan documents management expectations of the internal audit function. It identifies specific studies to be performed in financial and operational areas. The plan assigns priorities to internal audit activities based on management needs and assessed risk. It identifies staffing levels to ensure effective completion of internal audit programs.

The objectives of evaluating internal audit planning include assessing

- The appropriateness of criteria used to establish audit coverage;
- Planning effectiveness for short-term and long-range planning horizons;
- The risk factors, so that the internal auditors can establish audit objectives and write programs;
- The extent of input and review by management and the external auditors in the planning process;
- The internal audit plan approval process;
- The frequency, format, content, and distribution of audit results; and
- The extent of coordination between internal audit activities and external audit tasks.

Audit planning requires a thorough understanding of an organization's internal controls. Internal audit should have criteria for assigning audit coverage based on the control system's complexity, data sensitivity, and history of associated problems. Risk factors used to establish audit priorities may be related to potential monetary losses, inadequately trained personnel, and transaction-processing volumes. Audit planning of computer-based systems should consider risks related to data, physical site, and program security.

Successful audit plans incorporate reviews by management and the external auditors to ensure management concurrence with audit priorities. Results of these reviews should be appropriately documented. The audit plan should be approved by the audit committee, senior management, or the board of directors prior to implementation. By ensuring that the plan reinforces overall management objectives, senior management and the audit committee establish detailed standards against which actual audit performance can be measured.

Long-range audit planning should consider effective staff utilization. The long-range audit plan should define required staffing levels for timely completion of activities. The plan should be integrated with the audit department budget and should also be coordinated with the scheduled activities of the external auditors. Clearly documented, the long-range plan requires approval by the audit committee and senior management.

Audit planning requires flexibility to reassign resources as priorities shift and to report those changes to involved personnel. How audit progress is monitored and reported to management should also be assessed, as these changes should be followed by management approval.

Audit Performance

Audit performance includes all aspects of executing the audit plan. Activities begin with developing detailed audit programs and conclude with reporting and follow-up on recommendations. Audit programs identify specific controls and tests to be evaluated and performed. Programs provide the outline for workpaper preparation and other documentation. Effective audit performance is measured by the efficiency demonstrated in executing the program. It is also based on the confidence that management and other key users place on the findings and reports.

The objectives of evaluating audit performance include determining that

- Auditing fieldwork is conducted in a controlled, efficient manner with adequate staff supervision and review of results;
- Testing and evaluations are documented and support conclusions and recommendations;
- Actual performance is monitored against plan estimates to evaluate staff efficiencies and performance; and
- Management and the external auditors place reliance on audit reports and workpapers.

Effective audit performance results from compliance with established policies, procedures, and standards. Auditing policies should reflect accepted standards, such as those of the Institute of Internal Auditors, Inc. They should be comprehensive, clearly defined, and periodically reviewed and updated. Auditing policies should be consistent with overall corporate policies and integrated with more detailed departmental procedures. When necessary, procedures should be written using standard terminology and should be communicated to staff prior to conducting the audit program.

Audit programs should identify overall objectives, auditing issues, and risks.

These programs should include resource estimates by area, task, and person. Audit budgets, actual performance statistics, and variance analyses should be used to evaluate audit effectiveness.

Workpaper documentation can indicate if activities were effectively supervised and if findings were sufficiently reviewed. This material should be logically organized so that persons not directly involved may review audit status and identify the basis of audit findings.

Effective reporting is the key communication tool of the internal audit department. Reports should document audit results and responses to audit findings. Although content may be dictated by report type, it should be consistent with industry standards and approved by management. Reports should be evaluated for clarity, conciseness, and completeness. The extent to which management and the external auditors rely on these reports may indicate the quality and completeness of internal audit's work products.

An effective internal audit department should have procedures for monitoring responses to report findings and for ensuring timely follow-up by appropriate personnel. Procedures should state how responses will be structured to include pertinent information and should include criteria to assess the adequacy of those responses. Procedures should exist to evaluate and distribute replies and to complete required follow-up.

Organizational Independence

An effective internal audit department must have organizational independence. Audit reports and findings are useful to management only to the extent that internal audit operates without interference from groups or individuals with potentially conflicting interests. Effectiveness increases when the audit function has direct and frequent access to the audit committee and senior management. Free access to information required to achieve stated objectives also increases internal audit effectiveness.

The objectives of evaluating the organizational independence of the internal audit function include determining that

- Reporting relationships support the accomplishment of audit objectives;
- Internal audit has access to all necessary records and resources;
- Management and the audit committee have a commitment to internal audit activities, as indicated by the frequency and content of responses to reports; and
- Conflicts of interest are minimized.

Reporting relationships with management and the audit committee should enable internal audit to achieve its objectives without interference or diminished objectivity. Management commitment to internal audit independence is demonstrated by the direct reporting of internal audit to a high-level financial officer or chief executive. The department preferably should not report directly to an operating executive with daily responsibility in other financial function areas, such as treasury or accounting.

Any special projects assigned to the internal audit department should be assessed for their impact on objectivity in performing future work. Projects requiring auditors to assume operating or design responsibilities should be noted; subsequent audits should be reviewed to ensure that auditors are not assigned to audit work that they previously performed.

ASSESSING THE CONTROL FRAMEWORK

Controllers complete their assessments of effectiveness when they move beyond a function-specific review to look at the larger control framework of their organizations. The control framework includes the policies, organization, and procedures that dictate how the financial organization should work. Tools for structuring and documenting this review are included as Appendix E - Attributes for the Control Framework.

Assessment of the control framework in the financial organization should consider

- How effectively policies are established, communicated to employees, monitored, and enforced;
- Whether the organizational structure, productivity, staffing levels, and staff development are adequate to support business needs; and
- Whether procedures accurately reflect work flows, identify internal controls, and are effectively communicated to, and applied by, employees.

Policies

To remain competitive in today's marketplace, organizations require a solid framework to plan, execute, and manage financial function activities. Strategic plans generally provide a foundation for such a framework. Implementing those strategies effectively requires appropriate policies and procedures to guide the execution of strategic directives. Since effective strategies are responsive to environmental change, policies and procedures must also be flexible to change. In this regard, policies and procedures should be designed to promote shifts in actions, behaviors, and practices to support changing strategies.

Policies and procedures, which should be designed in concert with business strategies, enforce strategy implementation by

- Promoting the uniform handling of similar activities so that tasks are coordinated and redundancies are minimized,
- Limiting independent actions by setting guidelines for the type and direction of actions to be taken,
- Aligning actions and behaviors to strategies throughout an organiza-

tion to minimize conflicting practices and to promote a unified approach to strategy implementation, and

- Acting as an automatic decision maker by formalizing precedents for resolving issues.

When properly established and maintained, policies and procedures form the framework for institutionalizing strategy.

Guidelines and standards should be considered when reviewing corporate policies and procedures. Closely related to policies and procedures, guidelines and standards provide practical ways to make policies and procedures operationally effective. As advisory or directional aids, guidelines fit standard procedures to specific circumstances. They offer specific examples of how a procedure will affect a specific job or activity. Guidelines, along with procedures, communicate to staff how things should be done.

Useful for evaluating compliance with policies and procedures, a standard should be a specific, objective, measurable reading, obtainable during the normal course of business. Characteristics of standards should be documented with respect to

- Purpose, which describes the policy or procedure being measured;
- Specific objective and measurable data that indicate policy compliance;
- The optimal value of the standard to conclude policy compliance;
- The title of the position responsible for monitoring the standard; and
- The frequency recommended for monitoring the standard.

A method for monitoring each standard should be defined, and a reporting mechanism established for deviations from standards. This mechanism should identify escalating problems and notify individuals that their work is not up to standard.

When policies and procedures are impractical, corporate strategies cannot be effectively executed. Guidelines and standards provide practical methods to implement and control policies and procedures. They thus contribute to the overall effectiveness of the financial function by facilitating strategy implementation.

An effectiveness review of policies should consider

- Policy structure,
- Implementation, and
- Maintenance.

Policy Structure

For financial policies to support the critical business processes, they must provide specific guidance about roles and responsibilities in each area. Describing "what should be done," policy documents should

- Briefly describe the intent of the policy;
- Summarize the issues, reasons, and conditions forming the basis of the policy;
- Discuss the significant results that the policy statement seeks to produce;
- Identify the organizational units affected by the policy;
- Indicate responsibility for implementing and maintaining conditions set forth by the policy; and
- Identify existing company documentation supporting the policy statement.

The chief financial officer generally retains authority to issue policy, although the authority may be delegated to managers responsible for the functional areas where specific policies apply. Responsibility for maintaining policies should be clearly defined and the documentation procedures clearly specified.

Implementation

Policy effectiveness depends upon management success in implementing policies. Well-designed communication programs are necessary to ensure that employees understand existing policies, have timely information on policy changes, and understand whether they comply with policies.

Best understood if documented thoroughly and organized logically, policies should be grouped into manuals directed toward particular audiences. For each audience, manuals may be compiled based on staff level or organizational unit, depending on the size of the company. For a large company, a hierarchy of policy documentation may include

- A company-wide policy manual, containing company directives and a summary of the other manuals in the hierarchy. The primary audience is company-wide executives with cost-center responsibility.
- A function-wide policy manual, containing policies, guidelines, and standards that describe company positions on matters of development or operation of activities within the function. The primary audience is function-wide management.
- Department manuals, defining policy for the internal operations of a department. The primary audience is the department staff.

Training programs linking policies to strategic directives and interpreting their meaning to a particular organizational unit are important for policy deployment. Inadequate training may produce failure of an otherwise high-quality set of policies.

Maintenance

As economic, corporate, and market environments change, strategies will change and require the review and possible modification of policies. Dynamic environments dictate timely approval and implementation of policy changes.

To detect policy obsolescence, particularly if departments reorganize or department management changes, responsibility for monitoring policies should be centrally maintained. However, responsibility for policy maintenance should be allocated to the appropriate managers of each functional area. User areas responsible for preparing documentation should receive training and assistance as needed.

Steps for maintaining policies should be documented in the policy manual and should

- Identify the organizational unit responsible for policy maintenance;
- Serve as a guide for documentation activities;
- Ensure that changes to policy statements are reviewed, approved, and prepared in a standard format; and
- Provide basic documentation guidance to individuals with documentation responsibilities.

Organization

The financial function relies on the individuals comprising the financial staff to execute services effectively. Personal qualities, as well as technical and communication skills, should enable the financial staff to balance active involvement as a decision support resource with objectivity and independence. Organizational structure and policies provide an environment to challenge and reward staff and individual efforts. An effectiveness review of the financial organization should consider

- The organizational structure,
- Staff productivity, and
- Staff development.

Organizational Structure

Research to define an optimum organizational structure has suggested that there is no one "best" way to organize an operation. Organizational design or structure should be tailored to each situation. The most suitable structure for a given financial function organization depends on the internal and external environment affecting it.

To provide optimal benefits to operational units, good organizational structures

- Clearly identify individual responsibility and authority,
- Group similar business activities and duties into logical organizational functions,
- Dispose of jurisdictional conflicts between individuals,
- Prevent duplication,

- Decrease the likelihood of "run-arounds",
- Make communication easier by keeping channels clear,
- Identify promotional opportunities that encourage executive development,
- Provide a basis for performance appraisal and individual capabilities,
- Aid in wage and salary administration; and
- Permit operating expansion with adequate control.

In most organizations, the financial function provides input into operating and strategic decision-making processes. Concurrently, the financial function has fiduciary responsibility for accurate internal and external financial reporting and for safeguarding assets. This fiduciary responsibility requires the financial function to maintain independence from operating management. Because of conflicting operating management obligations, the financial function is challenged to balance these dual roles.

Evaluating financial function effectiveness requires assessing the risks associated with operational involvement and determining whether existing controls are capable of preserving objectivity and independence.

Staff Productivity

Since financial function expenses are largely for staff salaries, staff productivity is a key element in determining the effectiveness of the financial function. The financial function achieves optimum productivity by coordinating activities and tasks with proper staffing levels within appropriate spans of control.

Excessive layers of personnel are costly; hamper communication, planning, and control; and adversely affect morale. Functions performed at the lower levels of an organization are usually grouped according to similarity of activities. At higher levels, groupings relate to the interaction and exchange of information by management. Appropriate combinations of activities provide adequate internal control through a segregation of duties. Well-structured activities improve staff utilization and may create economies of scale.

Reviewing procedures used to perform financial activities is as important as analyzing the grouping of organizational activities. Procedures should represent the most efficient process for achieving desired results. Using work simplification techniques, each step of a procedure should be assessed to determine whether it could be combined with another step, simplified, or eliminated. Additionally, work standards for each activity should form a basis for staffing-level decisions, as well as performance monitoring and evaluation. Established work standards specify the amount of time required for an experienced employee to complete a job when following a prescribed method. Reviewing standards and their use by the financial organization is essential for assessing organizational effectiveness.

In many organizations, staffing levels evolve in reaction to various internal factors rather than as the result of an approved plan. Factors influencing staffing levels include

- Staff availability, ability, and experience;
- The variety and nature of staff activities;
- Delegated authority;
- The existence of policies and procedures;
- The rate of business change; and
- Business schedules and timetables.

An inappropriate mix of staff capabilities and support actually may hamper productivity, as well as produce redundancies and gaps in functional responsibility.

Many organizations staff the financial function to meet peak workload requirements. Overtime is typically an alternative to meeting these demands. The financial activities of most organizations follow a combination of workload patterns that include

- Routine functions,
- Cycle-intense functions, and
- Randomly intense functions.

Routine functions include activities such as payroll, customer billing, accounts receivable, and accounts payable. These activities often follow a reasonably uniform pattern of work throughout the year and peak toward the end of each accounting period.

A cycle-intense pattern refers to certain predictable periods of the year when the workload of the financial staff increases significantly. In addition to the month-end and year-end increases in routine work, cycle-intense activities may include monthly, quarterly, and yearly financial closings and analytical review. Profit planning and budget preparation and analysis are cycle-intense activities that can significantly increase staff workload.

Randomly intense activities such as acquisitions, special financial analyses, and capital expenditure planning can increase the workload significantly at unexpected times during the year.

Achieving optimum staffing levels requires consideration of peak workload requirements, as well as the organizational activities to be performed.

The span of control directly affects staff productivity. The span of control refers to the number of individuals who report to a manager, as well as the number of activities for which the manager is responsible. Productivity among financial staff members is optimized when the span of control enables responsible managers to effectively manage, motivate, and evaluate employee performance. The appropriate span of control will depend upon the abilities of managers and subordinates.

The span of control framework affects the shape of an organization and its communication channels. A relatively flat organization, which results from wide spans of control, shortens the communication channel from top to bottom. It may foster general supervision since managers may not be able to devote significant time to individual staff members. In contrast, narrow spans of control allow for close supervision but lengthen communication channels and may increase cost.

Staff Development

An effective financial function depends on finding, hiring, and retaining individuals with the capability and motivation to perform in a complex environment. Staffing jobs with the right individuals is a dynamic process. Proper staffing matches characteristics of the position with those of the individual. A company developing a strong financial function can recruit from other companies with reputations for having strong financial functions or develop its own talent. The first approach requires assimilating individuals into an established corporate culture.

The second approach may be time consuming and requires a substantial commitment of resources. Effective staff development begins with recruiting activities and encompasses initial placement, career development, and training.

An effective recruiting and selection process relies upon the exchange of valid, accurate information about the candidate and the organization. Ideal candidates should have appropriate educational or professional backgrounds, such as undergraduate or graduate degrees in accounting, finance, or economics, Certified Management Accountant (CMA) certificates, or Certified Public Accountant (CPA) certificates combined with a business background. Candidates should provide evidence of interpersonal skills and other relative attributes. In addition, managers should supply accurate job descriptions, requirements, and expectations.

The initial experiences in an organization are particularly important in shaping a long-term relationship between the individual and the organization. Initial placement should foster development of individual business skills and should improve technical skills in relation to the individual's background. Staff members should have realistic information, challenging work, and effective supervision.

Individual development is a vital part of supporting staff and increasing the effectiveness of financial services. Effective career development systems should consist of structured career paths supported by well-designed training, continuing education programs, and proficient personnel evaluation practices. Career paths should provide for promotions that expose financial staff members to other aspects of the company's operation so that they can broaden their business experience and improve their communication and technical skills. Career development should strive to match an individual's career aspirations with opportunities for achieving them. Moving financial personnel between the corporate level and divisions or operating units could be part of the career path design. Lateral transfers to other functional areas of the company may also enhance an individual's opportunities for advancement.

Influencing individual motivation and capability to perform specific jobs, training, and educational programs typically promote better performance. Training programs should place special emphasis on developing interpersonal skills and balancing the dual roles of the financial function. Training should include company-sponsored and outside technical programs. As for back-up support in the event of absenteeism or turnover, cross-training is a productive way to broaden an individual's knowledge of a function.

Successful development of financial staff members relies upon the financial manager's ability to assess fairly and accurately an individual's working characteristics and performance. Not all staff will possess or develop the necessary skills required for long-term success. Some characteristics are difficult to assess during the initial selection process and must be judged on the basis of subsequent performance. An effective personnel evaluation system should provide a formal analysis of an individual's performance on the job, as well as constructive feedback, to ensure that performance is sustained, modified, or improved. An evaluation program not only monitors the development of staff members, but should also provide historical information to assess what skills are required for long-term success in each job.

Procedures

Procedures document the approved steps for performing an activity. They always should be consistent with corporate policy.

Procedure Structure/Content

Procedures should describe the steps required to complete an activity in a manner consistent with corporate policy. Although procedure formats vary by company, every procedure should consist of several standard components. Effective procedures should clearly identify the objective and scope in a narrative format as a reference for readers. They should identify the input sources that trigger the steps within a procedure. Input may include hardcopy documents or events such as monthly cutoff. Output generated from procedure steps also should be identified with its destination(s). Procedure steps should include the title of the person responsible for completion. The bulk of a procedure should present detailed instructions for performing specific tasks. If company procedure formats permit, each procedure should include complete samples of each input/output document along with its source or destination. Each procedure should have an effective date, standard review date, and approval signature.

Approved procedures should be consolidated in a manual for distribution as an ongoing reference. For large companies, the hierarchy of procedure documentation may be structured to parallel the organization's lines of authority. The arrangement of the procedure manuals should be consistent with reporting relationships, responsibility assignments, and authority limitations of key individuals in each group.

Department procedure manuals contain the detailed procedures for a specific department with department staff as the primary audience. Department manuals may also contain policies for the department's internal operations and accepted criteria or measures of performance. The department manual may document a departmental organization, including a complete set of job descriptions.

Training for Procedures Implementation

To successfully implement procedures, users should have initial and ongoing training. Training will ensure that employees understand existing procedures, have timely information on changes, and understand how well they are complying with the approved procedures. Training programs to present procedures and provide feedback to management are essential to procedure development. Lack of or inadequate training can cause the failure of otherwise high-quality procedures.

Procedure Maintenance

Financial procedures require review and update over time. A maintenance process should enable changes to be approved, implemented, and communicated in a timely manner within the financial function. This process should minimize disruption and confusion within the organization. Procedures maintenance should be documented in the procedure manual. This documentation should

- Identify the organizational unit responsible for procedure maintenance;

- Ensure that procedures are reviewed, approved, and prepared in a standard format; and

- Provide basic documentation guidelines to individuals within the organization with documentation responsibilities.

To prevent procedures from becoming obsolete, responsibility for the manual should be assigned so that it is not neglected in the event of reorganization or management change.

Procedures should be grouped into manuals according to their intended audiences. Manuals may be compiled for a particular staff level, an organizational unit, or both, depending on company size. For a large company, a hierarchy for procedure documentation may be structured to parallel the organization. The arrangement of the manuals should be consistent with reporting relationships, responsibility assignments, and authority limitations of key individuals in each group.

CONDUCTING THE SELF-ASSESSMENT

The last section detailed what to look for in evaluating the key functions of the controllership. This section will concentrate on how to structure a comprehensive evaluation to help controllers assess

- What financial services are needed but not received,

- What financial services are received but not needed, and

- How effectively essential financial services are provided by the financial organization.

Controllers can better respond to management needs by conducting a self-assessment of their present organization, identifying key opportunities for improving performance, and developing and implementing action plans to take advantage of those opportunities.

Step 1: Confirmation

The self-assessment process should start by confirming understanding of three dimensions of the business: strategy, organizational structure, and essential business activities. These dimensions form the basis for evaluating the relevance, effectiveness, and productivity of specific transaction-processing and decision support activities.

As a start, controllers need to confirm their understanding of the business strategy of the organization. Understanding strategy enables the controller to define those activities and functions most important for business success. A review of company planning documents including strategic plans, operational plans, and annual budgets should provide a fundamental understanding of business strategy and related objectives.

Controllers must also understand the organizational structure of their businesses. A formal organizational structure defines entities and their reporting relationships. Regardless of specific approach, the controllership organizational structure should be consistent with the overall organizational structure. Where operating functions are highly decentralized, the controllership function should be sufficiently decentralized to support those operating functions.

Understanding essential business activities is the key to success in meeting the organization's information and financial service needs. Recognizing budget constraints, the controller must focus resources on supporting those activities essential to the success of the business. These essential activities are best determined by obtaining the perceptions of key financial and operating managers of the company. Based on their perceptions, a limited number of activities will be agreed upon as most crucial for long-term profitability, survival, and growth. The controller should focus improvement on services directly supporting those essential activities.

Evaluating Controllership Effectiveness

Step 2: Specification

Once controllers have completed the confirmation step, they should specify the key financial services required to support the strategy, organizational structure, and essential business activities of the business. These financial service needs are shaped by the requirements of operating and financial management. Comparing the financial service expectations of key operational and financial managers against the actual services provided identifies potential service gaps that the controller should address. The output of this step should be a list of key financial information and services that should be provided by the controllership functions.

Step 3: Assessment

An assessment of the key controllership functions follows specification. Each function is compared to the financial requirements specified in the previous step. Required financial services are evaluated to determine their adequacy based on known needs, as well as baseline service attributes and performance indicators, such as those delineated in the appendices to this statement. Next, key areas for improvement are identified. Areas for immediate improvement should focus on what is specifically needed to support the business strategy, organizational structure, or essential business processes.

Step 4: Implementation

Once the final assessment has been completed, plans should be developed to implement improvements. Responsibility for plan implementation should be assigned, and a timetable with measurable goals should be set. The final implementation plan may be presented to management if appropriate.

Step 5: Monitoring and Control

Finally, control schedules and status-reporting mechanisms should be developed to follow up on plan implementation. The progress of implementation should be analyzed periodically to identify accomplishments and resolve any problems.

SUMMARY

Controllers must ensure that their organizations can respond effectively to management expectations and needs. Measuring and evaluating the effectiveness of the controllership function can assist controllers in this responsibility. With an understanding of the business strategy, organizational structure, and essential business activities, controllers can ensure that they are providing essential financial services. By evaluating function-specific and control elements, controllers can pinpoint weaknesses and implement improvements. Although a comprehensive self-assessment requires effort, it yields an understanding of the key actions required to establish a strong financial organization that supports management in building and sustaining competitive advantage.

APPENDIX A
Service Attributes For Transaction Processing

A. General Accounting

1. Is the account code logically structured to define
   a. major and minor accounts?
   b. budget areas?
   c. products?
   d. cost or profit centers?

2. Is the account classification easily recognized through a systematic numbering scheme?

3. Can the chart of account codes be modified?

4. Can current and prior year data be retrieved for all accounts for
   a. the beginning balance?
   b. transactions by month?
   c. month-end and year-to-date balances?

5. Are all changes to prior-year actual and current-year budgeted amounts properly authorized?

6. Are journal entries edited prior to posting for balance and valid account numbers?

7. Are rejected entries reported, including the reason for the rejection?

8. Are edit and control procedures in place for entries from subsidiary systems to the general ledger?

9. Do closing timetables exist?

10. Are reports prepared on a timely basis and do they include
    a. a balance sheet?
    b. an income statement?
    c. a statement of cash flows?

11. Is accurate and timely information regarding cash disbursements, receipts, and transfers provided?

12. Are monthly reconciliations prepared for all bank accounts?

13. Are accounting methods consistent with generally accepted accounting principles and SEC regulations for the industry and type of business?

14. Do general accounting policies and procedures manuals exist?

15. Are suspense accounts monitored regularly and cleared in a timely manner?

16. Are intracompany and intercompany accounts reconciled monthly?

B. Accounts Payable

1. Have inventory management policies and procedures been established?

2. Is an inventory control system in place?

3. Do accounts payable and purchasing have a common vendor master file?

4. Are vendor file additions and deletions approved by appropriate individuals?

5. Are key item reports, including operational statistics reports, prepared regularly?

6. Have dollar limits been established for requiring purchase order use?

7. Have policies and procedures been established and forms designed to count, inspect, and record receipt of items?

8. Are receiving report, purchase order, and invoice data reconciled?

9. Are receiving reports, vouchers, and invoice registers numerically controlled?

10. Do procedures prevent processing of invoice copies?

11. Are invoices approved prior to payment in accordance with established procedures?

12. Are check signing, check mailing, and voucher approval duties adequately segregated?

13. Is the check stock renumbered and numerically controlled?

14. Do procedures prevent duplicate payments?

15. Are supporting documents physically canceled upon check signing?

16. Are adequate steps taken to investigate and eliminate recurring errors?

17. Are reasons for lost discounts adequately explained?

18. Do control procedures allow for timely reconciliation of the trial balance with general ledger reports?

C. Payroll

1. Are procedures documented for collecting and processing employee data?

2. Are personnel and payroll data integrated to permit compliance with federal and state regulations?

3. Is access to and backup of employee data secure?

4. Do payroll transaction validations exist?

5. Are policies and procedures maintained for reporting employee time and attendance information?

6. Is responsibility for the preparation and approval of time and attendance documents segregated from documenting, coding, and processing functions?

7. Are policies and procedures governing payroll adjustments maintained?

8. Does the payroll system support
    a. payroll adjustments?
    b. payroll deductions?
    c. net pay calculations?
    d. employee liabilities?
9. Are controls in place over the production and distribution of checks?
10. Are controls in place to ensure that payroll expenses are properly distributed to general ledger accounts?
11. Do payroll transactions posted to the general ledger meet detailed financial reporting requirements of the organization?
12. Are budget projections of payroll expenditures prepared?
13. Are guidelines and criteria for processing and rejecting payroll transactions formally documented and updated on a regular basis?
14. Are policies and procedures maintained for submitting and processing claims for job-related expenses?

D. Accounts Receivable

1. Are billing activities segregated from accounts receivable activities?
2. Is there adherence to established credit memoranda procedures?
3. Are there credit policy and procedures for credit investigation, approval, and limits prior to adding a new customer to the master file?
4. Is customer master file maintenance centralized to ensure authorized file changes?
5. Are invoice preparation and accounts receivable posting activities segregated?
6. Is there an audit trail of all transactions posted to customer accounts?
7. Are cash receipts processing and payment adjustment authorization segregated from accounts receivable posting?
8. Are there policies and procedures for
    a. customer statement generation?
    b. delinquent account follow-up and collections?
    c. write-off approval?

E. Cash Management

1. Are cash collection and disbursement methods documented and analyzed?
2. Are internal processing costs identified, monitored, and regularly reviewed for each collection and disbursement method?
3. Is a formalized netting system used for intercompany payments?
4. Is there a formalized pooling system?

5. Are automated cash management systems used?

6. Are counterpart services and limits reviewed on a regular basis?

7. Can the number of bank accounts be rationalized?

8. Is there an effective reporting system for bank balances?

9. Does management of disbursements optimize float time?

10. Are customer payment practices regularly examined, especially with respect to major customers?

11. Are lock boxes used at regional collection sites?

F. Fixed Asset Management

1. Are assets tagged at the time of receipt and acceptance?

2. Are capital transactions readily traceable to feeder systems and source documents?

3. Are transactions strictly monitored and audited to ensure the propriety of capital treatment?

4. Are policies and procedures in place for capital treatment?

5. Is the capitalization approach consistently applied?

6. Are asset records sufficiently detailed for property identification?

7. Are asset movements routinely identified and recorded?

8. Are periodic audits taken of deeds, titles, and lease contracts to certify ownership?

9. Is equipment needing regular maintenance identified and schedules established?

10. Are asset utilization and productivity reviewed?

11. Are depreciation methods and assumptions periodically reviewed in light of current economics?

12. Are analyses made for
   a. investment tax credit (ITC)?
   b. ITC recapture?
   c. gain or loss?
   d. state and local asset apportionment?
   e. replacement cost?
   f. leases?
   g. cost and reserve activity summaries?

13. Is financial statement footnote information routinely obtained for significant asset commitments, write-downs, and procedural changes?

14. Are there policies and procedures for retirement approvals and methods, gain/loss and investment tax credit recapture calculations, and partial write-offs?

15. Are fixed asset reports generated and distributed in a timely manner?

16. Are periodic physical inventories taken of assets?

APPENDIX B
Performance Indicators For Transaction Processing

A. General Accounting

1. Ratio of correcting to total journal entries per month.
2. Average posting backlog for journal entries over the last twelve months.
3. Total hours per month to correct posting errors.
4. Total working days per month to close accounts and generate reports.
5. Average time between period-end and availability of budget variance analyses.
6. Total qualified/disclaimed audit opinions.

B. Accounts Payable

1. Average time between invoice receipt and vouchering.
2. Total monthly backlog of unpaid invoices.
3. Total checks returned and credit memos received for duplicate payments in the last twelve months.
4. Total monthly rejected invoices due to incorrect account distributions.
5. Percentage of manual checks to total checks issued per month.
6. Total monthly voided checks.
7. Total processing errors per month.
8. Number of lost discounts per month.

C. Personnel and Payroll

1. Ratio of rejected transactions to total transactions for payroll data in the past year.
2. Total monthly payroll adjustment errors as a percentage of total monthly payroll adjustments.
3. Average delay in payroll processing.
4. Total reconciling items to accurately reflect general ledger payroll distributions in a typical pay period.
5. Amount by which withholdings exceed payroll deduction maximums for the past twelve months.
6. Total monthly adjustments to correct employee withholding amounts.
7. Average time between

a. payroll check generation and issuance.

b. incorrect paycheck cancellation and corrected paycheck reissuance.

D. Accounts Receivable

1. Total monthly customer complaints regarding invoicing.

2. Total monthly hours to correct the invoice edit register.

3. Total monthly errors in the

    a. billing/general ledger interface.

    b. accounts receivable/general ledger interface.

4. Average time between identification and correction of suspense transactions.

5. Total monthly customer complaints regarding customer statement errors.

6. Average backlog of customer discrepancies to be reconciled over the past year.

7. Total write-offs for uncollectibles as a percentage of total sales for the past twelve months.

E. Cash Management

1. Average time between

    a. completion of the sales transaction and customer invoicing.

    b. check receipt and bank deposit.

    c. customer invoicing and payment receipt.

2. Average internal processing cost for collection and disbursement methods for

    a. checks.

    b. bank transfers.

    c. direct debits.

    d. cash.

3. Monthly transaction volumes for automated cash management systems.

4. Total hours monthly for bank account reconciliations.

5. Total interest collected on overdue accounts in the past twelve months.

6. Total dollars of invoices paid more than two days before due date over the past year.

7. Total purchase discounts taken in the past year.

8. Total purchase discounts available but not taken in the past year.

F. Fixed Asset Management

1. Total accounting errors in project accounting and accounts payable as a percentage of total monthly transactions.

2. Dollar amount breakpoint for capitalized and expensed items.

3. Physical inventory frequency.

4. Frequency of audits of deeds, titles, and lease contracts.

5. Average lead-time for requests for asset acquisitions.

6. Average unreconciled difference between fixed asset registers and the general ledger as a percentage of the average general ledger balance.

7. Total amount of investment tax credit (ITC) recapture in the past twelve months as a percentage of total ITC originally taken on the retired assets.

8. Average time between period-end and availability of key fixed asset management reports.

9. Ratio of inventory adjustments to book value of inventory.

APPENDIX C
Service Attributes Checklist For Decision Support

This appendix provides sample questions for evaluating the controller's decision-support functions.

A. Planning

1. Do plans present and evaluate all realistic alternatives?

2. Do plans analyze the impact of changes in key assumptions?

3. Are plans consistent with organizational goals and objectives?

4. Are plans prepared in accordance with management directives?

5. Are new plans linked to old plans?

6. Are plans from different departments integrated?

7. Do plans contain sufficient information to monitor and manage the business?

8. Is responsibility for plan preparation clearly defined to ensure appropriate accountability?

9. Is responsibility for providing key assumptions and components clearly established?

10. Are key planning assumptions clearly stated?

11. Are planning procedures formalized and documented?

12. Is full management backing and participation present?

B. Capital Budgeting

1. Is there a formal annual budgeting process that receives management approval?

2. Are capital budgets linked to facilities requirements and strategic plans?

3. Does the planning horizon encompass completion of moderate-length acquisitions?

4. Are budgets segmented by replacement/expansion and essential/discretionary expenditures?

5. Are phased completion schedules used and independently monitored for all capital projects?

6. Are objective economic evaluation methods used to value proposed projects (e.g. discounted cash flows, internal rate of return)?

7. Is the degree of risk associated with projects identified and evaluated?

8. Is sensitivity analysis performed to test variations in key assumptions?

9. Are comprehensive project status reports prepared on a regular basis?

10. Are postacquisition appraisals (forecasted vs. actual cost/value analyses) conducted for projects?

C. Operational Budgeting and Expenditure Control

1. Do unit managers participate in budget preparation?

2. Does top management review and approve all budgets?

3. Are budget development procedures fully documented?

4. Are automated budgeting and modeling systems used?

5. Are standardized forms used to develop routine budget components?

6. If budgeting assumptions change, how quickly can revised budgets be prepared?

7. Are budgeting responsibilities clearly defined and documented within all organizational units?

8. Are operating budgets coordinated with capital budgets?

9. Are operating budgets consistent among organizational units?

10. Is the coding structure for budget line items consistent with the chart of accounts?

11. Are the levels of authorization required for expenditures appropriate for the relative size of the expenditure request?

12. Are formal procedures in place to document expenditure requests?

13. Are automatic budget checks made to assure a sufficient balance prior to posting expenses?

14. Do management reports reflect the impact of sales forecast changes on budget and operating plans?

15. Are profit centers accountable for their operations and production as well as their profits?

16. Are nonmonetary measures of performance used (e.g., personnel statistics, market share, manufacturing reject rates)?

17. Are financial targets measured (e.g., return on inventory, days sales outstanding)?

D. Cost Accounting and Cost Management

1. Are annual budgets used as the basis for cost control?

2. Is budget information integrated with financial reporting systems for comparison to actual results?

3. Do budget control reports allow various management levels to review and revise aggregate budget data?

4. Is information provided for
   a. pricing and cost estimating decisions?
   b. efficiency and yield reporting?
   c. monitoring product cost changes?

5. Are there separate cost elements for
   a. direct labor?
   b. indirect labor?
   c. material?
   d. freight/duty?
   e. outside processing?

6. Is overhead separately identified as variable and fixed?

7. Are production and labor reporting data recorded on the same source document?

8. Are labor hourly rates sufficiently detailed by
   a. plant?
   b. cost center?
   c. job class?
   d. operation?
   e. individual?

9. Is there a single inventory record-keeping system for financial and manufacturing systems integration?

10. Is material usage by product and raw material available for performance measurement?

11. Are adjustments to inventory that are charged to cost of sales explained adequately?

12. Are direct labor rates, utilization, and efficiency values used for performance measurement?

13. Are overhead spending and capacity utilization monitored?

14. Can budgeted overheads be updated rapidly in response to actual changes in volume?

15. Does the cost allocation process support

    a. operating decisions for manufacturing management?

    b. pricing decisions for marketing management?

16. Are production and nonproduction costs clearly visible?

17. Does reporting support analysis of cost trends?

18. Is reporting timely enough for use by operating management?

19. Are inventory valuation methods (Last-In, First-Out, First-In, First-Out) consistently applied?

E. Financial Analysis

1. Do managers initiate variance analysis for their organizational units?

2. Do variance analyses aggregate both upward and downward?

3. Are reasons for budget variances identified and categorized?

4. Does variance analysis initiate budget modification?

5. Are favorable variances investigated to identify opportunities for performance improvement or better planning?

6. Are current period, prior period, and year-to-date information reported for comparison?

7. Are financing decisions related to the overall corporate plan, capital expenditure plans, and operating cash needs?

8. Does financial analysis reflect a cost of capital that is consistent with the current and projected capital structure as well as related costs of debt and equity?

9. Are appropriate financial ratios prepared and used for evaluating business performance?

F. Acquisitions and Divestitures

1. Is there a link between the corporate plan and the acquisition and divestiture (A & D) policy?

2. Are A & D criteria explicit?

3. Are the following criteria considered

    a. size?

    b. ownership?

    c. line of business?

    d. geography?

    e. regulatory considerations?

    f. financial stability?

    g. tax implications?

    h. cash flow impact?

    i. financial condition?

4. Is there communication with the outside investment community to identify potential A & D candidates?

5. Are operations, treasury, legal, marketing, accounting, and tax groups all involved in the A & D process?

6. Is there a formal process for evaluating A & D candidates?

7. Are there established procedures for pricing A & D candidates?

8. Are procedures in place to separately value divisional components?

9. Are formal postacquisition (divestiture) reviews conducted to analyze projected versus actual impact?

10. Are analytical methods evaluated when postacquisition (divestiture) review suggests unplanned impact?

11. Are specific plans in place for integrating the acquired company into the parent company for administrative and operations functions?

G. Special Projects

1. Are there defined channels of departmental communication to request assistance for special projects?

2. Are project reporting procedures in place? Are these procedures followed?

3. Are studies completed and findings reported on time and within budget?

4. Is the potential impact of projects on other departments investigated and reported?

5. Are there procedures for assessing project priorities when multiple requests conflict?

6. Are steering committees and status meetings used for monitoring large projects?

7. Are time, money, and other resource budgets set for each project?

8. Are postproject reviews conducted to report and analyze variance from project budget?

9. Are mechanisms in place to charge departments for projects which they request?

10. Are procedures for hiring outside consultants implemented where appropriate?

TAX ACCOUNTING

H. Tax Function Environment

1. Are tax goals and objectives established?

2. Is the tax function structured to address

    a. federal tax compliance?

b. international tax compliance?

c. state and local tax compliance?

d. payroll, pension, and benefits compliance?

e. tax planning?

3. Does the tax group participate in advising line management, parent, or holding companies, etc., regarding tax activity and requirements?

4. Do tax responsibilities for federal tax include

a. calculations of tax provisions and analysis of effective tax rates?

b. analysis of current and deferred liability accounts provisions, including cushion analysis?

c. reviews of key ledger accounts and consolidating entries that affect tax liability?

d. cost of goods sold and inventories?

e. preparation of consolidated and separate returns?

f. Schedule M-1 and Schedule M-2 reconciliation?

g. estimated federal income tax payments?

h. monitoring of compliance for domestic joint ventures?

i. research and development tax credits?

j. fixed asset tax control reviews?

k. revenue agent examinations?

l. dividend, interest, and miscellaneous income reports (form 1099)?

5. Do responsibilities for international tax compliance include

a. DISC and FSC reporting?

b. foreign corporations?

c. U.S. and foreign sales and expense reviews?

d. subsidiary or branch foreign returns?

e. joint venture, partnership, and noncontrolled foreign corporation compliance?

f. foreign tax credit and gross-up?

g. revenue agent examination?

h. boycott reporting?

i. U.S. companies controlled by foreign shareholders (form 5472)?

6. Do responsibilities for state and other tax compliance include

a. state return preparation and extensions?

b. state apportionment data?

c. state license, franchise, property tax, etc.?

d. sales and use tax?

e. excise and severance tax?

f. personal property tax?

g. real property tax?

h. revenue agent examination coordination?

i. unitary taxation?

7. Do responsibilities for payroll, benefits, and pension compliance include

a. federal unemployment tax (FUTA), FICA, and federal withholding deposits and forms?

b. state and local payroll tax reporting?

c. additional compensation reporting?

d. unemployment filings and data?

e. Forms W-2 and W-4?

f. WIN and jobs tax credits?

g. employee benefits compliance with ERISA and tax rules?

h. expatriate tax advice?

8. Are job descriptions current and complete for activities performed by the permanent tax group?

9. Are tax procedures documented? Do they accurately document the scope of tax activities?

10. Are outside tax specialists used to meet tax needs, when there is a lack of available internal resources or specialized skills?

11. Is general ledger integration adequate for accessing tax impact accounts at the legal entity and organization levels?

12. Are controls adequate over transaction flows from subsystems to the general ledger, when these flows affect tax records and compliance reporting, such as payroll?

13. Do data collection methods and information systems help accumulate financial information for tax compliance and planning?

I. Tax Policy, Procedure, and Compliance

1. Are tax policies approved by top management?

2. Does tax policy specify responsibilities for tax compliance?

3. Do tax procedures define responsibilities of tax and other financial personnel for availability, quality, and timing of required tax functions for tax compliance and planning? Do they

a. include periodic review of general ledger accounts to ensure proper tax treatment?

b. reflect low materiality limits consistent with tax compliance requirements?

    c. include reconciliation of company-wide account totals from management reporting to legal entity formats?

    d. define responsibilities for producing accurate tax-related data and for responding to outside audit requirements?

4. Do procedures and controls enable the tax department to monitor any tax activities outside the department's direct control?

5. Do tax administrative procedures provide

    a. training plans to maintain competence of the tax staff?

    b. periodic review of tax software to increase the effectiveness of tax services?

    c. steps to update current tax procedures?

6. Is supporting documentation maintained for all tax filings?

7. Does the company have recurring problems with late filings of returns, assessed penalties, or late payment of taxes?

8. Have audits performed by any taxing authorities resulted in significant adjustments?

9. Is adequate documentation maintained to settle issues raised by taxing authorities?

10. Do estimated taxes paid routinely exceed taxes payable?

11. Are federal income tax estimates and payments prepared on time?

J. Tax Planning

1. Are tax deferral and reduction techniques adequate to optimize the organization's effective tax rate?

2. Do reviews of legal entity tax provisions and liabilities identify opportunities to improve operating results?

3. Are tax strategies periodically reviewed using alternative operating scenarios and conditions?

4. Does tax planning consider the effects of corporate reorganizations with respect to

    a. tax strategy?

    b. close-down reserves and start-up costs under various reorganization scenarios?

    c. the tax impact of pending reorganizations?

5. Does tax planning include analyses of the tax impacts of proposed mergers, acquisitions, and buyouts?

6. Does tax planning include monitoring merger, acquisition, and buyout activities to prevent tax problems and to meet reporting requirements?

7. Are transaction reviews conducted to determine tax impacts of proposed agreements, such as joint ventures, licenses, royalty, etc.?

8. Are controlled foreign corporations structured to optimize tax benefits?

9. For foreign subsidiaries, are tax accruals and liabilities integrated into overall corporate plans?

10. Are international operations structured to optimize tax benefits from practices such as intercompany pricing and cost allocations?

11. Do tax personnel based in the U.S. participate in foreign tax planning and compliance activities, including examinations by foreign tax authorities?

12. Together with the human resource function, does tax planning adequately participate in developing and improving employee benefit programs to ensure optimum tax treatment for the organization and employee?

13. Together with the human resource function, does tax planning communicate compensation and reimbursement programs to expatriates to minimize U.S. and foreign tax costs?

APPENDIX D
Service Attributes For Internal Audit Activities

A. Scope

1. Is a formal policy statement maintained for the internal audit function?

2. Does the internal audit policy statement describe

    a. the purpose and objectives?

    b. overall responsibility?

    c. the source of authority?

3. Do upper management and the audit committee approve the internal audit policy statement? If not, where is approval obtained?

4. Is the internal audit policy statement consistent with management objectives, including strategic and business plans?

5. Is the policy statement periodically reviewed and revised?

6. Do internal audit activities include

    a. evaluating manual and computer-based control systems?

    b. verifying operational efficiencies against budgets, business and strategic plans, and other performance standards?

    c. monitoring compliance with policies and procedures, industry guidelines, and regulations?

7. How are internal audit activities documented?

8. Do internal audit activities include financial and operational audits? Do audits include key computer-based systems?

9. Does internal audit have sufficient access to upper management and the

audit committee? What is the quality and frequency of internal audit communication to those groups?

10. Is management responsive to internal audit findings and recommendations? Does operating management

    a. cooperate fully with internal audit activities?

    b. complete corrective steps recommended by internal audit in a timely manner?

11. Is the internal audit function regarded as technically competent, objective, and comprehensive by

    a. upper management?

    b. the audit committee?

    c. operating managers?

    d. the outside auditors?

B. Audit Planning Attributes

1. Does audit coverage for organizational units and functions consider

   a. historical problems?

   b. data sensitivity?

   c. the complexity of control systems?

   d. transaction volumes?

   e. staff turnover?

2. Are previous audit plans reviewed when establishing audit coverage?

3. Does operating management participate in establishing audit coverage?

4. Is the emphasis on financial, operational, and computer-based audits consistent with the scope of internal audit activities?

5. Is audit coverage for computer-based systems adequate to verify data, physical, and program security?

6. Do internal audit activities include a review of information system designs?

7. Does internal audit perform information system control reviews?

8. Does the internal audit function include a long-range audit planning cycle?

9. Does the long-range planning cycle include adequate planning schedules and plan updates?

10. Is the internal audit long-range planning horizon consistent with the organization's planning horizons?

11. Does the long-range plan approval process include frequent and extensive reviews?

12. Does the long-range plan delineate staffing requirements?

13. Is the long-range plan integrated with internal audit department budgets?

14. Are procedures and systems in place to monitor internal audit progress against planned activities?

15. Are progress reports rendered frequently enough for timely detection of deviations from schedules and planned activities?

16. Are staffing levels and audit objectives reassessed as part of the progress reporting for internal audit programs?

17. Are material changes to audit plans communicated to the appropriate personnel?

18. Are internal audit programs coordinated with activities performed by outside auditors? Does this coordination include

    a. overlapping coverage of high risk areas?

    b. coordination of report findings and recommendations?

19. Are internal audit schedules coordinated with operating management to consider

    a. production cycles?

    b. financial reporting cycles?

    c. systems design and implementation schedules?

C. Audit Performance Attributes

1. Is audit fieldwork conducted efficiently with adequate supervision and review of results?

2. Are auditors briefed on special risks and the nature of key controls?

3. Do auditors review prior-year audits and have access to sample records?

4. Are prior-year audit findings used to identify areas for improvement and to document audit deficiencies?

5. Does the audit program include

    a. a description of overall objectives?

    b. an assessment of issues?

    c. budgets developed by task, area, and staff?

    d. clearly defined tasks?

    e. updates to address special conditions and scope changes?

6. Are budgets established for all audit programs?

7. Are audit personnel involved in developing budgets?

8. Are standard budget forms used?

9. Is time reporting sufficiently detailed to monitor actual results against budget?

10. Are budgets approved by management?

11. Are variance analyses used to explain deviations from budget?

12. Are prior-year variances factored into the budgeting process?

13. Is workpaper documentation consistent from year to year?
14. Are internal audit documentation and standards consistent with
    a. corporate requirements?
    b. industry standards?
    c. professional standards?
15. Are internal audit reports consistent with industry and corporate standards with respect to
    a. content?
    b. clarity?
    c. support of findings by workpaper documentation?
16. Is audit report distribution
    a. approved by management?
    b. controlled by established procedures?
17. Does audit report follow-up include steps for
    a. verifying assigned responsibilities?
    b. logging and distributing audit responses?
    c. auditing corrective activities performed in response to audit findings?

D. Organizational Independence Attributes

1. Does internal audit have solid line reporting relationships to any of the following
   a. upper management?
   b. the board of directors?
   c. the audit committee?
2. Does internal audit have dotted-line reporting relationships to other organizational units? Identify those relationships.
3. Does the internal audit director have full responsibility for all internal audit activities?
4. Does management respond in a timely manner to implement internal audit recommendations?
5. Is the internal audit function centralized?
6. Do reporting relationships affect
   a. audit coverage?
   b. staffing levels?
   c. quality control?
7. Does the internal audit department have access to
   a. financial, operational, and personnel data?
   b. organizational guidelines and procedures?

    c. computer-based information systems?

    d. internal correspondence and reports?

8. Does the internal audit department have restricted access to information? Describe that restricted information.

9. Does the internal audit staff perform special projects that could create future conflicts of interest, such as

    a. performing operating assignments?

    b. writing or approving department procedures?

    c. designing information or internal control systems?

10. Do formal and informal reporting relationships with the internal audit department have the potential to create conflicts of interest? Describe those reporting relationships and potential conflicts of interest.

APPENDIX E
Attributes For The Control Framework

A. Financial Policies

1. Do financial policies support implementation of corporate strategies?

2. Do financial policies address each financial function (controlling, performance reporting, treasury, internal audit, and tax)?

3. Are policy statements timely and adequate?

4. Do policies satisfy the related elements of business needs, management objectives, and any management agreements?

5. Are policies complete according to the standard components of a policy statement?

6. Is policy language clear and understandable?

7. Is there consistency between components of a policy with respect to

    a. purpose and background?

    b. objectives?

    c. consistency of scope?

    d. responsibility of the policy?

8. Are policies that address ratios or other economic indicators stated to allow for changes in the financial environment without requiring that policies be revised?

9. Do procedures and activities required by financial policies conflict with existing policies in other functional areas, such as marketing or production?

10. Is the chief financial officer responsible for review and final approval of all financial policies?

11. Do independent auditors review significant management controls for selected policies, guidelines, and standards?

12. Do managers of each user area review and approve new policies, to ensure that these policies

    a. are supported by the results of a policy review?

    b. satisfy business needs and management objectives?

    c. state the policy clearly and concisely?

13. Does a group responsible for policy maintenance monitor and coordinate documentation activities throughout the company?

14. Do objectives of the documentation group ensure

    a. consistent use of a standardized approach for documenting policies throughout the company?

    b. effective review of all policies?

    c. the proper coordination of all policy documentation activities?

15. Do responsibilities of the policy maintenance group include

    a. establishing a consistent and standardized documentation approach?

    b. establishing methods to monitor documentation activities?

    c. recommending documentation priorities to management?

    d. preparing a master plan for documentation activities?

    e. coordinating and monitoring documentation projects?

    f. providing assistance and documentation expertise to areas with documentation projects?

    g. assisting in the ongoing maintenance of documentation?

    h. performing special projects as requested by company management?

    i. refraining from preparing documentation for user areas except under special circumstances?

    j. refraining from performing internal audit functions?

16. Do responsibilities in the documenting policy include

    a. user areas responsible for reviewing policies and standards, and for preparing documentation?

    b. managers of each user area responsible for review and approval of new policies and standards?

    c. the chief financial officer for review and final approval of all policies?

    d. independent auditors responsible for review of significant management controls for selected policies and standards?

17. Are policy manuals compiled in accordance with the corporate organization structure?

18. Are manuals distributed according to the physical location of the readers?

a. does the structure of the manual follow the organizational structure of the department?

19. Are manuals organized to address the various levels of management and policy responsibility?

20. If there is a company-wide manual, does it

    a. articulate corporate strategies?

    b. summarize other manuals in the hierarchy?

21. If there is a function-wide policy manual, does it describe the company position on matters of general interest concerning the planning and development of operations within the function?

22. If there are department manuals, do they contain

    a. policies, guidelines, and standards for the internal operations of the department?

    b. detailed procedures for the department?

    c. a reference showing the organization of the department?

23. Are numbering schemes sufficiently flexible to identify

    a. the type of function?

    b. the type of manual?

    c. the section of the manual?

    d. the policy, guideline, or standard number?

24. Are policies numbered with corresponding policies and corresponding numbers? Do related procedures have corresponding numbers?

25. Do employees understand policies applicable to them, as well as the meaning of those policies?

26. Are policy changes communicated with timeliness to all affected employees?

27. Is feedback on policy compliance effectively communicated to all employees?

28. Are training programs used to communicate policy to employees, in a manner appropriate to the level of the employee?

29. Are inputs into the policy formulation monitored for

    a. the economic environment?

    b. the corporate environment?

    c. the market environment?

    d. the regulatory environment?

30. Is compliance with existing policies monitored?

31. Are causes for noncompliance identified?

32. Are corresponding guidelines and standards evaluated?

33. What is the role of the internal and external auditors in recommending policy change?
34. Are policies reviewed and changed regularly?
35. Are documentation activities planned?
36. Does a policy review process consider
    a. the assignment of review tasks?
    b. the appropriateness of the overall review organization?
    c. the role of internal audit?
    d. the documentation of a new policy and standards?
    e. circularization for comment?
    f. compliance with standard formats?
    g. the acceptance mechanism?
    h. publication?
    i. follow-through development of related procedures, standards, and guidelines?
    j. monitoring and control of each documentation project, including scheduled progress reporting?
37. Is policy manual issuance controlled with respect to
    a. distributing and recording the location of policy manuals?
    b. maintaining control logs and distribution lists of manual holders?

B. Organization Attributes

1. Is the finance organization's mission or purpose clearly defined?
2. Is the mission statement for all functional organizations prepared annually?
3. Are mission statements updated periodically?
4. Are responsibilities clearly defined and documented at all levels?
5. Is responsibility coupled with corresponding authority?
6. Are assigned functions and respective staffing reasonable?
7. Do staff members report to only one superior?
8. Are lines of authority within the organization clearly defined?
9. Is individual authority clearly defined?
10. Is absolute responsibility for acts of subordinates assigned to a higher authority?
11. Is authority properly delegated?
12. Are levels of authority maintained at a minimum?
13. Are reporting relationships clearly defined and understood?
14. Are reporting relationships structured to effectively perform functions?
15. Are reporting relationships clearly structured to avoid staff confusion?

16. Will planned changes to functional areas outside the financial function have an impact on the financial function?

17. What are the general attitudes toward change within the organization?

18. Does the financial function participate in operating business decisions by

    a. presenting information and analyses?

    b. offering guidance and advice?

    c. monitoring progress against plans?

    d. challenging plans and actions?

    e. recommending actions?

19. Does the financial function participate in strategic business decisions by

    a. presenting information and analyses?

    b. offering guidance and advice?

    c. monitoring progress against plans?

    d. challenging plans and actions?

    e. recommending actions?

20. Are there advantages to changing the financial function role in operating or strategic decision making?

21. What are the service expectations of the providers and recipients of financial services?

22. What are managerial expectations regarding the financial function role when key decisions are made for critical business processes?

23. Are there advantages to changing the financial function role when key decisions are made in critical business processes?

24. What responsibility does the financial function assume for

    a. annual planning and budgeting?

    b. long-range planning?

    c. capital-expenditure planning?

    d. periodic budget reviews?

    e. narratives of operations?

    f. personnel evaluations?

    g. incentive compensation?

25. What degree of decision-making authority (full, primary, or equal) do line and staff functions maintain over

    a. hiring?

    b. transfers?

    c. promotions?

    d. terminations?

e. salary adjustments?

f. bonuses?

g. setting work priorities?

26. Are there advantages to changing established lines of authority?

27. Are there duplicate or overlapping activities between the financial organization and other areas?

28. Have positions been established in response to

    a. discovery of fraud?

    b. defalcation?

    c. illegal payments?

    d. unexpected write-offs of inventory or receivables?

29. Do opportunities exist to increase staff productivity or reduce workloads by

    a. developing or improving computer-based systems?

    b. contracting out nonrecurring work?

    c. contracting out routine work?

    d. eliminating functions?

    e. consolidating functions?

    f. rescheduling activities?

    g. reducing the frequency of activities?

30. What are staff-meeting procedures with respect to

    a. timing?

    b. attendance?

    c. duration?

    d. context?

31. Are there financial areas requiring improved financial and operating controls to enhance the company's overall profitability?

32. Are there current activities of the financial organization that could be eliminated or performed elsewhere without adversely affecting the company's internal controls?

33. Can financial procedures currently be simplified and made more efficient?

34. Are work standards established?

    a. is employee performance measured against these standards?

35. Are current activities of the financial organization redundant due to the advent of computer-based information systems?

36. Have staff positions within the financial organization been created for reasons other than increasing workloads or new responsibilities?

37. Have inappropriate levels of personnel (numbers or types.) been assigned to perform activities within the financial organization?

38. Is each staff member's workload reasonably confined to perform a single function?

39. Are staffing levels appropriate for the time and frequency of special projects?

40. Are skill levels appropriate for the functions performed?

41. Are individuals frequently overly qualified for assigned tasks?

42. What existing constraints prevent or deter improved staff utilization?

43. What are the opportunities to interchange staff to increase utilization?

44. Where can capital expenditures be made to reduce operating costs and enhance staff productivity?

45. How does management philosophy affect the size and cost-effectiveness of the financial function?

46. Is routine and repetitive work so fragmented that unjustified higher-level staff perform it?

47. How do peak workloads or seasonality affect work utilization?

48. What additional resources would allow additional projects to be undertaken?

49. Have alternative levels of management been considered to enhance staff productivity within the financial organization?

50. How many positions are routinely coordinated by a single manager?

51. Are staff utilization reports or time analyses used as managerial tools?

52. What are the longer-term costs and impacts on the financial function if no efforts are made to improve staff productivity?

53. Where can managers "stretch" through assuming a wider span of control by supervising more than one function?

54. Where is more management attention required to protect assets or enhance profitability?

55. Does personnel documentation include

 a. current and complete job descriptions?

 b. minimum educational and experience requirements?

 c. unique job factors, such as annual overtime and promotability?

56. Are the following appropriate:

 a. the level of management responsible for hiring?

 b. interview procedures?

 c. formal orientation programs?

57. Are counselors assigned to each staff member?

58. Are regular performance evaluations conducted?

59. What internal and external training programs are used?

C. Financial Procedures Attributes

1. Do financial function procedures reflect the policies and standards of the company?

2. Do procedures include specific guidance about roles and responsibilities?

3. Are all procedures complete according to standard components of a procedure?

4. Is procedure language clear and understandable?

5. Is there consistency among components of a procedure with respect to

    a. purpose and overview?

    b. objectives?

    c. scope?

    d. responsibility for the procedure?

6. Are procedures organized as a set of steps needed to perform a task, and not as job descriptions for a particular person?

7. Are procedures or guidelines for ratios or other economic indicators stated to recognize changes in the financial environment without requiring that the documentation be edited?

8. Does the group responsible for procedure maintenance also monitor and coordinate all documentation activities throughout the company?

9. Do objectives of the documentation group include ensuring

    a. consistent use of a standardized approach for documenting all procedures?

    b. an effective review of all procedures?

    c. proper coordination of all documentation activities?

10. Do responsibilities for procedure maintenance include

    a. establishing a consistent and standardized documentation approach?

    b. establishing methods to monitor all documentation activities?

    c. recommending documentation priorities to management?

    d. preparing a master plan for all documentation activities?

    e. coordinating and monitoring documentation projects?

    f. providing assistance and documentation expertise to areas with documentation projects?

    g. performing special projects as requested by company management?

    h. refraining from preparing documentation for user areas except under special circumstances?

    i. refraining from performing internal audit functions?

11. Do other participants in the documentation process include
    a. users responsible for preparing and reviewing procedures, guidelines, and job descriptions?
    b. managers of each user area responsible for reviewing and approving new procedures, guidelines, and job descriptions?
    c. managers of the function responsible for review and final approval of all procedures, guidelines, and job descriptions?
    d. independent auditors who review controls within procedures?
12. Is the chief financial officer responsible for review and final approval of all procedures?
13. Do independent auditors review significant management controls for selected procedures?
14. Do managers of each user area review and approve new procedures to assure that they
    a. are supported by the results of a procedure review?
    b. satisfy business needs and management objectives?
    c. state the procedure clearly and concisely?
15. Does the procedure manual structure parallel the organization of the company?
16. Are manuals divided into separate volumes according to the physical location of users?
17. Are manuals divided into separate volumes addressing the various levels and responsibilities of users?
18. Do department manuals contain
    a. policies of the internal operations of the department?
    b. detailed procedures, guidelines, and standards for the department?
    c. a reference showing the organization of the department?
    d. a complete set of job descriptions?
19. Are numbering schemes sufficiently flexible to identify
    a. the type of function?
    b. the type of manual?
    c. the section of the manual?
    d. the policy, guideline, or standard number?
20. Are procedures, guidelines, and standards numbered to correspond to each other?
21. Do employees understand and can they perform procedures that apply to them?
22. Are changes in procedures communicated with timeliness to all affected employees?

23. Is feedback on procedures compliance effectively communicated to all employees?

24. Do training programs communicate procedures to employees, in a manner appropriate to the level of the employee?

25. Do training programs include refresher courses for existing and new employees?

26. If jobs exist that do not relate to an existing procedure, does this suggest obsolete job descriptions, or job descriptions providing de facto procedures?

27. Are processes used to monitor outside factors, such as regulatory change, which are inputs into the procedure formulation process?

28. Do changes in strategic direction and corporate policy prompt changes or additions to current company procedures?

29. Do the internal and external auditors recommend procedural changes?

30. Are procedures reviewed regularly?

31. Is procedure manual issuance controlled with respect to

    a. distributing and recording the location of procedure manuals?

    b. maintaining control logs and distribution lists of manual holders?

MANAGEMENT ACCOUNTING PRACTICES COMMITTEE
1989-1990
Chairman, Robert G. Weiss
Vice President and Controller, Schering-Plough Corporation, Madison, New Jersey

Robert N. Anthony
Professor Emeritus
Harvard Business School
Boston, Massachusetts

Diane M. Butterfield
Deputy Controller
Manufacturers Hanover Trust Company
New York, New York

Michael T. Cinalli
Manager, Accounting Policies and
*   Procedures*
E.I. du Pont de Nemours
Wilmington, Delaware

James P. Colford
Senior Consultant
I.B.M. Corporation
Stamford, Connecticut

Bernard R. Doyle
Manager, Corporate Accounting Services
General Electric Company
Fairfield, Connecticut

Neil E. Holmes
Vice President
The Marley Company
Mission Woods, Kansas

William J. Ihlanfeldt
Assistant Controller
Shell Oil Company
Houston, Texas

John J. Lordan
V.P., Business Affairs
Johns Hopkins University
Baltimore, Maryland

John C. Macaulay
Director of Operations Analysis and
*   Planning*
Dresser Industries
Dallas, Texas

Frank C. Minter
Vice President and CFO (Retired)
AT&T International
Basking Ridge, New Jersey

Timothy P. Murphy
V.P., Finance–Administration
GTE, Inc.
Stamford, Connecticut

John J. Perrell, III
V.P., Corporate Accounting and Reporting
American Express Company
New York, New York

Stanley A. Ratzlaff
V.P. and Controller
Pacific Enterprises
Los Angeles, California

L. Hal Rogero, Jr.
V.P., Administration
Publishing Paper Division
Mead Corporation
Escanaba, Michigan

John E. Stewart
Partner
Arthur Andersen & Co.
Chicago, Illinois

Norman N. Strauss
Partner
Ernst & Young
New York, New York

Edward W. Trott
Partner
KPMG Peat Marwick
New York, New York

NAA Staff
Louis Bisgay, *Director,* Management Accounting Practices
Wagdy Abdallah, *Manager,* Management Accounting Practices